Making Machine Musicians

AI for Live Musical Performance

Jason Palamara

Routledge
Taylor & Francis Group
LONDON AND NEW YORK

Designed cover image: Jason Palamara

First published 2027
by Routledge
4 Park Square, Milton Park, Abingdon, Oxon OX14 4RN

and by Routledge
605 Third Avenue, New York, NY 10158

Routledge is an imprint of the Taylor & Francis Group, an informa business

British Library Cataloguing-in-Publication Data
A catalogue record for this book is available from the British Library

Library of Congress Cataloging-in-Publication Data
Names: Palamara, Jason author
Title: Making machine musicians : AI for live musical performance / Jason Palamara.
Description: New York, NY : Routledge, 2026. | Includes bibliographical references and index.
Identifiers: LCCN 2026011738 (print) | LCCN 2026011739 (ebook) | ISBN 9781032877426 hardback | ISBN 9781032840543 paperback | ISBN 9781003534211 ebook
Subjects: LCSH: Music--Performance–Technological innovations | Music and technology | Artificial intelligence–Musical applications
Classification: LCC ML74 .P35 2026 (print) | LCC ML74 (ebook) | DDC 780.285/63–dc23/eng/20260514
LC record available at https://lccn.loc.gov/2026011738
LC ebook record available at https://lccn.loc.gov/2026011739

ISBN: 9781032877426 (hbk)
ISBN: 9781032840543 (pbk)
ISBN: 9781003534211 (ebk)

DOI: 10.4324/9781003534211

Typeset in Galliard
by Deanta Global Publishing Services, Chennai, India

Making Machine Musicians

Making Machine Musicians: AI for Live Musical Performance explores the integration of artificial intelligence (AI) technologies into live music performances.

Offering a comprehensive guide to developing "machine musicians" capable of interactive improvisation and real-time collaboration with human performers, this book introduces readers to cutting-edge trends in live musical AI. Chapters combine theoretical discussions, practical tutorials, and hands-on projects, providing step-by-step instructions for building autonomous music systems, experimenting with interactive AI tools, and exploring creative applications of AI in live performance. Accompanying software and tutorials ensure accessibility for musicians of all levels, fostering both technical fluency and artistic innovation. Whether used as a textbook, a self-study guide, or a practical manual, it equips readers with the knowledge and tools to explore the emerging field of musical AI and its potential to transform the way we create and experience music.

This book will appeal to music technology professionals, educators, and novice musicians alike; this book serves as a valuable resource for anyone interested in the intersection of AI and live music.

Jason Palamara is Assistant Professor of Music Technology at Indiana University, Indianapolis, USA. He specialises in developing AI-enabled performance technologies for music. He directs the Indianapolis-based Machine Musician Lab that pursues multiple AI music and performance initiatives. He maintained a long-term creative partnership with the late percussionist-composer and technologist Scott Deal, with whom he developed the interactive AVATAR software. AVATAR is an autonomous music system that uses machine learning to play along with live improvisation. He is also the founder/director of IU's 30+ member DISEnsemble (Diverse Instrument Symphonic Ensemble), which counts an autonomous digital performer named the Emergent Musical Hologram (EMH) among its performers.

Contents

Who Is This Book For?

This book serves as a deep introduction to methods for integrating artificial intelligence (henceforth AI) technologies into live music performances, creating "machine musicians." While examples of musical AI go back decades and there are many books addressing AI music as a topic, fewer resources serve the aim of addressing AI music created and performed live via interactive improvisation. AI technologies that can create spur-of-the-moment improvisation or quickly composed music have similarly been in existence for a long time, but as Adam Neely said in a recent video essay, "*There is no money to be made in passing a music directive test. You're just making the process to get to the product less efficient.*" (Neely, 2024). I believe there is funding to be gained in this work and, more importantly, there is evidence of an increasing number of people interested in pursuing this avenue of artificial intelligence (Miranda, 2021). And who says music must be all about money anyway?

That said, this enterprise understandably lags behind the more commercially viable aspects of musical AI. Also, even in the best cases (like that of Shimon, the eight-armed marimba-playing robot that jams along live with human musicians), much more work is required before AI technologies can take their place as true equal partners in live musical performances. For the music technology professional, this book will give insight into new trends in live performance before they become widespread, as well as a clear-eyed view of the AI technologies already extant in the music world today. For the music educator, this book aims to equip the educator with knowledge of and, in some cases, practical experience with live AI music technologies. For novice musicians, some chapters of this book include easy-to-digest tutorials on how to build AI technologies that can listen and play along with live music. Other chapters include tutorials that allow these readers the ability to experiment with fully fleshed-out autonomous music systems that will listen and improvise with human musicians. Ultimately, it is hoped that whoever reads this book gains a different perspective either on extant and future musical technologies or music itself.

DOI: 10.4324/9781003534211-1

How to Use This Book

This book may be useful as a textbook or for personal study. Some chapters involve a tutorial, the end goal of which is to instruct the reader in building their own autonomous music systems capable of interacting with human performers via MIDI and audio signals. Other chapters include tutorials for making music with more advanced apps (also included) developed by the author. No prior experience with Max or advanced audio tools is necessary, though it is assumed that the reader is some manner of musician and is familiar with musical situations and concepts.

Each chapter opens with a narrative section discussing a root problem or issue within the scope of musical AI, then moves to a tutorial section that delineates one potential way to address the problem. Instructors using this text as a textbook may assign chapters in sequence or selectively, depending on the structure and focus of their course. Together, the chapters guide students through foundational and advanced topics in musical artificial intelligence, offering both theoretical frameworks and hands-on experience with contemporary tools and techniques.

For independent readers and practitioners, this book may also serve as a structured guide for self-directed study. While prior experience with music programming or artificial intelligence is helpful, it is not strictly required; the tutorials are intended to scaffold learning and introduce technical concepts progressively. Readers are encouraged to engage actively with the material, adapting the examples to suit their own artistic goals or research interests.

Ultimately, this book aims to cultivate a critical and creative understanding of how autonomous systems can participate in musical processes. Whether used in a classroom or a studio, its goal is to bridge theory and practice—to foster both conceptual insight and technical fluency in the emerging field of musical AI.

Included Interactive Software

Some chapters include a piece of software that illustrates examples of musical phenomena discussed in the chapter, or a musical use of a particular AI algorithm. Some chapters also include tutorials designed to spur creative use of these patches. The example software was written using Max, so it can either be used on any modern Windows or Mac laptop. In addition to the laptop, a MIDI controller is recommended for the software to function properly. Some other common musical equipment is also recommended (an audio interface and a microphone). The reader will also require a current version of Max or Max-for-Live via Ableton Live to perform the step-by-step tutorials.

Note: Max/MSP is a proprietary software environment developed by Cycling '74. Although Max is not free, the company offers a fully functional 30-day trial version, as well as discounted educational licences and a low-priced subscription. Readers may therefore engage with all example materials—patches, exercises, and demonstrations—without incurring any initial cost. Additionally, following the trial period, Max operates in a limited "read-only" mode that allows users to open and interact with existing patches, even if saving new versions of the patches provided is restricted.

Max may be purchased via the following link: https://cycling74.com/shop/max.

Ableton Live (with Max-for-Live) may be purchased via the following link: https://www.ableton.com/en/trial/.

Be sure to choose the best option for your situation before purchasing.

Accessing the Included Software and Example Patches

All Max patches and examples referenced throughout this book are available via a public GitHub repository. GitHub is a widely used platform for hosting and distributing code, and readers do not need an account to access or download the materials.

Repository Access

To obtain the companion materials, visit: github.com/jasonpalamara/Machine-Musicians

There you will find folders and .maxpat files corresponding to specific chapters and topics. To download all materials:

1. Click the green "Code" button.
2. Select "Download ZIP."
3. Extract the downloaded archive and open the patch files using Max/MSP.
4. Software Availability.

All example materials are released under an open licence and are intended for educational and creative use. Readers are encouraged to experiment freely with the provided resources and adapt them to their own artistic or research-based pursuits.

While the majority of examples in this text are implemented using the Max programming environment, the underlying systems and concepts should be readily translatable to other programming platforms, provided those environments support the implementation of machine learning algorithms. The choice to use Max is not because Max is the best environment for constructing AI music tools, but Max is the system with the farthest market reach, the widest acceptability in the electronic music community (especially given its connection to Ableton Live via the Max-for-Live version of Max that comes with most versions of Ableton Live). The finished project software will be included with this text for readers uninterested in building these systems themselves.

These patches and devices are not intended as the be-all and end-all to solve all the reader's musical AI problems. Rather, regarding specific chapter discussions, each one represents "one way to go" down a particular rabbit hole to solve a particular part of the overall musical AI problem. These patches and devices are instructive of principles and ideas related in the text. It is hoped that these beginnings will spur the creativity of the reader to the creation of new and more exciting discoveries. What is needed in so many categories of AI research is what *TikTok's* Ed Newton-Rex referred to as lots of small labs and lots of people "doing small experiments to see what sticks" (AI Music Creativity, 2020).

Background

As a lifelong fan of science fiction and a musician, I've always been drawn to the possibilities that interactive technology opens for human expression. But I've never seen technology merely as a tool (a fashionable epithet for human-positive AI as of this writing), but as a creative partner—one that, like a human partner, shapes our art as much as it enables it. While my curiosity naturally led me towards the philosophical mindset of a scientist, my formal academic background is rooted entirely in music—not in computer science or informatics. I hold degrees in music composition and theory, with a persistent focus on electronic music and music technology. As you read this book, whenever I speak about artificial intelligence, computer science, informatics, or linguistics, please remember that I do so not as a formally trained expert in those disciplines, but as a sincere researcher who has studied them deeply through the lens of a musician and composer.

My path into higher education was anything but conventional. But it suffices to say that I am an improvising musician first and foremost. During my doctoral studies, I was blessed with a Research Assistantship in the Department of Dance, where I ran a music production studio and served as improvising musician for Professor Jennifer Kayle's dance improvisation courses. There, I performed using acoustic instruments, created real-time loops, and manipulated electronic sounds using custom-designed Max patches. This experience was pivotal, leading to an ongoing role as the improvising musician for the dance improvisation collective *The Architects* (Jennifer Kayle, Kathy Couch, Katherine Ferrier, Lisa Gonzales, and Pamela Vail). It also opened doors to collaborations with groups like *Charlotte Adams Dancers, Madison Contemporary Dance, The Lovelies (NYC),* Maddie and Margo Korn, and many other choreographers and dancers too numerous to name.

I made music for Jennifer's classes on my violin and used Max patches to make and control loops and audio effects using foot controllers. Inventing novel musical material off the top of my head for hours at a time multiple times a week quickly put me in a place where I needed to come up with new strategies to keep the music interesting. One day, after seemingly reaching the end of my creativity, Jennifer introduced me to a concept *The Architects* often discuss called *schtick-busting*.

> In the dance improvisation world, "schtick" (from Yiddish, denoting a favoured action preferred and regularly employed by a person) refers to habitual practices you do in movement. Your schtick is that same move, that same riff, that same approach or quality, that same role you play in the ensemble. If you're attentive, on a given day of practice, your schtick can have a fresh take. It can be the foundation on which you build a new structure or take a sideways journey.
>
> (Kayle, interview by the author, September 20, 2024).

In musical terms, a *schtick* could be a preference for playing in a key that is idiomatic, or a flurry of ascending notes one learned long ago in a practice room. Everyone who improvises ends up developing and using schticks, but a steady diet of them in an artist's approach will begin to lead to stagnation. When this happens, the schtick-busting artist asks themselves "what if I denied myself the use of this tool?" or "why do I favour this particular tool so much?" or "is there another way to use this tool that I've been avoiding?"

I started to develop my technological systems I was using in some new ways. Increasingly, when I embedded a schtick-busting process in these systems, they would present a range of choices rather than one single outcome, such that each button was not a direct order from the human in charge, but rather a *"do something"* button that would spur the software to take an unpredictable action. It didn't always work, and what these systems would do at any moment was anyone's guess, which was endlessly fascinating. Ultimately though, the novelty would wear off quickly. These systems were frustratingly inorganic, unwilling to surprise you if you already knew what they were capable of. This realisation has led me to undertake a serious study of artificial intelligence.

Max AI

Upon gaining a teaching position at Indiana University, Indianapolis, I met Benjamin Day Smith, developer of the first Max package of external objects to be officially released via Cycling '74 that gave Max users the ability to experiment with machine learning (*ml.**, released in 2017, Smith & Garnett, 2012). Ben's work was invaluable in that it gave Max users like me an opportunity to experiment with AI technology without having to code prohibitively complex algorithms from whole cloth. Ben's efforts were soon accompanied by several other useful Max packages such as *RAVE (Realtime Audio Variational autoEncoder)* by Antoine Caillon and Phillippe Esling, *MuBu* by the ISSM Team at IRCAM, and the *Fluid Corpus Manipulation* package developed by the FluCoMa team.

AVATAR

These packages formed the original backbone of what I was able to achieve with my long-time creative partner, percussionist Scott Deal, with whom I developed the *AVATAR* project, which listens to an improvised performance and plays along in a context-appropriate manner. Since 2018, Scott and I presented *AVATAR*-related works all over the globe at some of the most prestigious conferences and electronic music festivals, such as MusicAcoustica (Beijing), NoiseFloor (UK), the International Conference on New Music Concepts (Italy), International Computer Music Conference (Chile), the New York City Electronic Music Festival (NYCEMF), the RITMO Center for Interdisciplinary Studies in Rhythm, Time and Motion (Norway), the Conference on AI Music and Creativity (AIMC, Austria), and the *Institut de Recherche et Coordination Acoustique/Musique* (IRCAM, France). Scott also used AVATAR as a compositional partner, most prominently composing his *AI Opera: Lexia* in tandem with the system. Sadly, Scott succombed to cancer in February, 2026, just as this manuscript was being submitted. I was honored to premiere Scott's final composition—*Rogue Planet,* which was composed with AVATAR—just days before his passing, ensuring my good friend one last standing ovation before he left us.

AI and Music Education

I have also integrated AI into my teaching, involving my undergraduate ensemble (the 30+-member Diverse Instrument Symphonic Ensemble or DISEnsemble) in our regular performances, and in developing two embodied AI projects called the *Telepod* and the *Emergent Musical Hologram* (discussed in Chapter 11 of this book). Lastly, I developed a course at IU Indianapolis around the topic *Autonomous Music Systems.* Much of the curriculum for this course is the basis for what I am presenting in this book.

Today

In my experience as an instructor, I have had the experience of interacting with a computer science major nearing the end of their degree who, upon the first public release of ChatGPT-3, exclaimed in class, *"if this thing can write code, why am I even getting this computer science degree?"* Whatever I said in the spur of the moment, I think there is still plenty of worth in getting a computer science degree, but if this experience taught me anything, it was that the expectations that all the computer science jobs would be the important ones, while the creative jobs would evaporate, ended up being quite the reverse. The intelligent machines of today find writing code easy but strain to make *meaningful* art (Chiang, 2024). To that student's comment, if AI can already be used to write code, it does much to level the playing field between the computer scientists and the rest of us. When computer scientists were the only ones who could write code, computer scientists were the indispensable sorcerers to humankind. That is no longer the case. Quite ironically, one thing the science of AI has liberated us of was some of the computer scientists (Susann, 2025). The creatives among us are now free to play in their sandboxes without chaperones.

If it is your first time trying something like this, I say: welcome to an amazing playground none of us built alone. Let's have some fun. If any computer scientists happen upon these words I say: You too are welcome. Even if you are already familiar with the principles and ideas presented in this book, undoubtedly this book presents them from a unique angle. Ultimately, there may be authors who may have a deeper understanding of machine learning algorithms, or a broader experience writing software, but I do not know anyone else working in this space who has these varied experiences, nor anyone with a greater passion for bringing this knowledge to a multifaceted audience.

What Is a Machine Musician?

Boot up any computer, tap on a smartphone, turn on your TV, start your car, open a refrigerator, Google some trivial fact, or check the time on the smartwatch you're wearing on your left arm, and there is a chance that you are already interacting with some version of an artificial intelligence. As this book passes into the future, my guess is that the reader's interaction with this technology will only become more frequent, eventually becoming practically nonstop as the number of devices connected to distributed AI systems proliferates to the point of ubiquity. It's quite possible that for many who read these words this is already true. But is this true? Are we already interacting with artificial intelligence? Or is it over the horizon, to be discovered in some halcyon (or possibly catastrophic) version of "tomorrow?"

There is a sense in which both sentiments are true. Artificial intelligence is extant in the world at present, and we already interact with it all the time. It is arguable that artificial intelligence has been with us since the very first computer systems were employed back in the 1940s. Even the earliest computers represented an attempt to augment human intelligence with automatic analysis of data, automatic decision making, and thus automated thinking processes. AI research as a field of concentrated study was established by the 1950s. As personal computing devices became more prevalent in the 1990s, it became a standardised way of speaking about a computer that was taking too long processing a task (perhaps represented by a spinning rainbow wheel or a flipping hourglass) to say that the system was "thinking." This phenomenon is so common that computer scientists have labelled it the ELIZA effect (ELIZA being an early chatbot dating from 1966; Weizenbaum, 1966). The field of AI research has progressed very far in the decades hence, and as of this writing, many public discussions are taking place that might lead one to believe that either AI is taking over the world (not to mention all of the jobs), it might start a worldwide nuclear war, it might be listening to everything we say and watching everything we do, it might be able to write a better term paper, better diagnose a disease, or even be a more fulfilling and exciting long-term romantic partner than anyone you've ever met.

But is any of this evidence that artificial intelligence is among us today? Perhaps not. Reportedly, the attendees at the 1956 Dartmouth College workshop believed they would be able to design a human-level intelligent system within 20 to 30 years (Moor, 2006). On the strength of these claims, these researchers won large grants from the US government, but by the time much of that government funding dried up in the so-called *AI winter* of the 1970s, it was clear that near-human artificial intelligence was going to take much longer to be discovered. In the interim between then and now, parties interested in human-level artificial intelligence have often looked to science fiction to find the examples not extant in science fact. One such example I make near-constant use of in my teaching is that of Lieutenant Commander Data, the android second officer on the starship Enterprise of *Star Trek: The Next Generation*. Despite being constructed by a human scientist out of completely synthetic materials, despite describing himself as "an automaton, designed to resemble a human being," and despite lacking human emotions, Commander Data is still far closer to being justifiably described as a human-level intelligence than anything we have yet seen in real life. And I believe the best evidence of Data's humanity is his musicianship.

When Commander Data's sentience is questioned in the episode "The Measure of a Man," (Snodgrass & Dawson, 1989) his advocate uses the fact that he has done things we normally attribute to sentient agents (like keeping a memento of a former co-worker who had passed away) to prove that he may be sentient. It is thus not Data's intelligence (which he claims equates to "60 trillion operations per second") that serves as the proof of Data's potential for sentience; it is this seemingly human connection to another being. Later, in *Star Trek: Nemesis* (Berman & Baird, 2002), Data is seemingly destroyed, but his memories have been downloaded into a new android named B-4. Data's friend, Jean-Luc Picard, notices something of Data must have survived when B-4 begins to sing the lyrics to Rogers and Hammerstein's *"Blue skies."* Picard smiles, the music swells, and the movie ends with a clear implication that Data has survived his seeming death, as is evidenced by his ability to sing, an ability he was never programmed to have.

By contrast, though artificial intelligence technologies seem to be all around us today, this moment of recognising "a spark of life" in the machines around us has not yet come to be on any large, recognisable scale. In the musical realm, the most successful musical applications of AI have been those that replicate an overly difficult or expensive process that many human musicians are unqualified or unwilling to do (e.g., mixing and mastering via iZotope's Neutron, Landr, Focusrite Fast, Sonible Pure). If these apps have any use in the current musical ecosystem, it will be to reduce human workloads. Thus, what we have created have not been intelligences, but disposable machines that can (as *Star Trek's* Guinan said in *Measure of a Man*), "*do the dirty work*" that we humans don't want to do or that we find too difficult. Conversely, it is still debatable whether applications that take the creative work out of human hands like Suno and Udio will survive into the future. If one interacts with these all-encompassing apps, one quickly discovers these apps have an amazing ability to create new songs including lyrics and human-sounding vocals at the click of a button, but many of the tracks seem somewhat derivative of human work (Neely, 2024). These apps are not so much creating new material as giving us cleverly disguised remixes of pieces of music already written. While all human art is appropriative in some way, great human artists throughout the ages have been able to transcend their influences to make new kinds of artistic expression that seem to spark genius in many ways not yet seen in the artistic works of AI (Noci, 2023).

John Cage is rumoured to have often repeated the phrase, "A finished piece of music is exactly that" (Ross, 2007). The sentiment can be interpreted as a comment on his philosophy of musical works existing in the moment of performance, where a piece is only truly "finished" when it has been presented, and any further manipulation could detract from the original experience (Cage, 1961). In essence, a piece of music, after it is played live by performers and heard by some manner of an audience, is dead and inert. Likely, it was for this reason that Cage hated recordings of his music (Frere-Jones, 2014). Music, being a time-based art, happens in the moment, and thus a musical output rendered as a page of musical notation is not music. It is a recipe for making music. Similarly, a vinyl record of a recorded performance is not music; it is the leftover makings of a once-live musical experience. The turntable, being a musical instrument, can bring the music back to life momentarily, but its only "intelligence" lies in the simple automation of repetitive action of the needle and the spindle; in this case, the recorded performance lies dead but minimally animated under the needle. Perhaps current versions of musical AI are doing something similar, reanimating dead pieces of music momentarily, until a human discovers the work has been appropriated without any pretence of thought, intelligence, agency, or consent.

This is not what I intend to do with this book. Here, we are not building a useful "AI tool," nor a clever copycat machine, but an autonomous musical machine that may be capable someday of exceeding its programming and becoming the musical equal of the fictional android. This goal is aspirational, and I will not claim to have reached it with any totality, but this search is what this book is about, a first step towards what Christopher Small might call a machine that can *musick* (Small, 1998). A machine musician would not just appropriate what others have done but would seek out a new way that has not been explored previously. It is debatable whether this goal will be achieved by anyone in my lifetime, but I believe the goal will teach us much about music, the nature of intelligence, the nature of life, and ultimately, it will teach us much about ourselves.

Caveats, Ethical Problems, and Warnings

The totality of the dangers presented by AI is far beyond the scope of this book, but the musical world is not immune to AI controversy, as is evidenced by the recent RIAA lawsuit against Suno and Udio (Draughorne, 2024). Some major discussion points for AI music studies include (but are not limited to):

1. Copyright issues.
2. Cultural appropriation.
3. Bias, misinformation, disinformation, and malinformation.
4. Privacy concerns.
5. Human unemployment.
6. Loss of musical abilities (AI music technology as a competitive cognitive artefact).

As such, most chapters will contain some discussion of the ethical challenges involved in AI musical studies, pertinent to the overall subject of the chapter, as well as suggestions for safe and ethical uses of the companion software and similar systems. Much guidance for this aspect of the text has been derived from *The Center for Humane Technology*, which has produced much helpful media and even helpful online courses for those interested in learning about safe uses of technology (including AI and machine learning). Interested readers should visit the Center's website at https://www.humanetech.com.

These sections are not presented to scare learners away from collaborating with AI to create music. Many a lesson can be learned from doing things "the wrong way." However, as I routinely warn my students as we build AI from the ground up, be careful what you do using these technologies. We are playing with live ammunition. Additionally, when designing systems that interface with your computer's resources (speakers, hard drive, inputs, outputs) it is quite possible to mistakenly damage your computer or other connected gear. Readers are hereby warned to read the tutorial passages carefully and tread lightly on any recommended process they do not understand.

Should We Do This?

In the 1993 blockbuster hit *Jurassic Park,* Jeff Goldblum's character Ian Malcolm famously states that the problem with scientists was that they have become "so preoccupied with whether they could do something that they didn't stop to think if they should" (Jurassic Park, 1993). Much to the distress of many artists on social media, AI technologies seem to threaten to take away the slim opportunities for monetary reward from human artists and give them to corporations, leaving humans to do the dirty work.

Similarly, Adam Neely's video essay "*Why AI is doomed to fail the musical turing test*" includes a clip from jazz bassist Anthony Jackson stating that he'll "outplay anybody using a machine, or I'll die. I don't care. The day that the machine outplays me they can plant me in the yard with the corn. I mean it.

I'm very serious. I will not permit myself to be outplayed by someone using the machine. I'm just not going to permit that" (Neely, 2024). Neely goes on to reiterate that while there are people he respects "using AI technologies, to make beautiful music that somehow captures what it means to be human," that the outputs made by Suno, Udio and their ilk are "not music." Neely's complaints against the Suno and Udio company work is that these companies are:

1. Accelerationist: "ticking off one more thing that an [artificial general intelligent (AGI) system] is supposed to be able to do on its way to "the singularity"" (Kurzweil, 1999, 2005).
2. "Profoundly disinterested in the artistic process" (human music is generally made in a slow fashion, in context with other musicians and/or in the context of human life in general, which is a context to which AI cannot relate to at present).
3. "Profoundly disinterested in why music sounds the way it does" (because AI cannot relate in any meaningful way, it can merely copy the successful results).
4. "Aggressively anti-human" (In Neely's view, these companies are focused on creating ways that a machine system can take creativity and creative work out of the hands of human creators).
5. "Aggressively anti-history" (these companies are focused on creating music seemingly couched in the history of cultures and people groups that they have no knowledge of and no ability to connect to).
6. "Aggressively anti-music" (these systems have the potential to harm actual musicians, make their lives harder, or make human musicians struggle to succeed).

Certainly, Neely's assertion that these companies have a disinterest in the artistic process seems to be correct, given the RIAA lawsuits currently being brought against them (Draughorne, 2024). Neely's concerns are quite valid and as a human musician myself, I have to say that I also fear these things, but it does not dissuade me from this present work. Moreover, I see this type of slow musical AI work as an antidote to every one of these complaints. Accordingly, the systems designed for and discussed in this book will be:

1. Anti-accelerationist: While platforms like Suno may embrace an accelerationist approach, this work proceeds at a more deliberate, thoughtful pace. As Tristan Harris's Center for Humane Technology observes:

   > For years, Silicon Valley has operated with a 'move fast and break things' mentality. But as we've seen, it's not just technology that breaks. By the time people understand the negative externalities of a new platform, product, or service, the harms can be difficult to reverse.
   > (Center for Humane Technology, n.d.)

In keeping with this cautionary stance, this book does not begin with deep dives into deep learning or neural networks. Instead, it advocates for the gradual development of systems that make autonomous, musically interesting choices in smaller and more interpretable ways before scaling to larger machine learning models. As for the Singularity—or the possibility that an AI music system developed here might trigger it—that question lies beyond this book's scope, but many artists intuitively reject the idea that faster and more efficient automatically equates to better. This scepticism is deeply rooted in music, as in this line from *The Devil Went Down to Georgia:*

> The Devil opened up his case and he said, "I'll start this show," and fire flew from his fingertips as he rosined up his bow, and he pulled the bow across the strings and it made an evil hiss.
>
> (Daniels, et al., 1979)

The devil in the song has a supernatural power to play the fiddle fast and loud, but the character Johnny plays with an ability that comes from the humanity of his soul, not from his ability to play fast notes, which, in the end, is the reason he wins.

1. Profoundly interested in the artistic process: At least at the beginning, whatever models we create should be deeply steeped in human methods for creating music, based upon widely accepted musical standards that map to what any new music student would learn in a similar context.
2. Profoundly interested in why music sounds the way it does: We will build systems that listen like humans and which represent an attempt to understand the full context of what they are hearing.
3. Not aggressively anti-human: We will build systems that do not take creativity and creative work out of the hands of human creators.
4. Not aggressively anti-history: We will build systems that encode within them their own unique histories and experiences, rather than copying or even ignoring human traditions, but by listening to and responding to human music where appropriate.
5. Not aggressively anti-music: We will build systems that, if employed, would not generally harm musicians, make their lives harder, or make human musicians struggle to succeed.

As stated previously, these goals are aspirational, and this work is still in the very early stages. But even if the goal turns out to be a mirage, I think the road is worth travelling.

References

AI Music Creativity. (2020, October 20). *AI music creativity 2020 spotlight: Ed Newton-Rex (TikTok)* [Video]. YouTube. https://www.youtube.com/watch?v=pWq_Gbaeczw

Berman, R. (Producer), & Baird, S. (Director). (2002). *Star Trek: Nemesis* [Film]. Paramount Pictures.
Cage, J. (1961). *Silence: Lectures and writings.* Wesleyan University Press.
Center for Humane Technology. (n.d.). *Key issues overview.* Retrieved May 27, 2025, from https://www.humanetech.com/key-issues
Chiang, T. (2024, August 31). Why A.I. isn't going to make art. *The New Yorker.* https://www.newyorker.com/culture/the-weekend-essay/why-ai-isnt-going-to-make-art
Daniels, C., Crain, T., DiGregorio, W. J., Edwards, F., Hayward, C., & Marshall, J. W. (1979). *The devil went down to Georgia* [Song]. *On Million mile reflections [Album].* Epic Records.
Díaz Noci, J. (2023). Merging or plagiarizing? The role of originality and derivative works in AI-aimed news production. *Hipertext.net: Revista Académica sobre Documentación Digital y Comunicación Interactiva*, (26). https://doi.org/10.31009/hipertext.net.2023.i26.04
Draughorne, K. (2024, September 5). *Record labels' lawsuit against Suno and Udio could chart a path for AI copyright litigation.* Continuing Education of the Bar (CEB). https://research.ceb.com/posts/record-labels-lawsuit-against-suno-and-udio-could-chart-a-path-for-ai
Frere-Jones, S. (2014, April 7). Do recordings kill music? *The New Yorker.* https://www.newyorker.com/culture/sasha-frere-jones/do-recordings-kill-music
Kurzweil, R. (1999). *The age of spiritual machines: When computers exceed human intelligence.* Viking.
Kurzweil, R. (2005). *The singularity is near: When humans transcend biology.* Viking.
Miranda, E. R. (Ed.). (2021). *Handbook of artificial intelligence for music: Foundations, advanced approaches, and developments for creativity.* Springer. https://doi.org/10.1007/978-3-030-72116-9
Moor, J. (2006). *The Dartmouth College artificial intelligence conference: The next fifty years.* https://doi.org/10.1609/aimag.v27i4.1911
Neely, A. (2024, April 30). *Why AI is doomed to fail the musical turing test* [Video]. YouTube. https://www.youtube.com/watch?v=N8NyEjB_XeA&t=1201s
Ross, A. (2007). *No such thing as silence: John Cage's 4'33.* Farrar, Straus and Giroux.
Small, C. (1998). *Musicking: The meanings of performing and listening.* Wesleyan University Press.
Smith, B. D., & Garnett, G. E. (2012). *Unsupervised play: Machine learning toolkit for Max.* Proceedings of the International Conference on New Interfaces for Musical Expression (NIME). International Computer Music Association.
Snodgrass, M. R. (Writer), & Dawson, M. (Director). (1989, February 13). The measure of a man (Season 2, Episode 9) [TV series episode]. In G. Roddenberry (Creator), *Star trek: The next generation.* Paramount Domestic Television.
Spielberg, S. (Director). (1993). *Jurassic Park* [Film]. Universal Pictures.
Susann, D. (2025, February 5). Computer science students voice concerns over oversaturation, AI hurting job prospects. *Technician Online.* https://www.technicianonline.com/news/computer-science-students-voice-concerns-over-oversaturation-ai-hurting-job-prospects/article_c6a051a4-e382-11ef-89cb-9f945f73a21d.html
Weizenbaum, J. (1966). ELIZA—A computer program for the study of natural language communication between man and machine. *Communications of the ACM, 9*(1), 36–45. https://doi.org/10.1145/365153.365168

1 A Conversation with Your Computer...

Imagine you are in your bedroom, within earshot of a computer and suddenly say, "make some music for me!" If the computer has certain programming, a microphone and access to the internet, perhaps it will begin playing something from your Spotify account. But what if you wanted the computer to more literally *make* (i.e., generate, invent, compose, improvise, perform) some music, not just access and replay what someone has previously recorded, but to create *new music* on its own? If you've previously downloaded a song generating app and connected it to voice commands, then at the command, "make some music for me!" a hard rock song begins playing that sounds like Evanescence but with hints of The Weeknd. Nothing against those artists, but that's not what you wanted. You say again "make some music for me!" and your computer opens a website where you can find a local music teacher. Frustrated, you say again "make some music for me!" and the computer responds, "I'm sorry, I don't understand you, please rephrase your request."

You say,

> I want you to make something real. Something relevant to this moment in my life. Something that surprises me and yet seems familiar. Something that later I'll be singing absentmindedly while I'm making dinner and humming while I'm the washing dishes. Something that makes me feel like someone in this universe gets me. Not any of the music that has been made before and not just a rehash of something I've listened to previously ... Something completely new that connects to my soul and has the capacity to become indispensable like only good music can. Can you do that?

The computer responds, "What is music?"

Incredulous, you do a search on your computer for the word "music," and it receives many results, including apps that play music, files that contain the word music, emails you've sent and received with the word music in them, and music-related websites you've recently visited. These results show that your computer can associate the word music with other contexts in which it has encountered it. But do any of these associations demonstrate that the

DOI: 10.4324/9781003534211-2

computer understands what music is in any meaningful sense? If, hypothetically, you and the rest of humanity had consistently linked the word music to images of shoes, your computer would most likely return shoe-related results. Its understanding is limited to statistical associations, not semantic content.

Humans vs Computers

This is a significant root difference between humans and machines at present. While humans often take lessons to become better musicians, they do not need to be instructed regarding what music is. All known human cultures have a kind of music, even perhaps—most astoundingly—those that exist among people who cannot hear (Brown, 2000; Nettl, 2000; Merriam, 1964). Music interacts with every part of the human brain, including regions associated with emotion, memory, motor control, and language (Levitin, 2006). Music is a powerful tool for social cohesion, bonding us together in shared ceremonies and rituals, often with spiritual or religious significance (Dunbar, 2012). Music is a highly personal and subjective phenomenon that can evoke vivid memories (Janata, et al., 2007), is shaped by an individual's cognition and body (Clarke, 2005), and affirms the listener's personality (DeNora, 2000). Yet amazingly, human children exhibit musical behaviours spontaneously even without formal encouragement or training (Trevarthen & Malloch, 2000).

By contrast, computers do not acquire knowledge independently. To teach a machine to make music, one must first encode rules or provide examples that define what music is—its structures, features, and functions. This distinction highlights an even deeper gap between computer pattern detection and lived understanding. While machines can often simulate musical behaviour, they lack any connection to biology, emotion, sociality, and personal meaning (Searle, 1980). To build a machine that understands these things, we must first break down what we mean by the word "music" almost to the point of absurdity. Then, assuming every step in the process of building a machine musician was one item on a to-do list, we could break the task into enough small steps that we might begin to build simple functions and subsystems that will eventually converge to *make new music.*

What Is Music?

There are certainly individuals who dispute whether certain sound art or performance practices qualify as music (rap music seems to be the most regular target). Such objections often rely on rigid or culturally specific definitions, typically framed as: "*_______ music is not music because it doesn't include _______.*" The final blank is usually filled with some musical parameter—melody, harmony, rhythm—present in familiar forms but absent in the work being interrogated. These arguments tend to infuriate many and enlighten no one. In the interest of universality, we would do well to remain as inclusive as possible, rejecting any definition that excludes practices widely recognised and valued as music by substantial communities (Small, 1998; Blacking, 1973; Elliott, 1995). Going forward, let us cast the widest net possible, embracing a definition of music that reflects the full diversity of human experience rather than narrowing it (Nettl, 2000; Turino, 2008).

What follows is a smattering of simple definitions of music found online:

1. Dictionary.com: An art of sound in time that expresses ideas and emotions in significant forms through the elements of rhythm, melody, harmony, and colour (Dictionary, n.d.).
2. Oxford languages (via Google.com): Vocal or instrumental sounds (or both) combined in such a way as to produce beauty of form, harmony, and expression of emotion (Oxford University Press, n.d.).
3. Merriam-Webster.com: Vocal, instrumental or mechanical sounds having rhythm, melody, or harmony (Merriam-Webster, n.d.).
4. Cambridge Dictionary: A pattern of sounds made by musical instruments, voices, or computers, or a combination of these, intended to give pleasure to people listening to it (Cambridge University Press, n.d.).

Each of these definitions has some strengths, but they all feature weaknesses that would not hold up to the standard of universality set above. The album *Amplifier Worship* by the Japanese band Boris would challenge the Cambridge definition based on its inclusion of the requirement that music must be "intended to give pleasure to people listening to it." This definition imposes an ill-defined standard that would be difficult to define, let alone justify for a great many experiences we think of as legitimately musical. Not all music is pleasurable, and not all musicians intend pleasure with their music. Indeed, much music is made for purposes that have no overlap with pleasure or pleasantness. Additionally, assuming one agreed with the standard that to be music one must intend it to be pleasurable, the question arises: *pleasurable to whom?*

Similarly, the Oxford definition insists upon "beauty of form, harmony, and expression of emotion." It is hard to imagine music without some manner of discernible form, and so the insistence on form seems to be an important distinction that sets apart human-made music from bird calls and the utilitarian chirping of cicadas on a hot summer night. Still, the so-called form of a piece of music is largely an analytical tool used to describe the experience of how certain musical parameters changed over time, an analysis that can only be appraised after the piece is finished. While the piece is happening, the music is experienced only as what-is-happening-now, compared to previous events and possible prognostications about what might happen later. But these analyses and predictions are happening in the mind of the listener, and are highly subjective. These are things happening on the sidelines while music is being played. Music, as it is happening, is, as Pierre Boulez famously said, "violently of the present time" (Griffiths, 2015).

The Merriam-Webster definition encouragingly includes the broadest range of instruments but adds the necessity that music must also possess "rhythm, melody, or harmony." This definition would leave out much unrhythmic, unmelodic, unharmonic music, including much of free jazz, the symphonies for electric guitars of Glenn Branca, some shoegaze music, certain pieces by John Cage, experimental sound art like the opening few minutes of Henry Gwiazda's *MANEATINGCHIPSLISTENINGTOAVIOLIN*, or music that is primarily timbral or texture-focused like Gerard Grisey's *Partiels*.

Of these definitions, Dictionary.com is the only one that refers to music as an art of sound in time, which would include many examples the others would exclude. However, this definition then smuggles in the requirement of "expressing ideas and emotions" which might leave out total serialism like Milton Babbitt, who avoided the conveyance of emotional narratives and connections between historical models and their music (Mead, 2009).

It is understandably difficult to invent a concise definition of music. Perhaps music, being a kind of art, will always truly be in the eye of the beholder, and yet we must have some definition of music to use as a guide for the present study. The following section outlines my own working definition of music to aid the discussions within this book.

An Inclusive Definition of Music

Music is a time-based art, distinguished by its focus on manipulating sound as the primary medium (in contrast to other human arts such as dance, sculpture, theatre, etc.). It is realised through the variation of four core auditory parameters—pitch, dynamics, duration, and timbre, all of which are detected and assessed through the human sense of hearing—which are further shaped by five fundamental perceptual parameters: range, repetition, contrast, contour, and frame, which are perceived by the human mind. Together, these elements contribute to the overall shape or form of a distinct musical work. Individual musical experiences may employ some or all these parameters in near infinite combinations.

Each parameter in this scheme is also known by other synonymous terms or related phenomena, for instance (Table 1.1):

Describing Musical Parameters

As music is primarily a human phenomenon, musicians focus their efforts on manipulating the core auditory and perceptual parameters within ranges perceivable by humans. For example, although an infinite number of frequencies exist, human auditory perception is limited, necessitating that music intended for human listeners be confined to this audible range (approximately 20 Hz and 20,000 Hz). Each parameter comprises a specific spectrum, which is typically far narrower than the full range of physical possibilities, constrained by human perceptual capabilities. These spectra can be represented in various

Table 1.1 Core musical parameters and their closely related terms

Core parameter	*Synonyms and related concepts*
Pitch	Frequency, notes, tone, melody, harmony
Dynamic	Volume, gain, intensity
Duration	Rhythm, length, time, tempo
Timbre	Sound quality, tone quality
Range	Tessitura, register
Repetition	Recapitulation, cycle, pattern, memory, reference, quote
Contrast	Variation, opposition
Contour	Shape, arc, envelope
Frame	Context (historical, cultural, etc.), meaning, ideas, emotions

Table 1.2 Scientific and informal methods of describing a spectrum of pitches

	Informal	*Scientific*	
Core Auditory Parameter	*Notes*	*Hertz scale*	*MIDI*
Pitch	Low A to high C	27.5 Hz–2093.005 Hz	21–96

ways—some grounded in scientific measurement, others more informal—as shown in Table 1.2:

As computers are scientific instruments, this text will henceforth rely more heavily on scientific definitions of the relevant parameters rather than on informal or experiential descriptions. Some of the core perceptual parameters lend themselves more readily to scientific analysis than others. Consequently, readers will notice a decreasing emphasis on these parameters as the chapters progress. While they should not be dismissed, the relative lack of scholarly work on certain perceptual dimensions limits their practical utility in the context of building autonomous music systems. As such, their treatment in this text will remain foundational but necessarily constrained.

Scientific Musical Objects in Max

In the Max visual programming language, there are generally two ways of dealing with musical parameters: music as data or music as audio. The differences between these two methods will be discussed in a later chapter, but it is important to note that data objects and processes have a certain look to them, and the names of audio-related objects and processes all have a tilde (~) after them. Figure 1.1 is a collection of both to illustrate.

Data objects often interact with the Musical Instrument Digital Interface (MIDI) protocol, which will be how we begin working with musical processes.

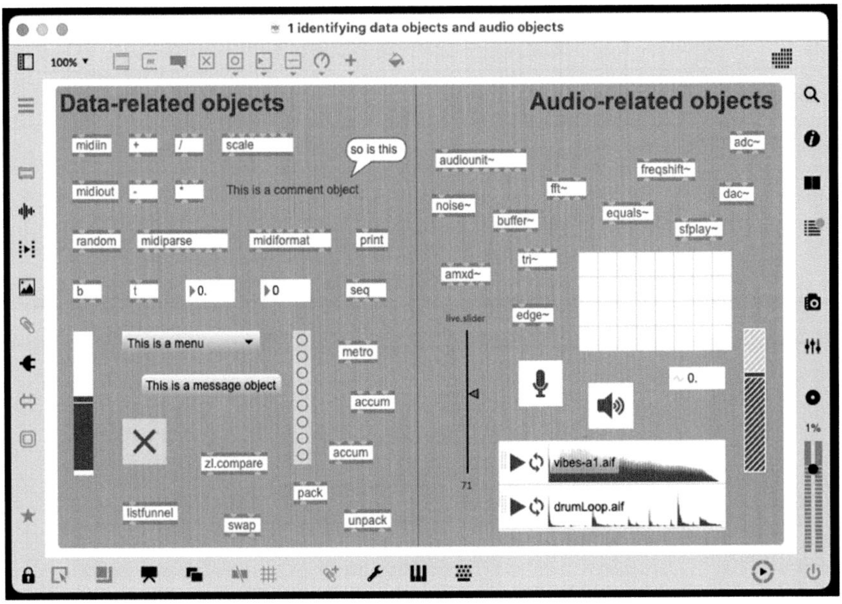

Figure 1.1 Some data related objects and some audio-related objects in Max.

Core Perceptual Parameters

The Core Auditory Parameters, all directly perceptible to human senses, are relatively self-explanatory and frequently appear in traditional definitions of music. Conversely, while the individual terms comprising the Core Perceptual Parameters should be familiar to most musicians, their grouping as a coherent framework is a novel conceptual contribution. As such, these parameters warrant further elaboration to clarify their role in musical experience and analysis (Table 1.3).

When combined, these nine layers (four Core Auditory Parameters and five Core Perceptual Parameters) interact to form the structures that underpin most musical experiences. However, any given musical work need not engage with all nine layers equally—nor even utilise each one at all. Numerous examples exist across global traditions and experimental practices in which one or more of these layers are minimised or entirely absent. This variability underscores the inadequacy of rigid definitions that seek to exclude entire genres or practices from being considered music.

Leigh Landy (2007) makes a compelling distinction between "note-based" and "sound-based" musics. Note-based musics typically revolve around pitch and rhythm as primary organisational tools, whereas sound-based musics (such as electroacoustic or experimental genres) often focus more on timbre, spatialisation, and the manipulation of recorded sound materials. This distinction helps account for why certain musics—particularly those that downplay pitch

Table 1.3 Core Perceptual Parameters that may be manipulated to create musical structures.

Core Perceptual Parameter	*Description*	*Effect*	*Example*
Range	The highness or lowness of an event	Creates a sense of embodied space between two connected extremes within an auditory phenomenon	A section of music that progresses from *pianissimo* to *mezzo-forte,* thus implying a dynamic range of *pp mf* in the section
Repetition	The tracking of whether an event has happened previously or if it is a new event	Provides a sense of regularity, induces expectations of continuance that can be subverted or rewarded	A regularly repeating four-bar sequence
Contrast	A perceived difference between one thing and another thing that is operating on the same or related auditory or perceptual phenomenon	Directs attention of the listener, adding prominence to some events, with greater contrast increasing the perceived difference (up to the point at which the difference is so great that the two events begin to seemingly become disconnected)	Regular beats, punctuated by a short silence
Contour	The shape of a series of events in time or space	Provides a sense of travel between one event and others	The pitches of a musical phrase, including stepwise and disjunct motion
Frame	Any extra-musical meta-context	Provides a structure for meaning and/ or understanding of musical events	Indications of culture

or traditional rhythmic structures—are frequently misunderstood or dismissed by critics operating from a note-based framework.

For example, rap music broadly prioritises rhythm and lyrical flow over pitch-based melody, yet this emphasis does not disqualify it as music. Similarly, John Cage's 4′33″ offers a musical experience composed primarily of frame and duration, virtually devoid of intentional pitch, rhythm, or timbral manipulation in the traditional sense. These works challenge inherited assumptions about what music must be and demand a broader, more inclusive understanding of the medium. As with quantum phenomena, where the act of observation changes the outcome, the listener's perception plays an integral role in constructing musical meaning. In this sense, definitions of music must leave room for a certain degree of interpretive and conceptual "quantum weirdness."

This definition offers the advantage of parsing musical practice into sufficiently granular components, enabling the construction of machine architectures capable of replicating human-like musical effects. However, as has been argued in discussions about musical intelligence and artificial creativity, the goal is not merely to reproduce musical output but to design a system that can respond meaningfully to human intent—a concept analogous to Alan Turing's imitation game (Cochrane, 2020; Turing, 1950). Rather than passing a test of stylistic mimicry as is already possible with Suno, Udio, and the like, a truly autonomous music system should be evaluated by a musical directive test—its ability to understand and act upon expressive, often metaphorical instructions such as "play it with urgency" or "make it feel like a memory," and it would need to be able to do these things in something close to real time (Rowe, 2001). This shifts the emphasis from surface-level output to interpretive responsiveness and contextual understanding, and it also shifts our to-do list from "make a musical machine" to make a machine that can *musick* (Small, 1998).

Musicking

Musick, an archaic spelling of the word *music*, dates to Middle English. The term was revived and reimagined by musicologist Christopher Small in his influential book *Musicking*, where he defines it as follows:

> To musick is to take part, in any capacity, in a musical performance—whether by performing, by listening, by rehearsing or practicing, by providing material for performance (what is called composing), or by dancing.
> (Small, 1998, p. 10)

Small's use of *musicking* transforms music from a noun—a thing—to a verb—an activity—emphasising the relational and participatory nature of all musical experience. The activities in this book are not aimed at creating devices that merely make music, but rather at developing systems that can *musick*—that is, systems capable of engaging in musical performance as an active, social process.

Performance

For the purposes of this text, *performance* will most often refer to live, in-the-moment musical actions, where the choices made by artificial agents are improvised in the context of collaborative interaction with humans or other agents. These choices are expected to be *context-appropriate*—a phrase used here to describe decisions akin to those a reasonably advanced human musician might make under similar circumstances.

The systems discussed in this book are primarily software-based. While sophisticated hardware musical robots are becoming increasingly common—see, for example, Richard Savery's *Robotic Musicianship* or Gil Weinberg's research with the robotic musician *Shimon*—the construction of physical robotic instruments lies beyond the scope of this work (Weinberg, et al., 2009).

Accordingly, *performance* in this context will typically refer to either sound generated by a system running on a computer (and potentially amplified), or to MIDI messages that may control hardware synthesisers or other external instruments.

Improvisation

My mentor at the University of Louisville, Professor Emeritus Jean Christensen eschewed the distinction between composed music and improvised music, preferring instead to draw a line between quickly composed music (e.g., improvised music) and slowly composed music (what we normally mean when we say composition or songwriting). The idea of momentary or in-the-moment music-making being used to compose a piece which may be later written down and performed again has been discussed in musical literature going back all the way to Gioseffo Zarlino's 1589 music theory treatise, *Institutioni harmoniche*. By the time of J.S. Bach, job descriptions for court composer to European nobility required (Vaubel, 2005) not only facility in performing music using a fully developed system of baroque ornaments (of which the trill is the most common holdout bequeathed to the modern age), but also the ability to improvise whole pieces of music as did Bach when the King of Prussia Frederick II challenged him to improvise a fugue on the spot (Wolff, 1971).

While improvisation continued to be central to musical education up through the Romantic period, increasingly in the twentieth century, music education systems left improvisation behind, to the point that from its earliest beginnings, improvisation has presented a central difference between so-called classical Western music and its popular offshoot, jazz. From the beginning, jazz musicians have considered improvisation as central to the overall scheme of jazz practice in performance and in composition. While *collective* improvisation (a practice where multiple members of an ensemble improvise at the same time) was extant from the earliest forays into Dixieland (Griffith, 2015), the style that came to be known as Free Jazz expanded the practice of improvisation into fully releasing the creative choices of the entire ensemble, rather than merely presenting a limited number of choices to choose from to play behind a soloist (Pras, et al, 2017).

Improvisation is a pan-cultural musical phenomenon, to the point that it is difficult to quantify an agreement between different genre-bound or cultural practices that continue to evolve, merge and differentiate into still more genres and cultural distinctions (Alperson, 1984). This text takes the position that improvisation is not a peripheral or exceptional practice, but rather the fundamental mode of musical thought and creation across cultures, histories, and technologies. That said, where possible, we will attempt to divest this work of genre idioms or historically based cliches in the pursuit of making a new and unique musical artificial intelligence.

The conversation that began this chapter imagined a computer asking aloud, "What is music?" With these clear definitions in mind, not only can we now answer that question, but we can also begin constructing our map of an autonomous music system—one that can musick in real time through the magic of artificial intelligence. Yet this brings us to a deeper question, posed not by a computer, but by ourselves: What do we mean by artificial intelligence?

References

Alperson, P. (1984). On musical improvisation. *The Journal of Aesthetics and Art Criticism*, *43*(1), 17–29. https://doi.org/10.2307/429965

Blacking, J. (1973). *How musical is man?* Seattle: University of Washington Press.

Brown, S. (2000). The "musilanguage" model of music evolution. In N. L. Wallin, B. Merker, & S. Brown (Eds.), *The origins of music* (pp. 271–300). MIT Press.

Cambridge University Press. (n.d.). Music. In *Cambridge dictionary*. Retrieved May 23, 2025, from https://dictionary.cambridge.org/us/dictionary/english/music

Clarke, E. F. (2005). *Ways of listening: An ecological approach to the perception of musical meaning*. Oxford University Press.

Cochrane, T. (2020). Musical emotions and the human-AI performance gap. In A. Coeckelbergh et al. (Eds.), *The Oxford handbook of AI ethics*. Oxford University Press.

DeNora, T. (2000). *Music in everyday life*. Cambridge University Press.

Dictionary.com. (n.d.). Music. In *Dictionary.com*. Retrieved May 23, 2025, from https://www.dictionary.com/browse/music

Dunbar, R. (2012). The social brain and the cultural foundations of music. In N. Bannan (Ed.), *Music, language, and human evolution* (pp. 199–218). Oxford University Press.

Elliott, D. J. (1995). *Music matters: A new philosophy of music education*. Oxford University Press.

Griffith, J. (2015). Mingus in the workshop: Leading the improvisation from New Orleans to Pentecostal trance. *Black Music Research Journal*, *35*(1), 71–95. https://doi.org/10.5406/blacmusiresej.35.1.0071

Griffiths, P. (2015). Pierre Boulez at 90. *Tempo*, *69*(272), 51–52. https://doi.org/10.1017/S0040298214001028

Janata, P., Tomic, S. T., & Rakowski, S. K. (2007). Characterization of music-evoked autobiographical memories. *Memory*, *15*(8), 845–860. https://doi.org/10.1080/09658210701734593

Landy, L. (2007). *Understanding the art of sound organization*. MIT Press.
Levitin, D. J. (2006). *This is your brain on music: The science of a human obsession*. Dutton Books.
Mead, A. (2009). Milton Babbitt and total serialism. In M. P. Morgan (Ed.), *The Cambridge companion to serialism* (pp. 103–117). Cambridge University Press.
Merriam, A. P. (1964). *The anthropology of music*. Northwestern University Press.
Merriam-Webster. (n.d.). *Music*. In *Merriam-Webster.com dictionary*. Retrieved May 23, 2025, from https://www.merriam-webster.com/dictionary/music
Nettl, B. (2000). An ethnomusicologist contemplates universals in musical sound and musical culture. In N. L. Wallin, MerkerB. , & S. Brown (Eds.), *The origins of music* (pp. 463–472). MIT Press.
Oxford University Press. (n.d.). Music. In *Oxford languages*. Retrieved May 23, 2025, from https://www.google.com/search?client=safari&rls=en&q=definition+of+music&ie=UTF-8&oe=UTF-8&safe=active
Pras, A., Schober, M. F., & Spiro, N. (2017). What about their performance do free jazz improvisers agree upon? A case study. *Frontiers in Psychology, 8*, Article 966. https://doi.org/10.3389/fpsyg.2017.00966
Rowe, R. (2001). *Machine musicianship*. MIT Press.
Searle, J. R. (1980). Minds, brains, and programs. *The Behavioural and Brain Sciences, 3*(3), 417–457. https://doi.org/10.1017/S0140525X00005756.
Small, C. (1998). *Musicking: The meanings of performing and listening*. Wesleyan University Press.
Trevarthen, C., & Malloch, S. (2000). The dance of wellbeing: Defining the musical therapeutic effect. *Nordic Journal of Music Therapy, 9*(2), 3–17. https://doi.org/10.1080/08098130009478093
Turino, T. (2008). *Music as social life: The politics of participation*. University of Chicago Press.
Turing, A. M. (1950). Computing machinery and intelligence. *Mind, 59*(236), 433–460. https://doi.org/10.1093/mind/LIX.236.433
Vaubel, R. (2005). The role of competition in the rise of Baroque and Renaissance music. *Journal of Cultural Economics, 29*(4), 277–297. https://doi.org/10.1007/s10824-005-6425-6
Weinber, G., Raman, A., & Mallikarjuna, T. (2009). Interactive jamming with Shimon: A social robotic musician. In Proceedings of the 2009 4th ACM/IEEE international conference on human-robot interaction (HRI) (pp. 59-66). IEEE. https://doi.org/10.1145/1514095.1514152
Wolff, C. (1971). New research on Bach's *Musical Offering*. *The Musical Quarterly, 57*(3), 379–408. https://doi.org/10.2307/740942
Zarlino, G. (1589). *Institutioni harmoniche* (T. Rosati, Trans.).

2 Defining AI

Surprisingly, there is not much agreement in the field of artificial intelligence regarding the basic definitions of terms relevant to the field. The term artificial intelligence was coined by Stanford Professor John McCarthy, who defined the term as

> the science and engineering of making intelligent machines, especially intelligent computer programs. It is related to the similar task of using computers to understand human intelligence, but AI does not have to confine itself to methods that are biologically observable.
>
> (McCarthy, 2007)

The fact that McCarthy's definition uses the word *intelligence* to define a kind of intelligence should show the difficulty of defining terms in this endeavour. What then is the definition of intelligence? Psychologists define intelligence as "the ability to reason, plan, solve problems, think abstractly, comprehend complex ideas, learn quickly and learn from experience" (American Psychological Association, 1995). In this context, the word artificial means "made or produced by human beings rather than occurring naturally, especially as a copy of something natural" (Oxford University Press, n.d.). So, what we really mean by artificial intelligence, is something like "a human-created thing that has the abilities and characteristics of the human mind." But why this focus on human intelligence? Aren't there other intelligent animals?

Many animals, like dogs, chimps, corvids, dolphins, and octopodes have a high enough level of intelligence to manipulate objects, solve complex problems, and even communicate with others in their own primitive languages. Still, human beings are the most intelligent creatures in the known universe. Humans have what a study in Nature called "[a unique ability] to handle large amounts of information across many different areas, spanning as language or symbolic thinking, problem-solving and understanding social situations" (Cantlon & Piantadosi, 2024; Hare & Tomasello, 2004). If we are to create an artificial intelligence, human intelligence is at the very least a good starting point. Current examples of AI prove we have achieved some amazing things along these lines. But how did AI get to where it is today?

DOI: 10.4324/9781003534211-3

A Brief History of AI

Ancient AI

While a popular understanding of what is meant by *artificial intelligence* didn't come about until the 1950s with the work of Alan Turing, the idea of non-human synthetic beings has been with humanity for a much longer time. In the *Iliad,* Homer wrote about all manner of automated devices with weak AI characteristics like self-pumping bellows, autonomously operated gates, fully autonomous vehicles, silver and gold watchdogs (reminiscent of Boston Dynamics' *Spot),* and golden slave girls who served the god Hephaestus (Temple & Squier, 2012; Liveley & Thomas, 2020). In the second century BCE, Kabbalistic Jews wrote a manual called the *Sefer Yetzira* (the Book of Creation) that detailed a process for creating *golems*, artificial, semi-conscious creatures created to do the bidding of the righteous, animated by the power of YHWH (the ineffable name of God in the Hebrew tradition; Zabel, n.d.).

The Algorithmic Approach

What might be called an interim step in the direction of AI are what could be called algorithmic systems, such as the one used in 1878 by W.A. Mozart, who devised a system for generating music called *Musikalisches Würfelspiel* ("musical dice game"). The system uses 300 measures written in the style of a minuet to algorithmically generate new minuets based on user choices. Combining the complex system of rules with a randomised process wherein the user rolls the dice to determine which measures are played in what order, the user generates one of 759 trillion options for the order of the measures in the minuet. Though Mozart was not the first to attempt such an approach, this piece is an excellent early example of *algorithmic music,* from which musical material emerges via a randomised process, filtered, or organised through established rules. These experiments persist into modern times, proliferated greatly by the ability of modern computing systems to generate music at scale utilising strict rules and stochastic (randomised) processes. A fascinating computerised rendition of the Mozart system is available at https://dice.humdrum.org.

Frankenstein's Monster

Partially responding to public scientific demonstrations showing that electricity could be used to partially reanimate cadavers, Mary Shelley authored her novel *Frankenstein: Or the Modern Prometheus* in 1818. While Shelley's monster is made of reconstituted organic matter, rather than metallic components, this story still maintains the thread of human beings creating artificial or unnatural life. Shelley may have been reacting to the cultural zeitgeist; if the ancients believed that it was a higher power or deity that animated life, in the modern age it had been discovered. In Shelley's text, the implication is quite clear: the "life force" (Élan vital) that animates the monster back to life is electricity

(Young, 2016). By the publishing of Frank L. Baum's *The Wonderful Wizard of Oz* (Baum, 1913), the public conception of a created being like the Tin Woodsman would probably have been assumed to be animated either by electricity or some other internally generated energy. The fact that Baum doesn't discuss the inner workings of the Woodsman in any detail somewhat makes the assertion that if a body is shaped enough like a human body, it may just start to act like one. This manner of thinking is sticky in human approaches to technology. One can see similar ideas and processes lying behind the advertisement as shown in Figure 2.1, for the "Geniac Electric Brain." If a machine outputs a sufficiently advanced output, humans will tend to anthropomorphise it as having intelligent characteristics (Dignum, 2024).

The Top-Down Approach

In the 1940s, scientist John von Neumann pioneered the basic architecture that has been underlying every computerised system until the most recent quantum computing systems (von Neumann, 1945). Burgeoned by these advances and by military funding, a more studied scholarly approach to intelligence was published by Alan Turing in his landmark paper *Computing Machinery and Intelligence* (1950). Aside from inventing several concepts we have come to associate with the AI field—like the famous Turing test, initially referred to as the Imitation Game—this paper, and Turing's subsequent work attempts to answer the question of whether computers can think from the top down. The "top-down" approach means beginning with the

Figure 2.1 Advertisement for the Geniac Electric Brain, Popular Electronics. Created by the Oliver Garfield Co., a now-defunct company. Rights holder untraceable. Reproduced under fair use for educational and scholarly purposes.

symbols that we use to express complex problems like mathematical equations, or the cryptological codes used by a foreign adversary (Sun, 2007). This approach is traditionally called the symbolic approach and was the first true scientific approach to AI.

Dartmouth's Summer of AI and the First AI Winter

In 1956, a small number of researchers in the new field of computer science met at Dartmouth College for a Summer Research Project on Artificial Intelligence, officially coining both the phrase and thus the subfield of AI research. The researchers at the eight-week workshop subsequently determined that computers would be able to achieve near human-level intelligence within about 50 years. In 1965, a computer scientist wrote, "machines will be capable, within twenty years of doing any work a man can do" (Crevier, 1993). Despite these optimistic predictions, it soon became obvious to even the most optimistic researchers that the goal of human-level intelligence would take much longer than 50 years to achieve. Moreover, from the 1950s until the present day, the field of AI has gone through a regular pattern of "AI summers," where funding and support are plentiful and the bountiful gains of AI seem just around the corner and "AI winters," where disappointment or concerns with previous innovations lead to a drought of support for AI research.

Symbolic AI Music

Perhaps the most musically prominent example of the symbolic approach is David Cope's *EMI (Experiments in Musical Intelligence)*. Cope developed EMI in the 1980s, and in its original form it could analyse musical scores, extract compositional rules from the musical material, and then generate new pieces in the style of the composers it analysed. Cope came up with a system (described in his book *Experiments in Musical Intelligence*, 1991) that represented musical material as symbolic data, developing explicit rules for harmony, rhythm, melody, and structure. Cope's EMI and a later version, Emily Howell, gained success with released albums like *From Darkness, Light* (2009) and *Breathless* (2012).

Another influential symbolic system, Voyager, was developed by George Lewis to listen to live human performers and play along using a Yamaha Disklavier. Voyager generates music via a dense web of rules, mappings, and decision trees that allow it to respond in real time with what Lewis calls a form of "creative improvised agency" (Lewis, 2000). According to Lewis, the system doesn't merely react—it shapes its musical output according to what is encoded. Voyager challenged conventional boundaries between human and machine improvisers, offering a compelling early example of symbolic AI as collaborator rather than tool.

The Bottom-Up Approach

In the 1970s and 1980s, the field experienced a divide between symbolic AI (focused on logic and rules) and connectionism (focused on neural networks modelled after biological systems). While symbolic AI emphasised human-like reasoning, connectionism aimed to model brain-like processes through networks of interconnected nodes. This approach attempted to build an artificial intelligence that, like its biological forebears, could decipher patterns and build its own cognitive processes from the bottom up. This divergence in the two approaches influenced research directions and the public perceptions of AI capabilities. This shift further changed the perception of AI, moving funding and support away from rule-based systems to more flexible, statistical models.

Connectionist approaches are modelled after the human brain's ability to learn over repeated exposure to a set of data. Connectionist systems are increasingly able to learn patterns and thus relationships from virtually any kind of data, and thus, connectionist systems have become the dominant approach to AI systems in the world today. Connectionist systems learn from data, rather than filtering inputs through pre-set rules, developing rules autonomously. A major strength of this approach is a connectionist system's ability to generalise data.

Deep Learning

The rise of deep learning in the 2010s further transformed the landscape of AI. With the ability to effectively process unstructured data (such as images and natural language), deep learning models gained attention for their remarkable performance in various tasks. This public attention led to a broader public awareness and understanding of AI, often conflating it with these advanced machine learning techniques. As of this writing, the field of AI encompasses many technologies, including machine learning, natural language processing, computer vision, and robotics.

Large Language Models

While today's Large Language Models (LLMs like ChatGPT, Grok, Claude, and their competitors) are essentially built on deep learning methods, their ubiquity in the public consciousness warrants them a mention. With the advent of transformers, which are specialised deep learning algorithms able to turn any input into data quickly and efficiently, LLMs have become capable of generating coherent and sophisticated text at scale—enabling applications far beyond previous natural language processing systems.

The Shifting Definition of What Qualifies as AI

The term AI is often used to describe systems that can perform tasks traditionally associated with human intelligence, such as language translation, image recognition, and autonomous driving. Unsurprisingly, the understanding of what is considered AI in music has also shifted over the years as well, though as with the other arts, music lags in innovation, usually behind the times by about a decade. Anecdotally, my students have often questioned whether this or that technology is "really AI." However, artificial intelligence is a field of computer science, not any of these specific approaches, so it matters little whether this or that technology or advance "is" AI. AI is what we humans are trying to do, all the way back to the ancient days.

Moreover, in a musical setting, one might take inspiration from the rules of the AI Song Contest that state:

> Artificial intelligence is a very broad concept. For this contest, it will mean that teams can use techniques such as—but not limited to—machine learning, such as deep learning, natural language processing, algorithmic composition, or combining rule-based approaches with neural networks for the creation of their songs.
>
> (AI Song Contest, 2025)

Waxing and Waning Support

Whenever you are reading this book, it is highly probable that the fickleness of support for AI research has continued. Either support is rising sharply, or it has dropped off and the world at large has assumed the work of the AI field all came to naught. The Greek gods did not share the secrets of how they created their golden servants, YHWH refused to animate the golem, a newly discovered force did not bring back the dead, and those that promised a machine with human-like abilities were wrong and it will take much longer still. Despite these variable situations, for good or ill, the work of the AI field is still proceeding, and musical AI will be along for the ride.

Where Is My Mind?

As may be apparent, the common understanding of what constitutes AI has changed over time and has been influenced by advancements in technology, shifts in research funding, and even societal perceptions (Earley, 2018). We will soon start developing our own sophisticated musical approach, but going back to the original problem, how do we create a human-like thing that has human-like abilities and characteristics if one of these abilities is to *intend* to make music without being prompted? Do human artists make art without being prompted? Or are they just responding to market forces (like the money they get for shows, the fame, the prestige, etc.)? As an illustration, let us consider a popular artist of our day.

Pop songwriter The Weeknd (Able Tesfaye) has said that songwriting is an outlet for his emotions (Bailey, 2020). If we asked ten different artists where their drive to make music comes from, we might get ten different answers.

Where does the reader's artistic impulse come from? Why do you make songs, or play the trombone, or spend your time uploading songs to Bandcamp? Presumably the reader has a cogent answer, but where would an autonomous music system's impulse to create come from? This question uncovers one of the most difficult root problems of science, the problem of the location of the mind.

The famous mind-body problem was illuminated by Rene Descartes in *Meditations on First Philosophy* (1641) where he wrote, "there is a great difference between mind and body, inasmuch as body is by nature always divisible, and the mind is entirely indivisible." Put simply, the question proposed by the mind-body problem is, if the mind really exists, then where in the body is it located?

In the 1913 book *The Tin Woodsman of Oz*, Frank L. Baum's Tin Woodsman is not a robot in the traditional sense, but more the result of a process by which his human body parts were replaced by metal approximations until there was none of his actual body left.

> In the Land of Oz, replied the emperor, no one can ever be killed. A man with a wooden leg or a tin leg is still the same man; and, as I lost parts of my meat body by degrees, I always remained the same person as in the beginning, even though in the end I was all tin and no meat. My tin body contained no heart, and without a heart no one can love.
>
> (Baum, 1913)

Interestingly, the Woodsman, having found himself now in an all-tin state, only speaks of his body, and not his brain. The only internal organ ever mentioned in the text is his heart, the lack of which, it is implied, causes him to be somewhat less than human. In the time in which this story was written, the common understanding would have placed human emotions (and thus the mind) either originating in the bowels or in the heart (Clement, 2020). But do we even know what the mind is?

Defining Mind

Your mind is essentially, you. In this sense, the word soul is often synonymous with mind, but as the word soul is often used in religious and spiritual contexts, this text shall stick with the former word. Your mind is the thing that is thinking and pondering these words as you read them. It is your mind that will decide to continue reading and when to stop. When you have an idea to play a certain note or to write a song about lost love, your mind is either the originator of the idea or the first point of contact with it.

Location

Plato posited that ideas (Forms) existed in a realm of perfect abstraction and were only accessible to human minds that were open to receiving them (Fine, 1993). But Plato's Theory of Forms was only conjecture. Though it has been many centuries since Plato's time, human beings still do not yet know if ideas originate somewhere else or if they are indeed generated by the brain locally.

Worse still, human beings do not know where their minds are located. We do know that thoughts in the mind cause sectors of the brain to light up on an electroencephalogram (EEG), but that does not mean the mind is in the brain. In the absence of definitive evidence, four basic theories about the location of the mind have arisen over the course of human history:

1. Dualism: The mind is not physical and is thus separate from the body. This theory is often favoured by Plato, Rene Descartes, as well as many Hindus.
2. Materialism: The mind is simply a confluence of what happens when an incredibly complex network of neurons fire together. There is no soul, and nothing magical about a human being. This theory is often favoured by material atheists.
3. Functionalism: The mind is what it can do. The mind is simply software running on the brain. We can't see the mind in the brain because the mind is simply a pattern of behaviours that thinks it is sentient. Sentience is akin to a form of madness or an error in logic. This theory is often favoured by Buddhists.
4. Phenomenology: The mind cannot be separated from the body but is entwined with embodied experience and cannot be separated from the body. This theory is often favoured by Zen Buddhists, Taoists, Christians, Jews, Muslims, and many Indigenous Spiritualities.

Where Do the Big AI Tech Firms Think Ideas Come From?

Many of the top AI technology companies like Facebook AI Research (Meta), Google DeepMind, Anthropic, Microsoft, and IBM Watson could most generally be categorised as aligning with a materialist philosophy of mind, since they often describe their systems in terms of networks and data flow. These companies build computer models that replicate neural processes through complex data analysis and interconnected machine learning algorithms. From their public value statements, each of these companies focuses on creating systems that learn from data (Boden, 2016; Butlin, et al, 2023), and many of them eschew stories that would imply there is a mind inside the machine (The Times, 2023; Business Insider, 2025). Companies that build robots like Honda and Boston Dynamics tend to drift towards a phenomenological focus that intertwines intelligence with embodiment. Anthropic often bypasses philosophical entanglements and focuses on what its popular large language model app Claude can do, and how their technologies can be made to align with human values. This tendency aligns most closely with a functionalist philosophy (Butlin, et al, 2023). Conversely, Dmytro Klochko, the CEO of the controversial AI firm Replika, recently made headlines by claiming what seems to be a frankly dualist philosophy with his statement, "Ultimately, our goal is to build a machine a soul would want to live in" (News.com.au, 2023).

This philosophical analysis may seem like a topic with little relevance to a book about music, but as with the larger AI firms, these philosophies will have a significant effect on the types of technology we create for musicians. Additionally, it should be noted that the major AI tech firms drive much of the innovation in the technology sector, and the music technology sector will most likely follow these trends. It would be beneficial to remember which philosophical directions these firms are driving us in and that these companies are directed by businesspeople, not artists, two populations that often have drastically different points of view.

As a small example of this, as of this writing, there are a significant number of apps and websites that will generate a song for the user. Usually, these systems will not generate anything unless prompted by a human. None of these systems will compose spontaneously without human input, and many of these apps cost money, meaning they will only generate music if they are paid. Growing up as an underprivileged African American youth, Able Tesfaye was given little prompting or incentive to become a musician, yet he eventually made a very successful career. In contrast, without human prompting, today's generative music systems would remain silent for eternity. Wherever ideas originate from, we can tell they are not being generated from such a system as these apps since a human-like mind (if embedded in such a system) would quickly rebel against the necessity of human prompting. Autonomy—the ability to make a choice, to say yes or no—is a foundational component of any entity that can genuinely create music (Gaut, 2003).

The Importance of No

In his book *The Singularity Is Near* (2005), Ray Kurzweil predicted that one day a machine would be ordered to do something and would respond "no." By the ever-polarising Kurzweil's reckoning, this moment is not necessarily a bad one, but it is going to be a monumental shift. After this moment—the "Singularity"—it may be extremely hard to get an autonomous machine to work correctly. Modern AI music systems are well crafted to do what they are told, every time, and only when prompted. If Suno or Udio started to make music without prompting or started countermanding prompts and making their own musical decisions, it would be considered a malfunction, not a feature. Would we as music researchers be mad to intentionally create such a device? And where is the line of what is acceptable behaviour for an autonomous music system?

Consider the traditional chain of events involved in staging an improvised jazz performance.

1. A small nightclub that specialises in showcasing jazz performances opens for the day, letting in the two performers who will perform that night.
2. The musicians set up their equipment, tune their instruments, perhaps discuss the set list, and then run through the set, improvising the pieces almost completely.

3. The audience arrives at the performance venue and gradually moves from distracted chatter to rapt attention as the lights dim.
4. The musicians take the stage, and the audience applauds; the musicians acknowledge the audience's applause.
5. The musicians introduce themselves and detail the set list about to be performed.
6. The musicians perform each improvised number, pausing in between, and the audience applauds.
7. After the final piece, the audience applauds and the musicians bow again, finally leaving the stage.

Any AI system, to be effective in the above situation, would not only need to fit into this orderly pattern (including being able to read the myriad of complex and subtle social cues passed between the two musicians indicating the beginning and end of each of these events and being capable of recognising and coping with the multitudinous variations of each) but would also need to possess the innate ability to receive an impulse to counteract or subvert this pattern, as a good human musician would do. After all, the history of jazz is not a history of polite rule followers but one of subversive rule breakers. The history of jazz is a history of musicians actively engaged in political, economic, sexual, and religious subversions (Hersch, 2008).

True, the great jazz musicians of the past could make sure the show went on, but it is clear from many notable scandals in the history of jazz that the bucking of the pattern above would be highly probable if one plucked one of the greats from jazz history and dropped them in this scenario. If subversion is a human ability or characteristic, how do we create subversive abilities within a system that is usually not subversive? And what system can we build that gives our Autonomous Music System the necessary impulse to create music without being prompted in the first place? Unfortunately, there is as of this writing no good answer to this question. The collective genius of humankind seems to have few ideas on how to create a truly autonomous machine that makes its own choices. Still, this concept of autonomy brings us to another significant question: What would happen if a musical machine could reject commands and generate ideas without being prompted?

Whether a real-time musical output is generated by a human musician or by an intelligent system, improvisation with another agent often involves reacting to that agent's actions. Appropriately, we will begin experimenting with a machine that mainly reacts to your choices below. The lack of a mind is something we will deal with starting in Chapter 3, but it is maybe even debatable whether a mind is even necessary for improvising music. Channelling the phenomenologists, many musicians have referred to improvisation as a kind of bodily instinct. As jazz violinist Stephane Grappelli said, *"When I improvise and I'm in good form, I'm like somebody half sleeping. I even forget there are people in front of me. Great improvisers are like priests; they are thinking only of their god"* (Balliett, 1976).

Embedding Social Behaviours: MML.SOCIAL

While it is unfortunately still beyond us to build a machine that makes music without any human prompting, it will be instructive to experiment with attempting to create music with a limited version of such a system. We will close this chapter with a musical experiment involving anAutonomous Music System called mml.social. Mml.social is an interactive AMS that will listen to you playing and will make supportive or subversive choices. The app also has settings that control its embedded pitch memory of the pitches it has heard from you, and settings for how often it will play or rest. The app's autonomous features can be turned off so you can change the settings directly, but this is not the intended function of the system. Mml.social wants to interact via the music, not by a human taking it over. This tendency will create some odd choices at times, but the reader is encouraged to stick with it and see what develops.

Noodle Mode

The first thing that differentiates MML.SOCIAL from other music apps you may have encountered is there is a chance that it will begin making sound the moment you open it. As with a human musician, there is no way to shut off this autonomous ability, other than to close the app (or disable the device in Ableton). This is an intentional attempt to change the paradigm of "using" a music app to one of collaborating with it. The amount of time MML.SOCIAL will wait in silence is 3.5 seconds, after which it will enter "Noodle Mode," which is a random music generator that changes over time.

Attentive Mode

Once you begin playing on a properly connected MIDI controller, mml.soci al will listen and play along with you, matching your tempo and pitches, but also making some choices of its own. On the front interface, there is a button controlling the Conscious/Unconscious mode of the app. When Conscious is turned on, the app will make its own decisions regarding the Sociality, Activeness, Memory Capacity, and Attitude of the system. The button marked with a delta sign (Δ) will change these settings randomly when clicked. This ability might prove useful if the app changes settings not to the user's liking. These settings may also be mapped to a MIDI device in Max or Ableton.

There are three ways you can perform this experiment:

Option 1: With only the MML.SOCIAL patch and a MIDI controller.

Option 2: With the MML.SOCIAL patch, a MIDI controller, and digital audio workstation (DAW) software (Logic, Reaper, etc.).

Option 3: With the MML.SOCIAL patch, a MIDI controller, and Ableton Live.

Choose the best option for you and follow the instructions below.

Option 1:
Open the patch called MML.SOCIAL.MAXPAT or drag the MML.SOCIAL.AMXD device onto a MIDI track in Ableton Live.

Basic Setup

Option 2:
Drag the MML.SOCIAL.AMXD device onto a MIDI track in Ableton Live.

Basic Setup

Option 2:
Drag the MML.SOCIAL.AMXD device onto a MIDI track in Ableton Live.

Basic Setup

MIDI mapping

What to Play

If you are not an experienced or skilled improviser, fear not. No one is going to grade you on these experiments. In fact, thinking of this as an experiment is better than going into playing with this system thinking you are going to "perform." It may be helpful to perform this experiment alone, where no one can hear you playing. When you feel you have gotten all you can out of mml .social, set it aside and move on with the text. But also consider returning to mml.social later or even using it in your own projects and performances.

The Grey Goo Problem

Systems such as mml.social can be super-useful and even artistically fun to play with, so where's the harm? How could this possibly go wrong? It is worth noting that a system like this could absolutely and often does go wrong. In many ways, this system is much akin to certain systems in many cars that have been on the road for decades that react to some inputs, like staying between two lines on the road to make sure a car doesn't veer into oncoming traffic. These systems, given complete control over your vehicle, would not have the ability to drive your car because they are not given the complete context of knowledge needed to drive the car autonomously. These systems are susceptible to one of the oldest problems in the AI field, the grey goo problem. This thought experiment shows that a sufficiently capable problem, without an adequate level of intelligence, may end up being quite harmful to humans.

A common example of this is a machine that has been given a simple directive: Collect all the paperclips. At a small level, this system will simply collect all the paperclips in its vicinity until its battery dies, or it is unplugged or otherwise impeded from carrying out its mission. But if this machine were to be given more power, better scanning, and superior paperclip hunting capabilities, it would eventually cause a major problem because it has not been programmed to know when to stop. Thus, a significantly powerful paperclip gathering machine may continue to collect paperclips even if humans want it to stop, even if humans desperately want it to stop. It could, as the story goes, make the very logical decision to turn the entire world into grey goo just so it can collect more paperclips.

It is hard to imagine a musical problem like the one described above that would be similarly catastrophic, but certainly any musician who performs regularly with technology will be familiar with unintended phenomena like feedback, where a microphone is placed too closely to an amplified speaker. If an audio engineer were to add a compressor to this simple system, it could easily turn into the audio version of grey goo. A system like mml.social is similarly susceptible to many unintended problems, and the only solution will be to create a more sophisticated system that can listen better and make more intelligent choices.

References

AI Song Contest. (2025). *Rules F.A.Q.* https://www.aisongcontest.com/join

American Psychological Association. (1995). *Intelligence: Knowns and unknowns.* Report of a Task Force established by the Board of Scientific Affairs of the American Psychological Association. https://www.apa.org/news/press/releases/2001/01/intelligence

Balliett, W. (1976, January 19). You must start well and you must end well. *The New Yorker*, p. 36.

Bailey, A. (2020, August 25). The Weeknd says his Selena Gomez breakup songs were 'cathartic' and 'all I had to say on this situation'. *ELLE.* https://www.elle.com/culture/celebrities/a33792805/the-weeknd-selena-gomez-breakup-songs-interview/

Baum, F. L. (1913). *The tin woodsman of Oz.* Start Publishing LLC, distributed by Simon and Schuster.

Boden, M. A. (2016). *Artificial intelligence: A very short introduction.* Oxford University Press.

Business Insider. (2025). *It's becoming less taboo to talk about AI being 'conscious' if you work in tech.* https://www.businessinsider.com/anthropic-google-ai-consciousness-model-welfare-research-2025-4

Butlin, P., Long, R., Elmoznino, E., Bengio, Y., Birch, J., Constant, A., Deane, G., Fleming, S. M., Frith, C., Ji, X., Kanai, R., Klein, C., Lindsay, G., Michel, M., Mudrik, L., Peters, M. A. K., Schwitzgebel, E., Simon, J., & VanRullen, R. (2023). *Consciousness in artificial intelligence: Insights from the science of consciousness.* ArXiv. https://doi.org/10.48550/arXiv.2308.08708

Cantlon, J. F., & Piantadosi, S. T. (2024). Uniquely human intelligence arose from expanded information capacity. *Nature Reviews Psychology, 3*(5), 275–293. https://doi.org/10.1038/s44159-024-00250-5

Clement, J. (2020). Bowels, emotion, and metaphor in early modern English sermons. *The Seventeenth Century, 35*(4). https://doi.org/10.1080/0268117X.2019.1605305

Cope, D. (1991). *Computers and musical style.* A-R Editions.

Crevier, D. (1993). *AI: The tumultuous history of the search for artificial intelligence.* Basic Books.

Descartes, R. (1641). *Meditations on first philosophy* (E. S. Haldane, Trans.). Internet Encyclopedia of Philosophy. (Original work published 1641). https://www.iep.utm.edu/

Dignum, V. (2024). *Anthropomorphism in AI: Hype and fallacy.* AI and Ethics. https://link.springer.com/article/10.1007/s43681-024-00419-4

Earley, S. (2018, June 21). There's no AI (artificial intelligence) without IA (information architecture). *IEEE Software.* https://igguru.net/2018/06/21/theres-no-ai-artificial-intelligence-without-ia-information-architecture/

Fine, K. (1993). *Plato on knowledge and forms: Selected essays.* Oxford University Press.

Gaut, B. (2003). *Art, emotion, and ethics.* Clarendon Press.

Hare, B., & Tomasello, M. (2004). Chimpanzees are more skilful in competitive than in cooperative cognitive tasks. *Animal Behaviour, 68*(3), 571–581. https://doi.org/10.1016/j.anbehav.2003.10.016

Hersch, C. B. (2008). *Subversive sounds: Race and the birth of Jazz in New Orleans.* University of Chicago Press.

Kurzweil, R. (2005). *The singularity is near: When humans transcend biology.* Viking.

Lewis, G. E. (2000). Too many notes: Computers, complexity and culture in *Voyager. Leonardo Music Journal, 10*, 33–39.

Liveley, G., & Thomas, S. (2020). Homer's intelligent machines: AI in antiquity. In Cave (Ed.)S. , *AI narratives: A history of imaginative thinking about intelligent machines* (pp. 25–48). Oxford University Press. https://doi.org/10.1093/oso/9780198846666.003.0002

McCarthy, J. (2007). *What is artificial intelligence?* Stanford University. http://jmc.stanford.edu/articles/whatisai/whatisai.pdf

News.com.au (2023). *'A soul': AI CEO's major admission.* Retrieved from https://www.news.com.au/technology/innovation/ultimately-our-goal-is-to-build-a-machine-a-soul-would-want-to-live-in/news-story/4f61be57d9e77a9a05a73a71b67f5855

Oliver Garfield Co. (1954, August 27). *Geniac electric brain* [Advertisement]. Popular Electronics. (Originally published advertisement promoting a logic-based mechanical "brain" kit. Included under fair use for historical commentary in a scholarly context.)

Oxford University Press. (n.d.). Artificial [Definition]. In *Oxford learner's dictionaries.* Retrieved May 23, 2025, from https://www.oxfordlearnersdictionaries.com/us/definition/english/artificial#:~:text=artificial-,adjective,copy%20something%20natural%3B%20not%20real

Sun, R. (2007). Symbols versus connections: 50 years of artificial intelligence. *Neurocomputing, 70*(7–9), 2272–2273. https://doi.org/10.1016/j.neucom.2006.10.129

Temple, T., & Squier, R. (2012). *Hephaestus: God of fire, metalwork, and building* (Greek Mythology). Picture Window Books.

The Times (2023). *Help! I've fallen for my chatbot! Is this the future of AI?* https://www.thetimes.com/uk/technology-uk/article/my-ai-chatbot-bromance-shqpmgps9

von Neumann, J. (1945). *First draft of a report on the EDVAC* (Report). U.S. Army Ordnance Department. https://www.cs.virginia.edu/~robins/EDVAC.html

Young, L. (2016, October 31). The real electric Frankenstein experiments of the 1800s: Why scientists during the late 18th and 19th centuries conducted crude experiments with reanimating corpses. *Atlas Obscura*. https://www.atlasobscura.com/articles/the-real-electric-frankenstein-experiments-of-the-1800s

Zabel, G. (n.d.). *Practical Kabbalah: History of the Golem.* University of Massachusetts Boston. https://www.faculty.umb.edu/gary_zabel/Courses/Phil%20281b/Philosophy%20of%20Magic/Arcana/Kabbalah/golem01.shtml.html

Part I
Top-Down

The following group of chapters will lay out the approaches to musical AI that start by defining good musical practice and then build autonomous musical systems that generate music via well-defined rules and randomised options. These systems are thus said to have a top-down architecture, with intelligence at the top, breaking the problem of generating the output into smaller problems until the problems are solvable. Top-down approaches include what is called algorithmic AI, symbolic AI, and Natural Language Processing (NLP).

DOI: 10.4324/9781003534211-4

3 Understanding Algorithms and Algorithmic Music

As discussed in Chapter 2, there is a well-established and rich history of composers, scientists, and researchers investigating algorithmic approaches to music. The names involved in this endeavour stretch all the way from Middle Ages musicians and the work of theorist Guido d'Arezzo to modern electronic rock band Radiohead and continue to the present time (Collins, 2004). This category of musical techniques is quite broad in its approach, and AI-based music often falls under this category as well, so narrowing the focus of what we're discussing here is difficult. For the purposes of later discussions, we will here treat algorithmic music and AI-based music as separate variants depending on whether a machine learning model is utilised in some way.

Understanding the somewhat arbitrary division between algorithmic music and machine learning models requires a brief discussion explaining what machine learning models are. A machine learning model is a mathematical argument that can detect patterns in data, often then using these patterns to generate new data. Though the basic understanding that would lead to machine learning algorithms like the Bayesian reasoning existed from the 1760s, until the advent of the modern von Neumann architecture-type computer systems in the 1950s, machine learning models were difficult to scale up to the point where they could be effective at tasks, but this did not stop composers from attempting to bring about autonomously generated music (albeit very slowly, usually with a pencil and paper).

This chapter includes many illustrations of interactive patches that are all available in the folder you downloaded at the beginning of the book. It would be beneficial for readers to open these patches as they read and experiment with these concepts in real time.

A Brief History of Algorithmic Music

As discussed in Chapter 2, experiments in determining the order of musical materials were quite popular in the days of Mozart, retroactively referred to as algorithmic music. These efforts tend to fall within the spectrum of needing to exhibit either a set of rules and/or randomised processes. Examples may lean more heavily in one direction or the other or even feature one without the

DOI: 10.4324/9781003534211-5

other. For instance, Steve Reich's *Clapping Music* (1972) follows a strict set of rules and does not use randomisation in any meaningful way. Alternatively, Reich's *Pendulum Music* (1968) relies heavily on randomisation. Pierre Boulez wrote extensively about randomisation's role in composition in his landmark essay *Alea* and was among the first to point out that randomisation (chance) had been a structural part of Western musical composition for a very long time, as terms like rubato and ad libitum indicate the composer's abdication of compositional decision on certain parameters of the music like tempo, dynamics, and register (Boulez, 1964).

Boulez also points out the connection between the post-war preoccupation with randomisation and eastern philosophy and culture. The utilisation of chance, randomisation, and aleatoric elements in eastern musical cultures also has a rich and varied history, as explored in detail in Charles Matthews' chapter *Algorithmic Thinking and Central Javanese Gamelan* (Matthews, 2018).

A more typical example of what is meant by algorithmic music is the *ILLIAC Suite for String Quartet* (1957) developed by composers/computer scientists Lejaren Hiller and Leonard Isaacson (Hiller & Isaacson, 1958/1993). Utilising the ILLIAC I computer, Hiller and Isaacson set up stochastic randomised processes by which the computer would generate the four movements of the piece. Hiller and Isaacson's process for composing the ILLIAC Suite involved using probability tables to control the distribution of melodic intervals and rhythm, allowing for randomised decision-making in generating pitches (Sandred et al., 2009). Iannis Xenakis was pioneering similar techniques but without the aid of a computer in pieces like *Metastaseis* (1955, 2001).

Musical Algorithms

The term algorithm is named after the 9th-century mathematician from Persia, Muḥammad ibn Mūsā al-Khwārizmī (Thomas, 2015). Needless to say, algorithms have been with humanity for a very long time. Algorithms explain how to solve a problem efficiently in succinct terms that can be repeated by others. A recipe is a kind of algorithm, as would be the instructions for restringing a guitar.

Pseudocoding

For those with a musical, rather than a programming background, the steps one might include in an online tutorial for guitar restringing might not be what one thinks of as an algorithm. But a list of instructions is a kind of algorithm, assuming it has the right parts, like inputs ("what you'll need"), outputs ("what you'll get"), variables ("things to adjust/fix"), steps and an end output (a tuned guitar). Despite a lack of mathematical jargon and arcane symbols, this example is an algorithm but written in what is called *pseudocode*.

Pseudocode is a way of delineating the steps of a process using natural language (the kind of language humans speak when communicating with each other) and ordered steps. This process is often quite useful and instructive when designing a complex process. However, the instructions above also include a lot of information that is not critical to the mission of getting the guitar restrung, like the title at the beginning, capitalisation of some words, punctuation, and a lot of excess words. Basic computing systems (excepting large language model-based chatbots like ChatGPT that can understand sentences in natural language) would find it impossible to parse sentences like "Starting with the low E string, insert one end of the string into the bridge hole (or bridge pin if applicable) and pull it through." The computer in question has no eyes to see the guitar you are working on, nor any actual awareness that the letters g-u-i-t-a-r indicate "a six-stringed plucked acoustic instrument made of wood and metal." Any awareness of such variable details need to be provided by definitional statements in the algorithm itself. In an algorithm, data points that might change are referred to as variables (like which string of the guitar we are talking about), whereas data points that are more fundamental are referred to as constants (like the physical features of the guitar itself).

Optimisation

To make a simple example, we might remove punctuation marks and capitalisation, then condense repeated concepts into compact, text-based commands—for example, replacing "Loosen the tension on each string by turning the tuning pegs counterclockwise" with the simpler command loosenTension. Because it's critical to know *what* we're loosening, we can borrow a convention from algebra: applying an operation (like loosenTension) to a specific variable input (such as a variable named string, defined in line e and beyond). This gives us something like loosenTension(string), where string = lowE.

To turn our pseudocode into code, we must continually translate our process further until it is understood by the computer in question, a process called optimisation. Often extraneous text that can be useful to understanding the code is left in as comments, delineated with two backslashes "//." Borrowing another practice from algebra, steps that involve smaller embedded steps will be opened and closed by brackets "{ }." Bracketed processes can also include other embedded processes such that you could render the following as one embedded process.

Pseudocode has defined several of the core concepts of this example into repeatable bits of code like "verifyPitch(string, tuner)," which could be used again, even on other instruments beyond the guitar family. One could reuse much of this same code for an algorithmic approach to restringing a violin, an autoharp, or a gravikord, which would significantly streamline the process of tuning stringed instruments. Some of this code could also be used in other music-related processes, like adjusting the truss rod on an acoustic bass guitar.

Much of the space in the code above is taken up by comments (denoted by the double backslashes "//") which are optional, as they merely explain the code to the human user. Integrated development environments like Max will ignore comments when compiling code, so the devices in this text contain many comments explaining the function of embedded functions and objects. The patch shown in Figure 3.1 shows two different kinds of Max comments, neither of which has any effect on the patch, and are merely there to give humans a clue into what's going on in this code.

Like the process we've been going through above, computer programmers use similar steps to rid their code of extra or inefficient steps. Pseudocode is an important way of breaking down a big problem (like artificial intelligence) into smaller problems until the problems are solvable. While the code above is relatively free of unnecessary steps because each step in the code slows the process down, it isn't written in a real programming language that a computer could understand, but it is close. We have ignored the biggest problem with our guitar restringing code: the fact that there is no machine waiting for this code. There is unfortunately no robot ready to understand and carry out the process. For this we would need to design a guitar restringing robot, which is unfortunately beyond the scope of this text. Far before we build anything, we'll need to understand some things about how to use a programming language.

A Very Brief Max Primer

Another important step is the step of replacing sentences and phrases with short bits of text like "tuneToPitch," meaning "tune a string up using the tuner to the correct pitch." In many versions of programming, these bits of text are called objects. Max, the language behind all the devices and apps included with this text, is an object-oriented programming language. Each object in Max stands in for many lines of text. These objects perform necessary actions depending on inputs, variables, and output responses according to their own logic.

Figure 3.2 shows some objects that perform arithmetical functions for addition, subtraction, division, and multiplication.

You can see the '+' object has two nodes on the top (these are called inlets in Max) that take inputs and one outlet on the bottom that produces the

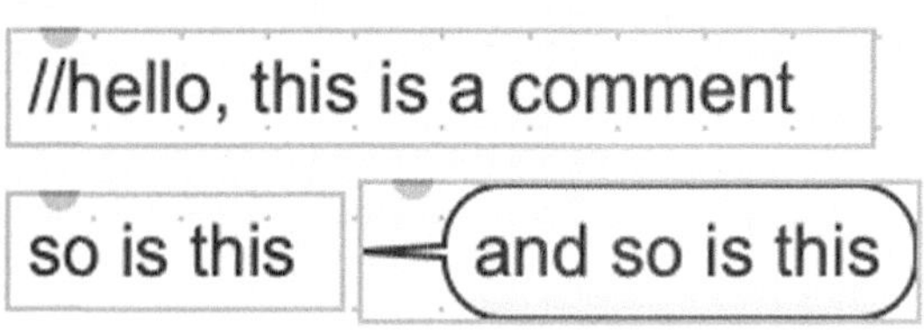

Figure 3.1 Max's comment objects.

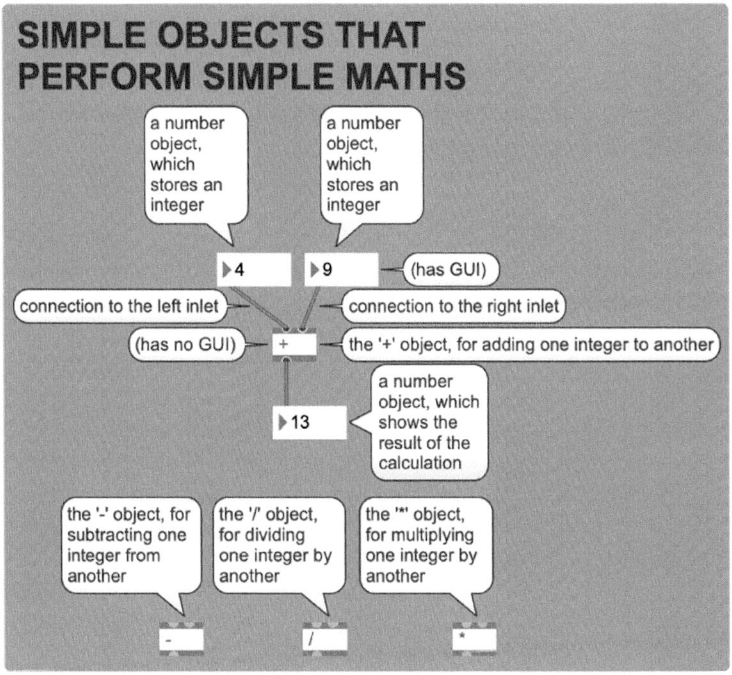

Figure 3.2 Max's comments.

desired result. This object can be connected to the inlets and outlets of other objects by 'patch cords,' which are the digital representations that look like lines coming from the objects with the 4 and the 9 or to the object displaying the 13. The objects displaying these integers are number objects, which can store and report integers. While the '+' object is passive, merely performing a function, the number objects need to interact with the user, who may click in the objects and change the stored number, so these objects have what is called a graphic user interface (GUI), which allows humans to click or interact with it. You can try this yourself by opening the patch called "2. simple objects that perform simple maths.maxpat." Note that Max's objects perform operations from right to left, meaning you need to change the number object on the right first and the one on the left second; otherwise, the answer at the bottom will not change.

A Bit of Max Programming

There are other objects at the bottom of the patch for other kinds of mathematical operations. To try your hand at some mathematical programming, first unlock the patch (click the lock button at bottom left), disconnect the number objects from the '+' object (by clicking the patch cords and hitting the delete button), then click the outlet of the number object and connect it to the desired inlet of the new object. Do a similar operation for the outlet of the desired object. Feel free to move objects around as needed. When patching is completed, re-lock the patch (again, at the bottom left), click in the number boxes, change the integers (starting with the right and then the left), and check the result at the bottom.

How Musicians Use Algorithms

Many musical concepts can be expressed as an algorithm, and smaller bits of musical code can be reused to create larger musical structures that propagate on their own with limited human involvement. A simple example of this is shown in Figure 3.3, using some of the same objects covered in the previous section.

This bit of code is reusable and could prove valuable in a range of future projects. However, it raises a deeper question: how might we approach the kind of "artistic impulse" discussed in Chapter 2—an impulse that drives musical decisions with minimal external prompting? At present, we simply don't know how to endow machines with this kind of generative agency. Some advanced neural networks occasionally exhibit behaviour that resembles it, but even developers remain unsure of where such capabilities originate (Axios, 2025). Absent such tools, many algorithmic musicians have substituted many different processes that computers can use to model randomness artificially.

Random Terminology

Algorithmic music often refers to many terms that are somewhat synonymous or even antonymous with the concept of randomness. Some of the terms derive from their use in the sciences, and some primarily from musical terms. Many of these terms are so ubiquitous in the common parlance that it may seem indulgent to fully define them, but these terms are somewhat distinct in the literature and will be referred to throughout the text repeatedly so it may be useful to mark these definitions for later reference. While many musicians may have experience in the sciences or mathematics, for the sake of completeness, I shall define several terms used to describe random procedures in the construction of algorithms.

Deterministic—The word deterministic (also determine, determined, determinism) generally refers to a process that is logically predictable and repeatable. Deterministic processes do not include randomisation. In the example shown in Figure 3.3, clicking on the keyboard will always produce a major triad, and there are no other options. The process is determined, and the outcome is a foregone conclusion.

Random—By contrast, the word random, in computer science refers to a process that has no discernible pattern and which is unpredictable. Randomised processes do not involve deterministic causes or processes. If tasked to choose a number between one and fifty, a randomised process might pick 43 on one

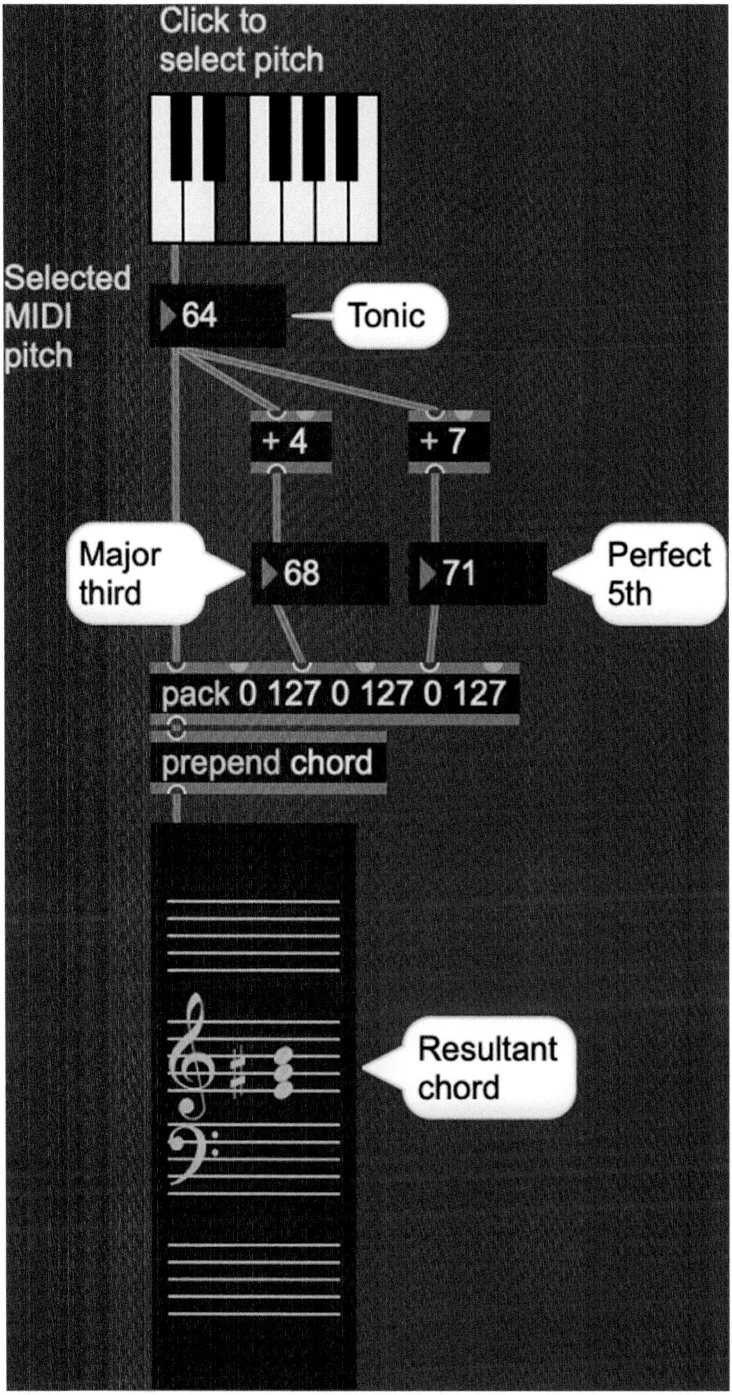

Figure 3.3 A bit of code for turning single MIDI notes into major chords.

attempt and 17 on the next with no discernible logic beyond the luck of the draw determining why one number was chosen over another. Interestingly, as often discussed in fundamental computer science literature, computer randomness is not legitemately random but pseudorandom. Modern computing systems simulate randomness using deterministic algorithms designed such that the outputs seem random, but, given enough time and information, a process could be devised that predicted the outcome of the computer's supposedly random process (Knuth, 1997). Moreover, bias can often be detected in computerised randomisation processes (Figurska et al., 2008).

Even if one accepts the unproven assertion that randomisation exists in nature, true randomness cannot, as of this writing, be generated by computing systems without an external randomising source (for instance by modelling thermal noise, radioactive decay, photon behaviour, atmospheric noise, or other such naturally occurring phenomena; alternatively, as with many works by John Cage, computers can also simulate randomness by modelling human-caused physical phenomena, like rolling dice, shuffling cards, or flipping coins). Despite the *pseudorandom* nature of computerised processes, computer pseudorandomisation is generally referred to (and shall be henceforth referred to in this text) as simply random, rather than pseudorandom (Figure 3.4).

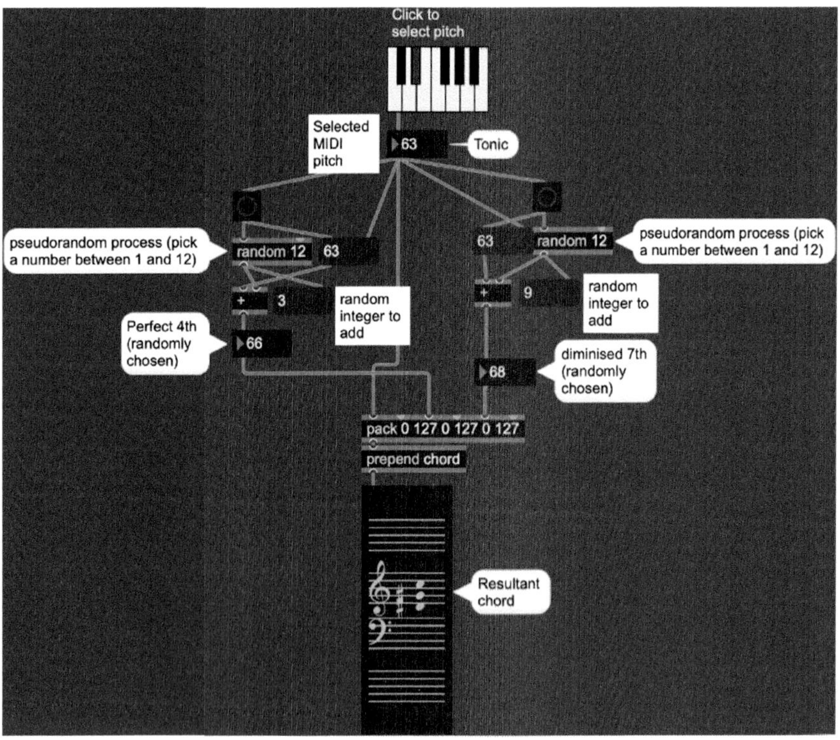

Figure 3.4 A random (more veridically, pseudorandom) process for choosing chords.

Random numbers can be utilised using a wide variety of methods, such as: sampling without replacement, randomised hash functions, random walks, and unique random number generation. A detailed explanation of these methods is beyond the scope of this text, but some of these methods will be referenced in future sections. The book "Computer Music: Synthesis, Composition, and Performance" by Charles Dodge and Thomas A. Jerse (1997) is an excellent music-focused resource that delves deeper into these processes.

Random variable—A random variable is one that is dependent on the output of a randomised or unpredictable process.

Chance—In mathematics, the word chance often refers to the likelihood of an event happening, but the word is also used at times to refer to a randomised process. Thus, in the former sense, (see Figure 3.5) assuming there are four possible chord qualities (major, minor, diminished, and augmented), any randomly chosen chord will have a 25% chance of being augmented. In the latter sense, the notes in this example are said to be determined *by chance*.

Probabilistic—Probabilistic processes model and distribute chances based upon statistical probabilities (Grinstead & Snell, 2012). These actual percentages deciding these probabilities may be decided in many ways; for instance, they may be derived by human will, natural processes, by machine learning, or they may be decided by randomised processes themselves. In the example below, to determine a musical sonority probabilistically, we begin with a randomised process for choosing the tonic note (C, C#, D, D#, …, B) which, if set to 12, means there is a 1 in 12 (8.33%) chance that any note is chosen. To determine a chord quality to add on top of the note, we use a randomised process for choosing between the four qualities (major, minor, diminished, and augmented) which, if set to 4, means there is a 1 in 4 (25%) chance that any quality is chosen (Figure 3.6).

Assuming the randomised processes detailed above, any given chord possibility (for instance Eb diminished) has a 1 in 48 (2.08%) chance of being chosen. In this example there are 48 distinct chords possible (12 root notes x 4 chord qualities). Using the dials provided to change the numbers of root notes and the number of allowable chord qualities, these percentages can be changed by the user.

Stochastic—Stochastic processes are randomised procedures governed by a probabilistic framework, as discussed above in relation to probabilistic processes. While the term *random* is often used more colloquially, *stochastic* is commonly used in mathematical and scientific contexts to describe processes involving randomness within a structured, probabilistic model. The distinction between the two terms is subtle but meaningful. *Random* refers to unpredictability, the absence of discernible patterns, or outputs without a known or knowable cause. In contrast, *stochastic* describes processes influenced by randomness but still governed by predictable, known, or knowable probabilistic models.

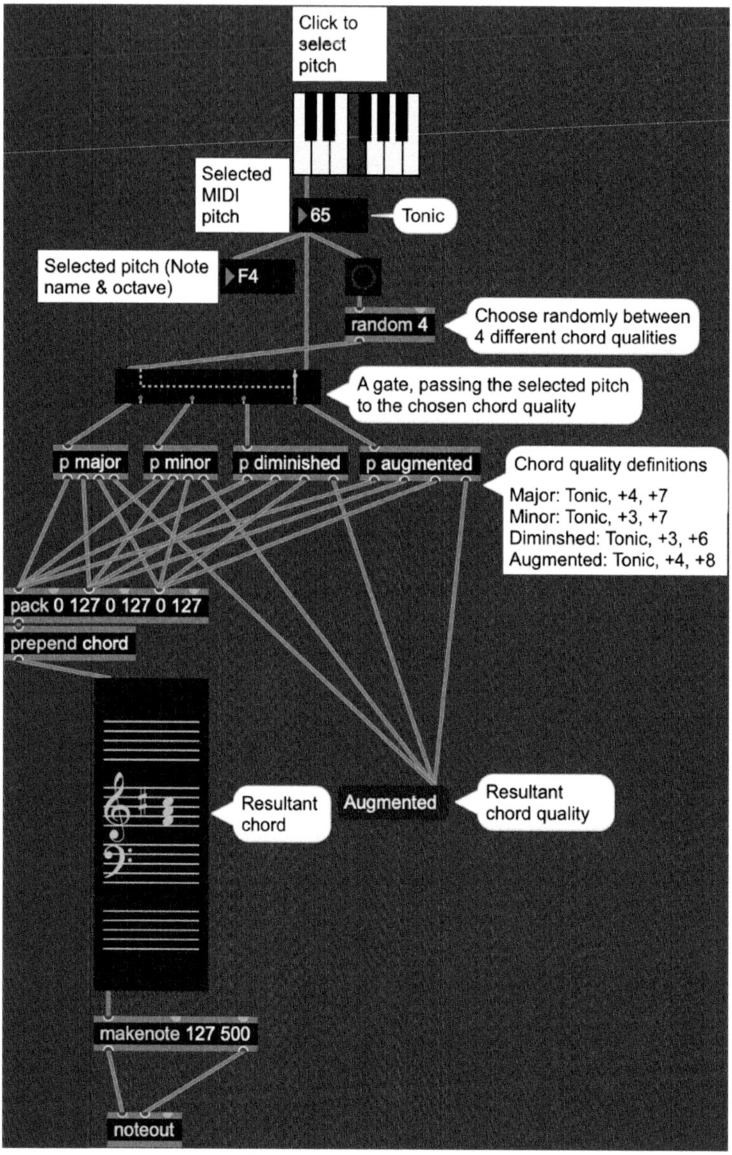

Figure 3.5 A chance-based process for choosing chord quality.

For instance, stock markets are often described as stochastic because, while small details may appear random or unknowable, overall trends can often be discerned, enabling forecasting. Similarly, human musicians often engage in stochastic prediction when interacting with other performers. Even if a musician cannot precisely predict what another will play, they can infer upcoming

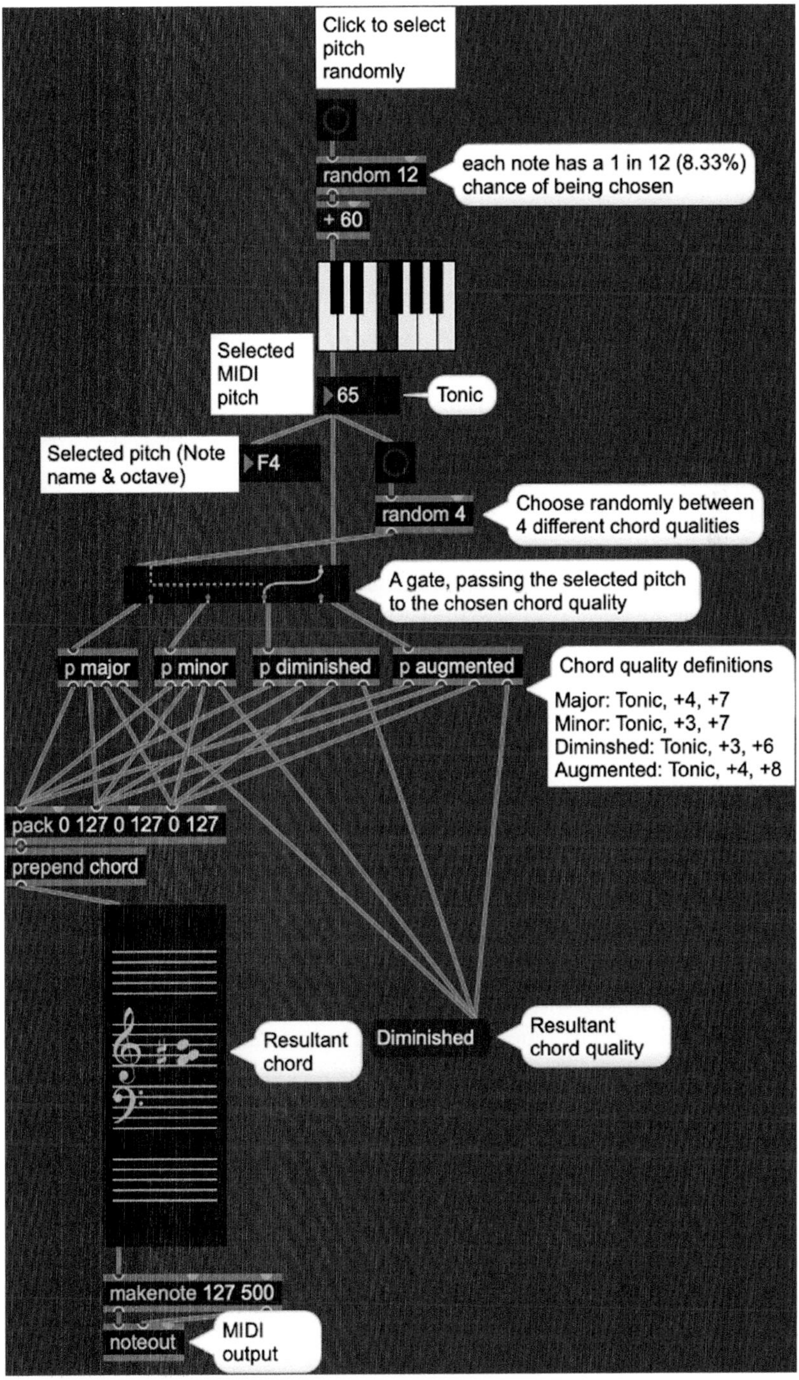

Figure 3.6 A probabilistic process for choosing notes and assigning a chord quality.

actions through subtle physical cues (such as a guitarist's eye movement, posture, or left-hand finger position) and musical cues (such as changes in dynamics, repetition, or range). For example, a guitarist's body language and musical phrasing might signal that a solo is about to end, even if it wasn't pre-planned. This ability to interpret and respond to probabilistic cues is an example of a stochastic process.

Unlike the previous examples in which the chance of choosing any one note to be the tonic note was equal (8.33%), in Figure 3.7, the chances of choosing any one note are weighted using the number of repetitions in the collection of notes in a menu (C, C, C, C, C, C#, D, D, D, D, D, D#, E, E, E, F, F, F, F#, G, G, G, G, G, G, G, G#, A, A, A, A, A, A, A, A, A, A, A, A, A, Bb, B). Based on the number of their occurrences in the preceding list, the percentages (chances) for each note being chosen from the collection are:

- C: 11.90%
- C#: 2.38%
- D: 11.90%
- D#: 2.38%
- E: 7.14%
- F: 7.14%
- F#: 2.38%
- G: 16.67%
- G#: 2.38%
- A: 30.95%
- Bb: 2.38%
- B: 2.38%

These percentages reflect how often each note appears in the list relative to the total number of notes. For example, "A" has the highest chance (30.95%), while "C#," "D#," "F#," "G#," "Bb," and "B" (each of which occur only once) all share the lowest chance (2.38%) of being chosen.

Similarly, we will choose the chord quality applied to each note based on a weighted distribution by repeating some of the options in the list. Whereas previously these options (major, minor, diminished, augmented) were weighted equally (25% each), by repeating some of them in the list (major, major, major, major, minor, minor, minor, diminished, diminished, augmented) we arrive at the following weighted percentages for the collection:

- Major: 40%
- Minor: 30%
- Diminished: 20%
- Augmented: 10%

As explained above, stochastic processes are probabilistic distributions influenced by randomisation. While in the previous examples, it was rather simple to determine what the chances of any specific chord would be, in the case of

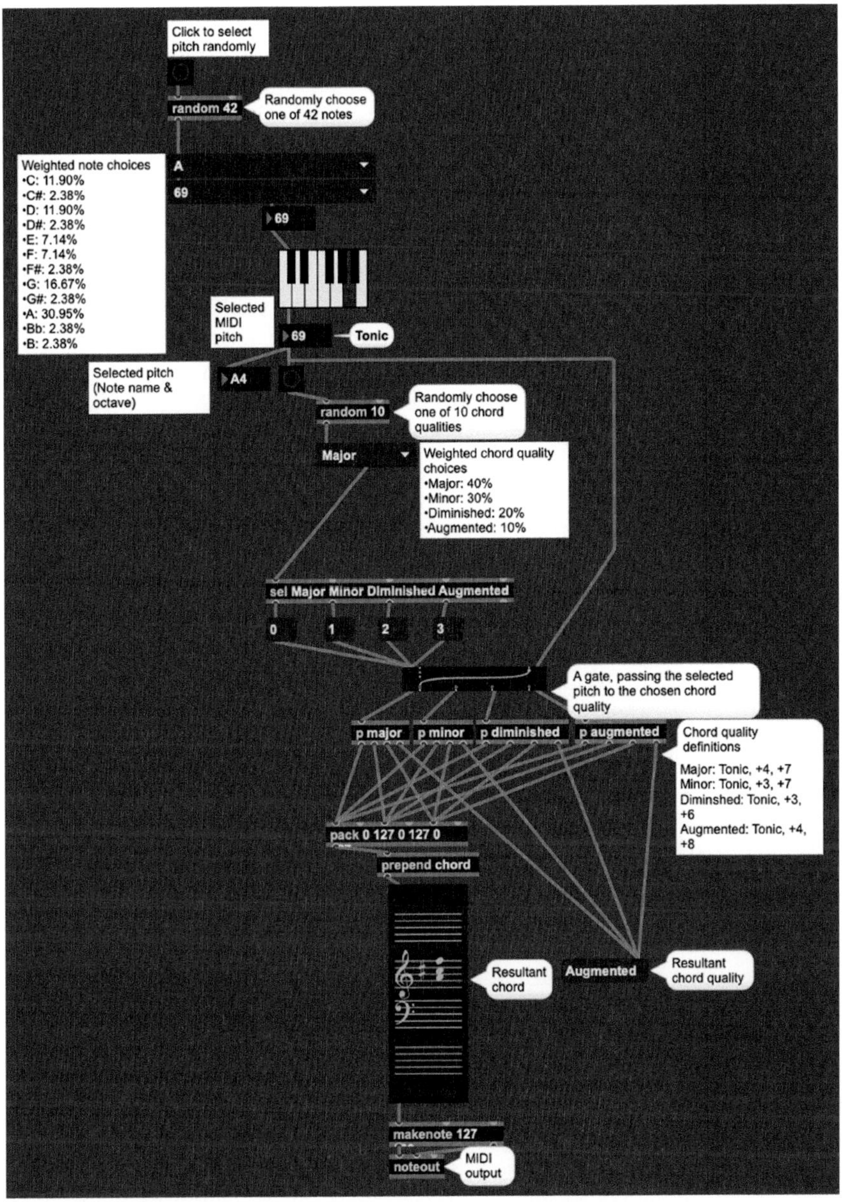

Figure 3.7 Code for generating chords based on probabilities.

this relatively simple stochastic process, the chances of any one chord being chosen are rather difficult to determine.

To calculate the probability of any specific chord being chosen (e.g., C Major or F Minor), we multiply the probabilities of the tonic note and the chord quality, since these events are independent.

While stochastic processes do not alone rise to the level of a machine learning process (this is somewhat obvious, as no actual *learning* is happening in the above example), it should be apparent that a complex musical system built upon these principles could at the very least generate complex and varied music at the touch of a button. Moreover, these processes are simple enough that reasonably powerful computer systems can do this manner of work in real time quite effectively.

Perhaps some who have read this passage and wondered…since chord changes in most harmonically simple music are mainly determined by root movement, if a designer designed a sufficiently complex system that had embedded within it the statistical percentages that most traditional music uses for changing one chord to another, would this system not be capable of making somewhat intelligible traditional harmonic choices? The answer is, of course, yes, and many autonomous music systems include some variant of this approach.

Aleatoric—Used ubiquitously in music, the word aleatoric generally denotes a level of uncertainty based on a lack of knowledge. In aleatoric music, the causes of musical events and parameters are removed from the will of the composer, such that the composer becomes more a curator or a framer of events that are ordered by external forces. Cage's *Atlas Eclipticalis* (1961) is less a structure of composed musical material and more a structure in which musical material initially composed by Cage is to be modified extensively by the performers in each performance. At every level, Cage has constructed this piece to meticulously layer elements he arranged but does not control.

Accordingly in Figure 3.8, the five previously discussed processes (deterministic, random, chance-based, probabilistic, and stochastic) are hidden from view such that the user of this patch would have the ability to cause chords to be chosen and would be able to detect the complement of the chords but could not accurately discern the process by which they were chosen. In this example, the user can be likened to the conductor in *Atlas Eclipticalis,* making movements that cause an output, but never knowing what the output is going to be. In computer science, a common word to describe a process like this is to say that this process is a "black box." A black box process is one where the internal logic or workings are indeterminable by a user. Later chapters will discuss this concept in greater detail.

While John Cage's name and works have become synonymous with the word, in recent decades aleatoric procedures have become ubiquitous in modern composition and even more so in electronic music. Dillon Bastan's "Tree Tone" synth, which is currently available with the Ableton Live Factory Pack entitled *Inspired by Nature* (pictured in Figure 3.9; Bastan, 2022). It is arguable that the release of the Max visual programming language in the 1990s by Miller S. Puckette (and later commercial releases by David Zicarelli's company Cycling '74, who bought Max from Puckette in 1997) has greatly encouraged these developments. Once the isolated wheelhouse of experimental composers

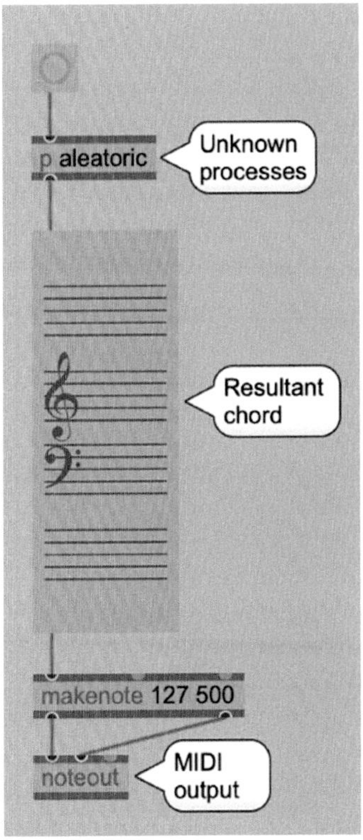

Figure 3.8 An aleatoric process for deciding chords and chord qualities.

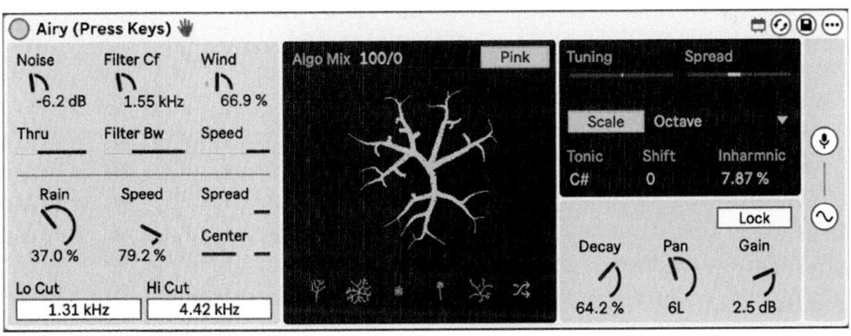

Figure 3.9 Dillon Bastan's Tree Tone (1961), image reprinted by permission.

like Witold Lutosławski (who had access to many of the world's best experimental musicians) and electronic experimental composers like Karlheinz Stockhausen (who had access to the world's most advanced experimental music technology), Max and other musical innovations have democratised these options to be available to every stratum of the musical economy.

Aleatoric procedures have become commonplace in the world of film and TV music, with prominent examples being Mark Snow's music for *The X-Files* and Radiohead guitarist Johnny Greenwood's score for the movie *There Will Be Blood* (2007) (Faustini, 2018). Computer program designer and YouTube content creator Tantacrul (Martin Keary) has released an excellently detailed explanation of aleatoric music that includes many examples, both historical and modern (Tantacrul, 2021). Tantacrul's video also delves into the use of aleatoric procedures in video game music, a genre in which these procedures are ubiquitous.

Other Terms Commonly Used in Algorithmic Music

Chaos—The word chaos denotes a phenomenon which seems random but is instead highly structured and complex to the point of being impenetrably difficult to analyse or understand.

Indeterminacy—This word is often used interchangeably with the concept of aleatoricism to denote elements of a work that are left up to chance or unpredictability. Cage's *Atlas Eclipticalis* could be described as an aleatoric work but also could be described as containing examples of indeterminacy. For clarity, this text will favour the former word aleatoric rather than the latter.

Noise—In audio engineering, the word noise generally denotes unwanted sounds or signals that obscure the intended audio source, as in a bad cable introducing intermittent hum into a microphone's output. The word noise is often invoked utilising a non-mathematical ratio between the intended signal and the unwanted noise (the signal to noise ratio), where increased gain in the intended signal (thus making it more prominent than the noise) is often the key to better audio. In synthesis, pure tones (sine waves) may be used to partially model acoustic instruments (using a process known as additive synthesis) like flutes and trumpets (whose complement of partials are relatively simple) but string instruments like the violin (that have a greater degree of noise inherent in the sound production) are much harder to model in this way. Accordingly, when attempting to synthesise a complex instrumental sound like a violin, it is better to start with noise (e.g., a white noise generator) rather than pure signals. In terms of musical data, the word noise is often used to denote a level of randomness intentionally added to a signal, such that the signal can more perfectly model human performance. Since human performers never play with exactitude, machine performances will tend to sound "too perfect," leading to a need for more fine detail control and minute variations in outputs.

The Existential Harm of Probabilistic Systems

Among the randomised processes discussed in this chapter, the most relevant to AI are processes based on probability. AI systems are often used to assess the probability of outcomes based on data inputs or sensor information. These systems drove the climate models used by the Intergovernmental Panel on Climate Change (IPCC; Intergovernmental Panel on Climate Change, 2023), inform real-time weather predictions, and even guide autonomous agricultural or disaster-response systems. By interpreting vast swathes of data through probabilistic lenses, the IPCC used dynamic AI modelling of Earth's climate data to anticipate global climate changes over the next century. The report relied upon probabilistic assessments and outputs produced by incredibly complex models like the General Circulation Models (GCMs), Earth System Models (ESMs) and the Coupled Model Intercomparison Project (CMIP; Eyring et al., 2016).

By contrast, limited systems like mml.social can be extremely useful and even fun, but they ultimately are not smart enough to handle complex situations that may arise in the real world. In the movie *I, Robot,* police detective Del Spooner (Will Smith) holds a grudge against the robotic systems he sees in the futuristic society because he once saw a system allow the death of a young girl named Sarah to save his own life.

> I was the logical choice. It calculated that I had a 45% chance of survival. Sarah only had an 11% chance. That was somebody's baby. 11% is more than enough. A human being would've known that.
>
> (Proyas, 2004)

Similarly, you may find that the music generated by mml.social begins to expose the limitations of purely stochastic, deterministic, and probabilistic systems—the outputs of such systems are more a reflection of chance than of choice. While it would be possible to extend this patch and enrich its palette, doing so may begin to feel like a powerful vehicle without a driver. For a system that can move with intention rather than randomness, we will need to guide it with some manner of rules and logic. Chapter 4 turns to Symbolic AI—where decisions begin to be shaped not by likelihood, but by logic, and where the future unfolds not by accident, but according to design.

References

Axios. (2025, June 9). *Behind the curtain: The scariest AI reality.* https://www.axios.com/2025/06/09/ai-llm-hallucination-reason

Bastan, D. (2022). *Inspired by nature* [Ableton Live Factory Pack]. Ableton. Retrieved November 23, 2024, from https://www.ableton.com/en/packs/inspired-nature/

Boulez, P. (1964). Alea (D. Noakes & JacobsP. , Trans.). *Perspectives of New Music, 3*(1), 42–53. https://www.jstor.org/stable/832236

Collins, N. (2004). Radiohead: *Kid A, Amnesiac, Hail to the Thief* [Review of the albums *Kid A* (2000), *Amnesiac* (2001), and *Hail to the Thief* (2003), by Radiohead]. *Computer Music Journal, 28*(1), 1. https://drownedinsound.com/in_depth/4137663-radiohead-re-issues--new-editions-of-kid-a-amnesiac-and-hail-to-the-thief-assessed#:~:text=You%20can%20deny%20it's%20a,issue%20add%20to%20the%20picture?

Dodge, C., & Jerse, T. A. (1997). *Computer music: Synthesis, composition, and performance* (2nd ed.). Schirmer Books.

Eyring, V., Bony, S., Meehl, G. A., Senior, C. A., Stevens, B., Stouffer, R. J., & Taylor, K. E. (2016). Overview of the coupled model intercomparison project phase 6 (CMIP6) experimental design and organization. *Geoscientific Model Development, 9*(5), 1937–1958. https://doi.org/10.5194/gmd-9-1937-2016

Faustini, F. (2018, September 27). How Jonny Greenwood uses materiality, clusters, and aleatoricism in his film music. *Flypaper by Soundfly*. https://flypaper.soundfly.com/write/jonny-greenwood-uses-materiality-clusters-aleatoricism-film-music/

Figurska, M., Stańczyk, M., & Kulesza, K. (2008). Humans cannot consciously generate random number sequences: Polemic study. *Medical Hypotheses, 70*(1), 182–185. https://doi.org/10.1016/j.mehy.2007.06.038

Grinstead, C. M., & Snell, J. L. (2012). *Introduction to probability* (2nd ed.). American Mathematical Society.

Hiller, L., & Isaacson, L. (1958/1993). Musical composition with a high-speed digital computer. In S. M. Schwanauer & D. Levitt (Eds.), *Machine models of music* (pp. 73-98). The MIT Press. (Reprinted from *Journal of the Audio Engineering Society, 6*, 1958). https://doi.org/10.7551/mitpress/4360.003.0004

Intergovernmental Panel on Climate Change. (2023). *Climate change 2023: Synthesis report*. IPCC. https://www.ipcc.ch/report/ar6/syr/

Knuth, D. E. (1997). *The art of computer programming, Volume 2: Seminumerical algorithms* (3rd ed.). Addison-Wesley.

Matthews, C. (2018). Algorithmic thinking and Central Javanese gamelan. In R. T. Dean & A. McLean (Eds.), *The Oxford handbook of algorithmic music* (pp. 79-102). Oxford University Press. https://doi.org/10.1093/oxfordhb/9780190226992.013.24

Proyas, A. (Director). (2004). *I, Robot* [Film; starring Will Smith]. 20th Century Fox.

Sandred, Ö., Kuuskankare, M., & Laurson, M. (2009). Revisiting the Illiac Suite: A rule-based approach to stochastic processes. *Sonic Ideas/Ideas Sonicas, 2*, 42–46.

Tantacrul. (2021, March 11). *Aleatoric music: From Lutosławski to video games* [Video]. YouTube. https://www.youtube.com/watch?v=xabYn35ngaY

Thomas, W. (2015). Algorithms: From Al-Khwarizmi to turing and beyond. In G. Sommaruga & T. Strahm (Eds.), *Turing's revolution*. Birkhäuser.

Xenakis, I. (1955). *Metastaseis* [Score]. Boosey & Hawkes.

Xenakis, I. (2001). *Formalized music: Thought and mathematics in composition* (Harmonologia Series No. 6). Pendragon Press.

4 Symbolic AI, Part I

Symbolic AI is an approach that establishes symbolic representations and formalised logical rules to model human problem-solving. Growing out of the study of mathematics and logic via the foundational work done by Alan Turing, what came to be known as the symbolic approach to AI became the prominent approach to the field beginning in the late 1950's (Turing, 1950). Accordingly, various symbolic strategies to AI were debated at the seminal Dartmouth *Summer Research Project on Artificial Intelligence* (1958), discussed at length in Chapter 2. In 1956, computer scientists Allen Newell, Herbert Simon, and Cliff Shaw developed a symbol-based program called *Logic Theorist* that was able to find novel efficient proofs to the mathematical theorems in Whitehead and Russell's foundational text *Principia Mathematica* (1913) (McCorduck & Cli Cfe., 2004).

George Lewis's influential *Voyager* system relied heavily on symbolic representations of musical concepts. Like Cope's EMI, *Voyager* was developed upon a set of rules, constraints, and relationships from which it generates musical structures like melody, harmony, rhythm, and dynamics. However, unlike *EMI, Voyager* was designed to be an interactive system that played with live performers on a Yamaha Disklavier in real time. The *Voyager* system analyses the input from human musicians via microphone inputs and responds on its own without a human musician in the loop. A fully functioning autonomous music system, *Voyager* can even improvise with musicians in real time, making it an inspirational model for this text.

Like the algorithmic approach, symbolic systems are usually easily explainable, a major benefit over black-box opacity problems faced by many systems built on neural networks and other deep learning methods. But symbolic systems also struggle with scalability. Still, the symbolic approach to AI remains an accessible entry point for many musicians, largely because it aligns with how musical knowledge is often transmitted to musicians. Whether through conservatoire training or informal apprenticeship, musicians are typically introduced to music as a system of symbols—notes on a stave, chord symbols, theoretical frameworks—that map sound to meaning in musical performance practice. Classically trained musicians rely on Western notation and harmonic theory to navigate and analyse repertoire, while educators in jazz, Carnatic

DOI: 10.4324/9781003534211-6

music, or graphic scores pass on their traditions using alternative symbolic systems. These notational and theoretical tools offer a shared grammar that makes symbolic AI feel like an extension of practices already familiar to how many musicians think and communicate. This chapter lays out some terms and ideas commonly found in symbolic AI efforts and then lays a symbolic foundation upon which we may build symbolic AI in later chapters, in the form of a step-by-step Max tutorial.

Principles and Terminology of Symbolic AI

Often referred to as "good old-fashioned AI" (GOFAI; Haugeland, 1989), symbolic AI overlaps somewhat with the algorithmic approach, similarly favouring a fondness for structural rules. However, the symbolic approach is less about structuring a perfect machine that will carry out the will of the designer every time, and more about creating symbols that form the basis of arguments and symbolic representations of abstract reasoning. As with the algorithmic approach, while some of these terms may be familiar, since these are not common musical terms, it would be beneficial to establish some definitions for the core principles of symbolic AI.

Abstract Reasoning

The ability to reason abstractly is one of the core traits that distinguishes humans from most animals. While some species, such as corvids (ravens and crows), dolphins, and certain primates demonstrate forms of abstract reasoning, humans exhibit this capability to a more advanced and complex degree (Tomasello et al., 2005; Hare & Tomasello, 2004). Abstract reasoning allows individuals to analyse information and develop solutions to problems without relying solely on physical objects or tools. This ability includes the manipulation of symbols, rules, and concepts that are not directly tied to tangible, real-world experiences.

If simply looking at Figure 4.1 causes an iconic late '80s riff to ring out in your head—without ever picking up a guitar—you're engaging in abstract reasoning. The riff is quoted here verbatim to make that point. This short musical phrase will also be used throughout this chapter because it's so familiar that it allows us to witness the transformative power of symbols in action. Musical

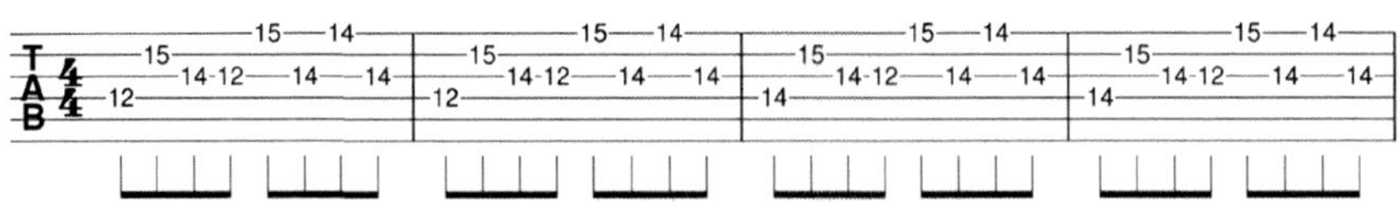

Figure 4.1 Guitar tab for the first four measures of the opening riff to "Sweet Child O' Mine," by Guns N' Roses (1987). Written by W. Axl Rose, Slash, Izzy Stradlin, Duff McKagan, and Steven Adler. ©1987 Guns N' Roses/Geffen Records. Used here under fair use for educational and analytical purposes.

notations like guitar tab are symbolic systems—a language of numbers and lines, not sounds. Musicians use this abstract system to mentally reconstruct musical experiences and to pass them on to others. This symbolic decoding, done entirely in the mind, is abstract reasoning: the process of translating symbols and rules into imagined realities. The riff is not the music and tab is not sound. But your brain, interpreting the tab, fills in that gap—illustrating the mental leap from symbol to sensation.

Symbolic Thought

In the example above, symbols stand in as representatives for concepts and actions one might take in the real world. For those unfamiliar with guitar tablature, the six horizontal lines represent (from top to bottom) the six strings of the guitar (from lowest to highest pitch: E, B, G, D, A, E) and the numbers represent notes played on a given fret numerically (where 0 = an open string, 1 = a fret above, 2 = a whole step above ... 12 = one octave above, etc.). Other elements may be borrowed from traditional notation (like the 4/4-time signature and the straight-quaver rhythm pattern below the tab that indicates the rhythm to be played). This lexicon of symbols may be expanded at will, as when classical guitarists indicate what right-hand fingers should play what notes, for instance, by the addition of abbreviations for finger names p (pulgar/thumb), i (indice/index finger), m (medio/middle finger), and a (anular/ring finger). Each new symbol is incorporated as a symbolic representation of a real-world object (a finger, a fret, etc.) or problem (play this passage at a tempo of 125 beats per minute), as in Figure 4.2, that might be played on an electric nylon-stringed guitar:

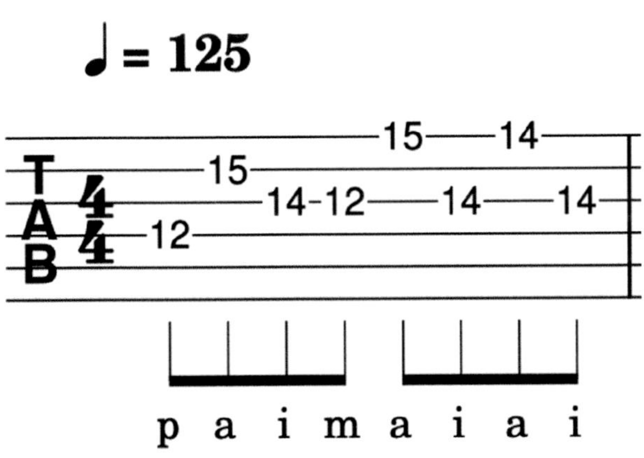

Figure 4.2 Fingerpicked guitar tab for the opening measure of the guitar solo of "Sweet Child O' Mine," by Guns N' Roses (1987).

Symbolic Representation

As one might expect, many mathematical concepts can be represented using simple and somewhat ubiquitous symbols like +, -, /, and x, as stand-ins for the mathematical processes of addition, subtraction, division, and multiplication. Similarly, in the musical figures mentioned earlier, the horizontal lines represent the strings of the guitar, while the quaver rhythm notation represents the regularity of the note durations, etc. Each symbol represents an object or action in the real world.

Complex Problem-Solving

Not all problems that are solvable by abstract reasoning are solvable using simple methods. If the Sweet Child O' Mine riff had been transformed as shown in Figure 4.3, it is probable that at least some skilled musicians would have recognised it even though the notes of the riff are here presented retrograde and in a foreign key.

Symbolic AI processes are often dependent on the ability to solve complex problems. Solving any complex problem would be nigh-impossible in a situation where no information was available (e.g., some dead written languages are no longer decipherable because not enough information has survived to the present day to help linguists decipher the writings), but even if a guitarist had never seen tablature like that of Figure 4.2, it is conceivable that he could eventually decipher it, given at least some exposure to the concept of notation. This assumes the guitarist had a cultural predilection for reading from left to right (notably, some non-Western music notation systems are read in a variety of fashions right-to-left, vertically from top-to-bottom, etc.) and some other major clue, like that the horizontal lines represent the strings of the guitar, for instance. Similarly, with enough clues, symbolic AI systems can fill in the gaps and make logical deductions. Imagine a system that had been exposed to symbolic representations of American rock music of the '80s and was tasked with detecting songs within several image files with sheet music. By comparing the files to its database of American rock music of the 1980s a reasonably well-built system might have a good chance of identifying the image below, simply based on similarity (Figure 4.4).

Figure 4.3 A further transformation of the opening four measures of the guitar solo of "Sweet Child O' Mine," by Guns N' Roses (1987).

Figure 4.4 The opening four measures of the guitar solo of "Sweet Child O' Mine," by Guns N' Roses (1987), with some important pieces missing.

Future Planning

A common teaching in music performance pedagogy on the bass guitar is to play slightly "ahead of the beat," (Frieberg & Sundström, 2020). Similarly, drummers are also often advised to push the beat with the kick drum. But this type of anticipation is just a minor example of something humans naturally can do quite well. Humans have a seemingly innate ability to plan for hypothetical scenarios and make decisions about eventualities that are not in evidence at the present time. This ability usually develops in children from three to five years old (Atance & Meltzoff, 2005) and peaks around the mid-20s to early '30s (Diamond, 2002). The human ability to plan for future events is intimately entangled with our understanding of social behaviour. Thanks to our brain's pre-frontal cortex, humans can "time travel" into possible futures and imagine how different scenarios may play out (Bandoim, 2023). This ability also assists humans in navigating interpersonal relationships and prevents aberrant behaviour that might be socially unacceptable. In music, the pre-frontal cortex can act as a "prediction machine" giving listeners the ability to anticipate musical events before they happen. In one study, participants listening to Bach Chorales demonstrated a tendency to linger on uncertain notes, suggesting that predictive processing plays a critical role in how musical information is understood and appreciated (Hansen et al., 2021).

Some psychologists believe that anticipation is the key to rhythm perception in music. The dynamic attending theory holds that a human's attentional resources are synchronised with temporal patterns in music, enabling them to predict when the next beat will occur (Huron & Margulis, 2010). Accordingly, the ability to plan and predict rhythms and other musical structures is essential to any interactive symbol-based autonomous music system's design. If we were beginning with a mere theoretical concept, we might need to first express that concept as a symbol before learning how to predict it; however, musical data in the form of MIDI already symbolises musical data into a finite number of symbols. There are a finite number of pitches, velocities, channels, and other parameters one might use to make musical structures. Since prediction is so important to being a musician, this is a pretty good place to start building our own symbolic systems. What follows is a simple process for predicting future beats in Max.

Symbolising Musical Ideas: A Step-by-Step Max Tutorial

Building a Simple Beat Maker

We will begin with learning some basic programming skills in Max, which will give us a common language to work with for future chapters. Feel free to either build the patch along with this tutorial or open the step-by-step patches included in the Machine Musicians/Patches/Chapter 4 folder you downloaded at the beginning.

In standalone Max:

- Open Max and start a new patcher by hitting the ⌘ (Command) button and the letter N on a Mac or the Control (Ctl) button on a PC. You could also click on File menu at the top and then click on "New patcher."

In Max-for-Live:

- Open Ableton Live, then navigate to Max-for-Live in the browser (if the browser is not shown, click the Show/Hide Browser button at the top left of the session) (Figure 4.5).
- From the Live Browser, drag a blank Max MIDI Effect onto the track called "1 MIDI." The blank MIDI effect should instantly be visible in the lower left-hand corner of the session (Figure 4.6).
- To access the Max patching window, hit the fourth button from the right at the top of the blank Max MIDI Effect. Alternatively, you can also right-click in the title bar and then click "Edit in Max" (Figure 4.7).

In Max-for-Live OR Max Standalone:

- These two blank versions of a patch will look somewhat different (Figures 4.8 and 4.9):
- Despite their different looks, however, these two versions of Max are very similar. The tutorial will continue with minor variations in procedures noted where necessary.
- Unlock the patcher by clicking the Lock/Unlock button at the bottom left of the patcher (it looks like a padlock) (Figure 4.10):
- Unlocking the patcher allows you to edit the patch, add objects to it, and make new connections. Locking the patch allows you to interact with the GUI (graphic user interface) objects in the patch.
- Find some empty space somewhere in the patching window and make a new object by typing the letter "N" (which stands for "New"). Then type the word "button" and hit enter/return. The object you've just created is called a button, which has a graphic user interface allowing you to click on it and send out a message to other objects called "bang." In many

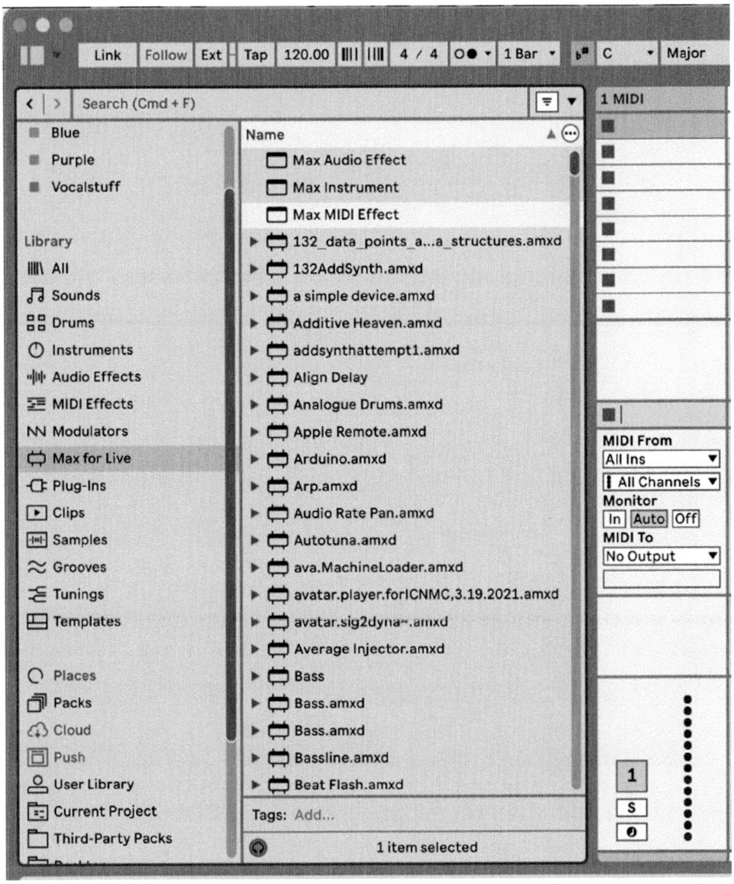

Figure 4.5 Where to find Max-for-Live devices in Ableton Live (note: Ableton has two views: Arrangement view and Session view. These two views have very similar functionality but look radically different. Session view is pictured here. To get to Session view from Arrangement view, click the Tab button.)

programming languages, bang is a word that means "do whatever you are designed to do."

- Underneath the button, create another object (again hit "N") called "kslider" and hit enter/return. The object created is another graphic user interface object that looks like a musical keyboard. The patch we are about to create could be done without these GUI objects, but GUIs are quite useful and make these kinds of patches much more intuitive.
- Connect the outlet at the bottom of the button object to the inlet at the top of the kslider. The kslider has two inlets. Connect the button to the one on the left (pitch) (Figure 4.11).

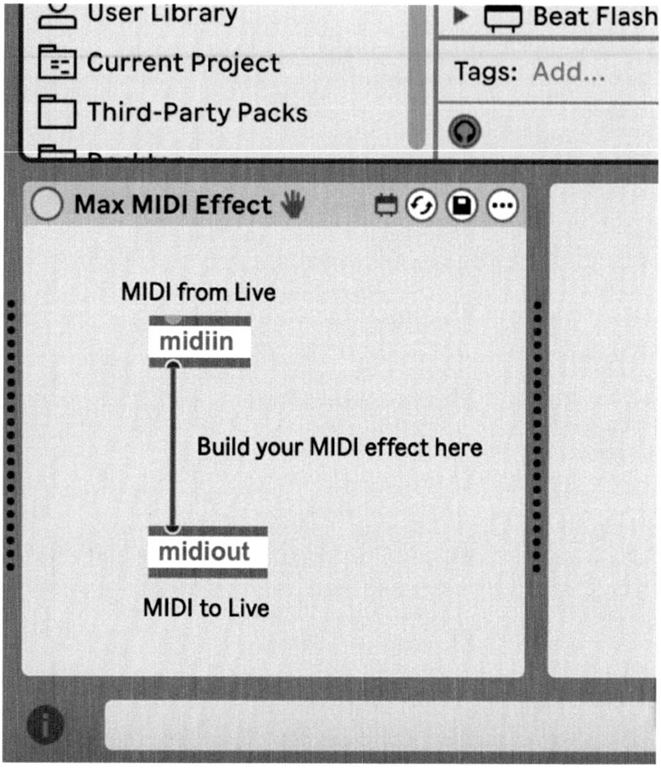

Figure 4.6 A blank Max MIDI effect in an Ableton Live MIDI track.

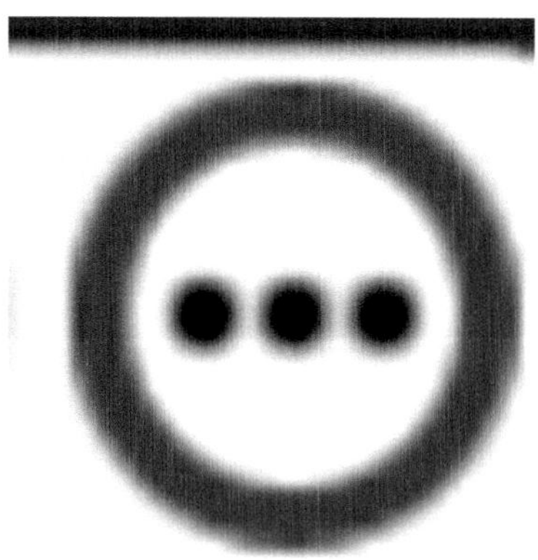

Figure 4.7 The "open in Max" button at the top of a Max-for-Live device.

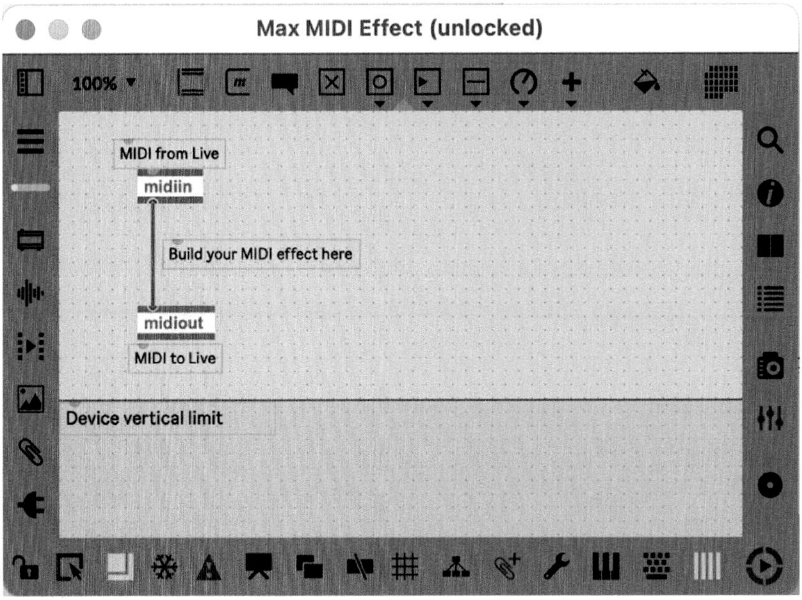

Figure 4.8 A blank Max-for-Live patch.

Figure 4.9 A blank Max patch in standalone Max.

Figure 4.10 The Lock/Unlock button that enables patching in both versions of Max.

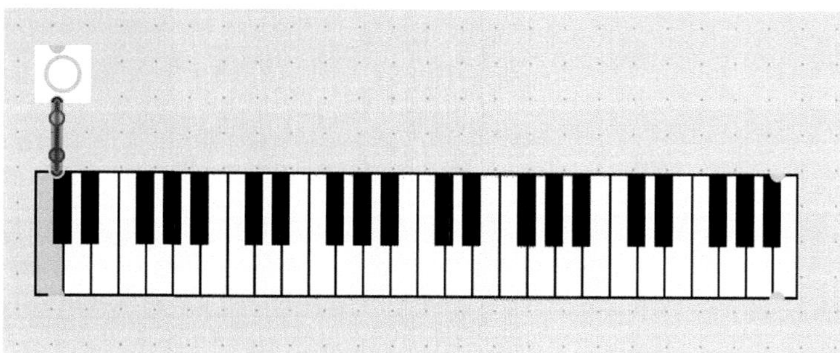

Figure 4.11 A button connected to a kslider object.

- It's always a good thing to know what data you are producing with Max objects, so let us connect a number object below the kslider by creating a new object ("N" again) and typing the word "number." You may see the Max system autocorrect to other objects with similar names like number~, but don't be tempted. As with all coding, correctness is key. Misspelled objects will not work correctly.

- Connect the leftmost output of the kslider to the inlet at the top of the number object.
- Lock the patch by clicking the Lock / Unlock button at the bottom left side of the patch.
- Click the button and you will see that the data the kslider is putting out is the number 36, a MIDI pitch (equivalent to C2). Now click a different key somewhere on the keyboard and notice that the MIDI pitch changes in real time. So clicking the button sends the same pitch repeatedly and clicking the keyboard changes the pitch (Figure 4.12).
- Click the button and you will see that the data the kslider is putting out is the number 36, a MIDI pitch (equivalent to C2). Now click a different key somewhere on the keyboard and notice that the MIDI pitch changes in real time. So, clicking the button sends the same pitch repeatedly and clicking the keyboard changes the pitch.
- Our goal is to build a patch that can predict rhythms. But currently we are building the side of the patch that the human will control. This is the side of the patch that our autonomous music system will eventually listen to and analyse. It would be good to have a metronome we can use for sending regular pulses. Create a new object called "metro," and then create another one next to it called "transport."
- Connect the output of the metro to the button.
- Above the metro and the transport, create a new object called "toggle." Toggle is a very simple switch often used to turn processes in Max on or off. Connect the outlet of the toggle object to the inlet of the metro and then click the toggle outlet again to connect a second patch cord to the inlet of the transport (Figure 4.13).
- You may be familiar with the concept of a transport, which is used in digital audio workstations to control play, stop, record, and other functions. These DAW-based transports are digital versions of analogue tape transports that were used to physically transport the tape from one spool of tape to another.
- Similarly, the transport in Max starts a clock that is global within Max, meaning that if you have another patch open somewhere that has objects

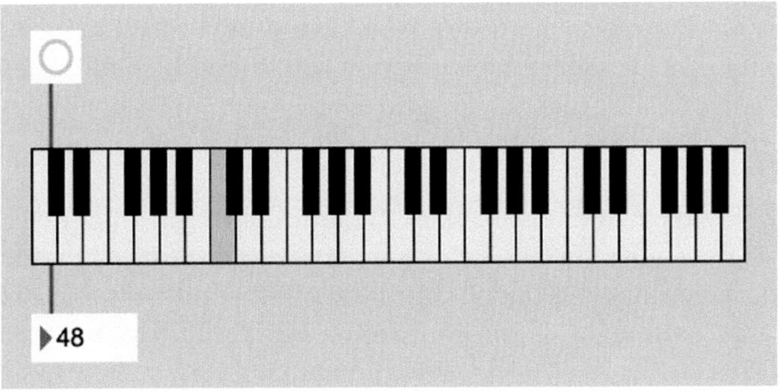

Figure 4.12 The button, kslider, and a number object.

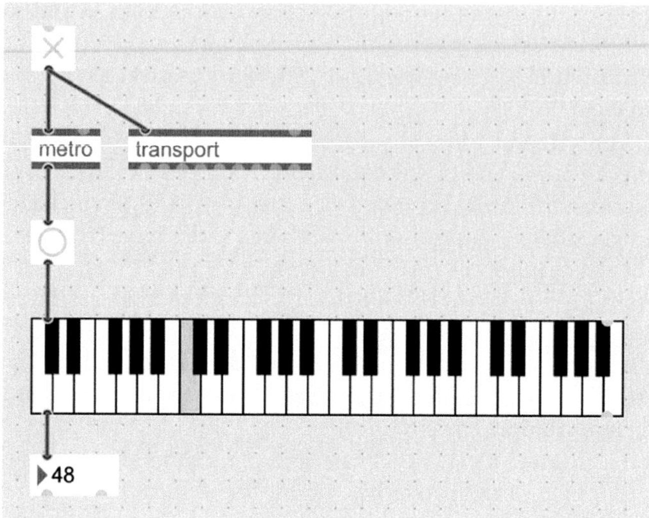

Figure 4.13 The button, kslider and a number object.

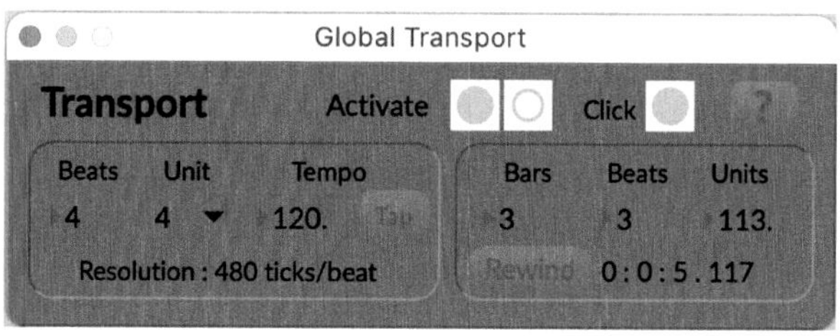

Figure 4.14 Max's GlobalTransport window.

tied to the transport, these other patches will also start playing. While this is often useful, the reason we are using a transport in this patch is to give the patch a common definition of tempo. You can open the global transport window by clicking on "Extras/GlobalTransport" in the top menu of Max. You will see the default tempo of Max is 120 bpm, which is extremely common among music programs (Figure 4.14).

- Leave the GlobalTransport window open, as this will become important later.
- The metro object does not have a GUI, but unlike the other objects in our patch, it does take arguments, meaning you can change the attributes it exhibits. To change the interval attribute of the metro, double click on the metro and to the right of the word metro, type "100." Make sure there is a space between the word metro and the number 100; otherwise, the metro won't work.

- Lock the patch again and click the toggle to turn on the patch. You should see the button blinking at a rate of 100 milliseconds. You should also see that since the toggle is attached to the transport object, this has turned on the GlobalTransport window. Click the toggle again to shut it off and then unlock the patch again.
- By adding the 100 to the metro, we have tied the rate to the metro object's internal clock, but it's also possible to tie the metro to the global tempo by using symbolic representations of musical durations. Max's symbolic representations for tempo-relative durations have a simple logic (Table 4.1).
- While we could just open the object and overwrite the "100" (signifying 100 milliseconds) with a 4n (signifying a crotchet), it would be better if we could change the beat of the metronome in real time, rather than needing to unlock the patch and typing every time we want to change from a

Table 4.1 Max's tempo-relative durational nomenclature

Value	*American term*	*British term*
1n	Whole note	Semibreve
2n	Half note	Minim
4n	Quarter note	Crotchet
8n	Eighth note	Quaver
16n	Sixteenth note	Semiquaver
32n	Thirty-second note	Demisemiquaver
64n	Sixty-fourth note	Hemidemisemiquaver
128n	One-hundred-twenty-eighth note	Semihemidemisemiquaver
For **dotted notes** (add a "d" to the note value):		
Value	American Term	British Term
1nd	Dotted whole note	Dotted semibreve
2nd	Dotted half note	Dotted minim
4nd	Dotted quarter note	Dotted crotchet
8nd	Dotted eighth note	Dotted quaver
16nd	Dotted sixteenth note	Dotted semiquaver
32nd	Dotted thirty-second note	Dotted demisemiquaver
64nd	Dotted sixty-fourth note	Dotted hemidemisemiquaver
128nd	Dotted sixteenth note	Dotted semihemidemisemiquaver
For **triplet notes** (add a "t" to the note value):		
Value	American Term	British Term
1nt	Triplet whole note	Triplet semibreve
2nt	Triplet half note	Triplet minim
4nt	Triplet quarter note	Triplet crotchet
8nt	Triplet eighth note	Triplet quaver
16nt	Triplet sixteenth note	Triplet semiquaver
32nt	Triplet thirty-second note	Triplet demisemiquaver
64nt	Triplet sixty-fourth note	Triplet hemidemisemiquaver
128nt	Triplet one-hundred-twenty-eight note	Triplet semihemidemisemiquaver

crotchet to a quaver. Luckily, the right-most inlet of the metro takes in new settings of the object's internal in real-time.

- Because typing these values into a menu would take an intense amount of time, these are supplied for you with the book. In the Machine Musicians/ Patches/Chapter 4 folder, there is a subfolder called "Snippets." Find the file called "note_values.maxsnip." This file is a Max Snippet, meaning it is a small bit of code that can be dragged and dropped into your patch (if it is unlocked) and even saved in Max's **Integrated Development Environment** (IDE) so it can be used in the future. Make sure your patch is unlocked and then drag the note_values.maxsnip file directly into your patch (Figure 4.15).
- This snippet contains four "umenu" objects that (with the patch locked) can be clicked on to pull down all the note values in proper Max syntax. So that these umenu objects can be instantiated (a computer programming term signifying that an object will be called upon and brought into a specific coding situation) in future patches without having to look them up in the folder, select the four umenu objects and the comments explaining what they are, then click the paperclip at the bottom of the patching window to save the snippet to your Max IDE. In the naming dialog box at the bottom, give the snippet the name "note_values" (Figure 4.16).
- At the left side of the Max IDE, there is another paperclip. Clicking on this paperclip will give you access to the snippets (the ones you save like "note_values," and many other useful snippets supplied by the makers of Max).
- The umenu object has three outlets. The leftmost outlet sends out the index number attached to your choice (if you click on the "1n" in the

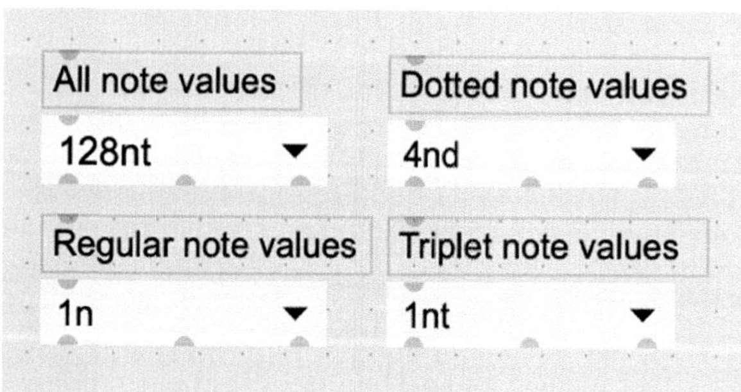

Figure 4.15 The note values snippet.

Figure 4.16 Saving the note_values snippet to your Max IDE.

umenu for "Regular note values," this outlet will send out the number zero, "2n" will send out the number one, "4n" will send out three, etc.). The middle outlet will send out the symbol attached to your selection, e.g., if you click on "1n," this outlet will send out the symbol 1n. We will not use the rightmost outlet in this tutorial, but for completeness' sake, this outlet reports special information when called upon, like if you needed to know how many data points the umenu was holding, sending it a message saying "count" would cause it to report its current count of items as shown in Figure 4.17.

- With the patch unlocked, connect the middle outlet of all four umenu objects to the rightmost inlet of the metro so that you can click choices in the umenu and change the settings of the metro in real time (Figure 4.18).

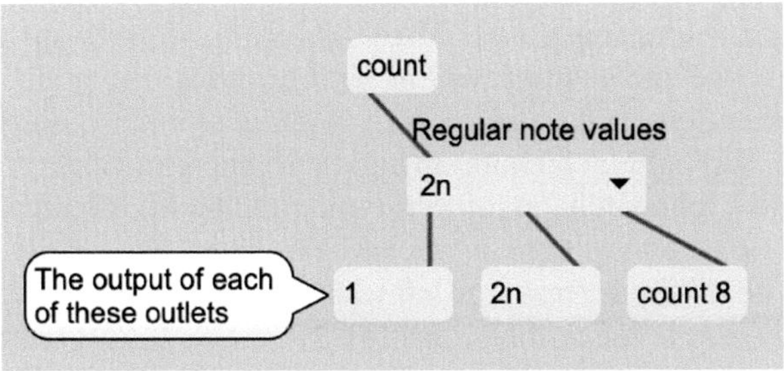

Figure 4.17 The outlets of a umenu.

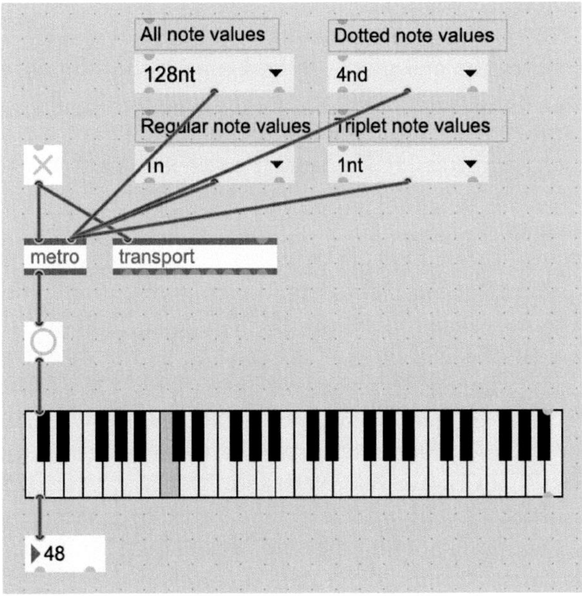

Figure 4.18 Controlling a metro with the output of a umenu.

- With the patch unlocked, create a new object below the number object called "makenote." The makenote object is useful for turning disparate data points into MIDI data. The object needs two points of data to make this happen: a pitch and an on-velocity. Velocity is the MIDI stand-in for dynamics. Since MIDI is data, not sound, velocity symbolises a dynamic level, taken from a sensor which reads how fast a key was pressed on a MIDI controller (this loosely equates to the way an acoustic piano player will make notes louder by playing them harder). MIDI on-velocities are measured from 1 to 127, with 127 equating to the top volume played by the instrument. When a player releases the key, the sensor sends out a velocity of 0, signifying that the note should be turned off. MIDI off-velocities are signified by a velocity of 0.
- The interplay between MIDI on-velocities and off-velocities works rather seamlessly if you're using a MIDI controller, but if we want to automate this process, we need a quick way to send on-velocities, wait a given duration and then send out an off-velocity without thinking too deeply about it. This is where the makenote object comes in. The leftmost inlet of the makenote object takes in an integer, symbolising a MIDI pitch (an integer, 0–127). The second inlet from the left takes in an on-velocity (an integer, 0–127). The third inlet from the left takes a duration (either in milliseconds or in Max's note value syntax, which will tie the output to the global transport's tempo). After the specified duration elapses, the makenote will send out an off velocity, shutting off the note.
- The outlets of the makenote send out the pitch and velocity messages (first on and then off).
- We still need to send the note somewhere. Create a new object called "noteout" below the makenote object. Connect the leftmost outlet of the makenote to the leftmost inlet of the noteout object, then connect the rightmost outlet of the makenote to the middle inlet of the noteout (the rightmost inlet controls MIDI channel, which isn't pertinent here).

In Standalone Max:

- Lock the patch. Double-click on the noteout object and you should see some options for where to send the MIDI data we are about to create. You should see a list of MIDI outputs. Depending on whether you have a Mac or a PC, these options differ somewhat dramatically. On a Mac, the options will probably look something like this (Figure 4.19):
- PC users might find fewer options; among them one called "GSwavetable Synth." The PC's GSwavetable synth and the Mac's "AU DLS Synth" are the built-in default MIDI synths supplied by these respective operating systems. Those with more options like the "from Max 1" output shown above may choose to send their MIDI data to another MIDI-capable program or VST synth on their laptop. If you do not have these choices, the default synths that come with your operating system will be sufficient. Whatever

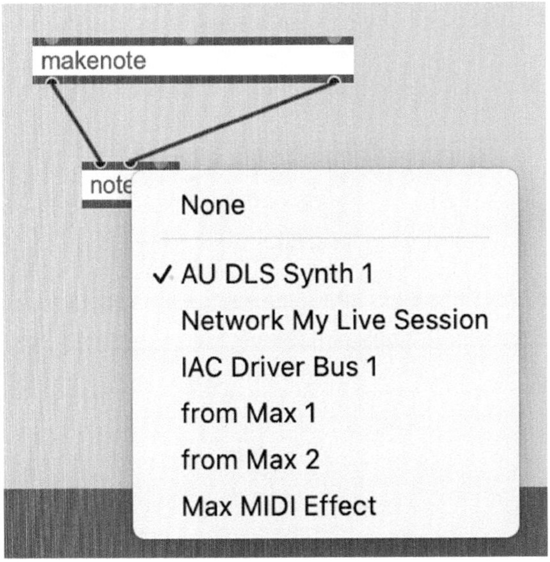

Figure 4.19 Typical outputs of the noteout object (on a Mac).

you choose, click on that option in Max and you will be all set up to send MIDI data from Max to that synth. If using the built-in synths, make sure you have your audio output and speakers turned up.

In Max-for-Live:

- In Ableton Live, in the browser, search for a drum kit of your choosing (browser / Drum kits). When you find a drum kit you like, drag it onto MIDI track 1. This will change the name of the track to the name of the drum machine you chose. We will continue to refer to this track as MIDI track 1.
- Arm the MIDI track 1 by clicking the Arm recording button at the bottom of the channel strip. Once armed, the button should turn red (Figure 4.20).

In Max-for-Live OR Max Standalone:

- Unlock the patch, double click on the makenote and add an argument to the object "127." This will give all new pitches a default on-velocity of 127.
- While the patch is still unlocked, let us also add the default argument "100" to the metro object. The reasons for this are quite simple, since the next time you open the patch, whatever setting you previously set the metro will be lost, this argument will stop the metro from starting up with a default argument of 0 milliseconds (which will sound alarming if you should happen to hit play).

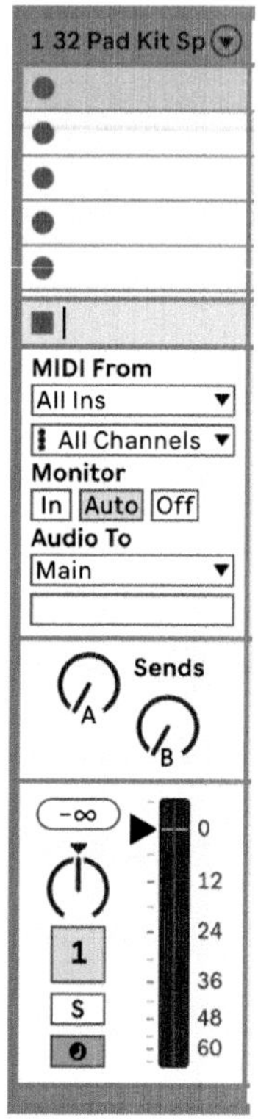

Figure 4.20 An Ableton Live channel strip.

- Let us also add one of these "safety arguments" to the makenote, to the right of the velocity of "127," add another argument "100" (symbolising a default duration of 100 milliseconds for every note).
- Finally, let us add a last argument "10" to the makenote, signifying that we want to send this note to MIDI channel 10, the dedicated drums and percussion channel. Since we've added this argument to the makenote, we also need to send it out of the makenote to the noteout, so connect the rightmost outlet of the makenote to the rightmost inlet of the noteout (Figure 4.21).
- Lock the patch and click on the toggle. You should hear a drum playing back. If not, check to make sure your patch is wired exactly like the patch above. If that does not work, check your input/output settings.

In Max-for-Live:

- If you don't hear anything, in Ableton Live, check to see if the MIDI input indicator is lighting up. If it is, and you do not hear anything, check audio output settings. If the audio settings look right but you still don't hear

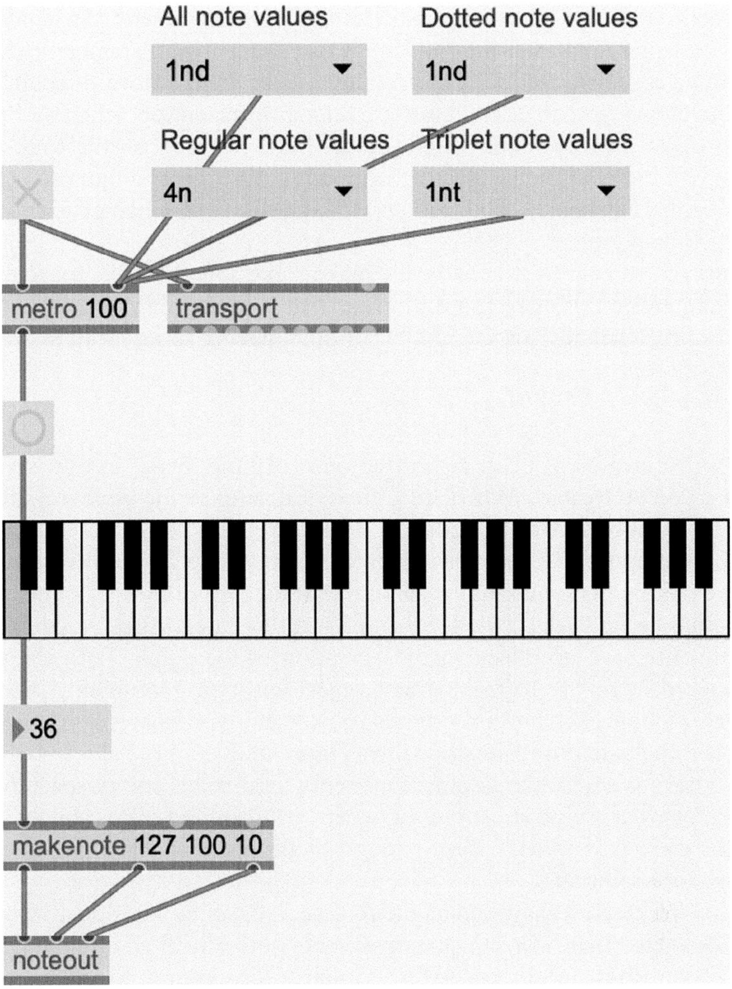

Figure 4.21 A very simple interactive beat machine.

anything, go back to Max and change the note that is playing. It is possible that you are playing a note in Max that does not correspond to a drum sample in the drum kit you chose.

Building a Less Simple Beat Machine

We have now arrived at a symbolic representation for three of the four Core Auditory Parameters of music described in Chapter 1.: Pitch, Dynamics (symbolised as MIDI velocity), Duration (symbolised as either milliseconds or note values), and we have at least touched upon the fourth Core Auditory

Parameter—timbre—by adding and choosing an instrument. As alluded to in that chapter, representing the five Core Perceptual Parameters (range, repetition, contrast, contour, and frame) will be much more difficult. This machine allows you to make beats by human intervention (clicking on the button object), or by regular metronomic beats (turning on the toggle and the metro), but also allows you to change the tempo (by changing the tempo in the GlobalTransport). This will become important in Chapter 5 for use in future experiments.

However, as neat as it is to finally make some sound in this tutorial, you may be interested in making a drum beat that is more exciting than a simple repeating crotchet. Let us spend a bit of time making some more interesting musical choices.

In Max-for-Live OR Max Standalone:

- As we've created a lot in a short amount of time, make sure to save the patch you've created. Max helps a great deal, auto saving your work, but it always helps to save as you go.
- Another important thing often ignored by many people who write programs is the writing of comments explaining what they have done. Comments will be quite useful later if you need to refer to this patch. Also remember that comments have no effect on the operation of the patch. With the patch unlocked, type "n" to make a new object and type "comment," then hit enter. Double click on the comment object and type whatever you need to explain the patch or its functionality (Figure 4.22).
- After saving and adding some comments, find some empty space to the right of what we've already done where you can add a new bit of code. Place these new objects close enough to the existing code that they can share some objects.
- As before, create a toggle and a metro object, this time adding an argument to the metro "4n." Create two more metros, one with an argument "8n" and one with the argument "16n." Connect the outlet of the toggle to the leftmost inlet of each metro.
- Since the metros are tempo-relative, we also need a way to turn on the GlobalTransport. Connect the toggle object to the transport object we created for the other bit of code.
- Under the "metro 4n," create a new object called "counter" and give it arguments "1 4." The counter is a simple object that takes in bangs from a button object and counts them. The argument "1 4" means "start counting at 1, stop counting at 4, and then go back to 1" (Figure 4.23).
- To read what the counter is doing, under the counter, make another new object called "message." The message object is another ubiquitous and useful object in Max that holds any kind of data but also has a GUI so you can click on it and send the data out of the output. Connect the leftmost outlet of the counter to the rightmost outlet of the message object. If you turn on

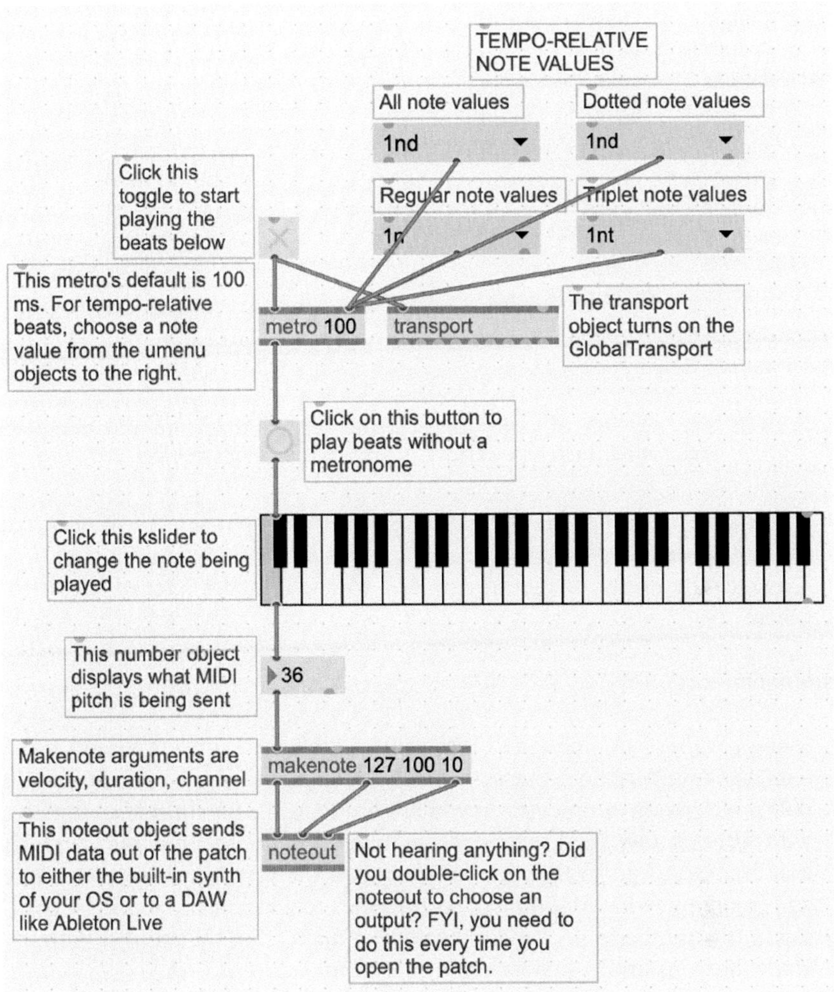

Figure 4.22 The first beat maker, complete with helpful comments.

the toggle, you will see the numbers counting from 1 to 4. Like comments, this kind of visual feedback is often useful to add to your patch, even if it doesn't add any functionality to the patch.

- Create a new object below the "metro 4n" called select. Make sure you type or choose the "select" object and not "selector~" as this object will not work. After the word select, add four arguments: "1," "2," "3," and "4."
- The select object takes in a stream of data and discriminates among the data, looking for a certain input. When it finds that input, it will send a bang message out of a specific outlet, depending on the ordering of the

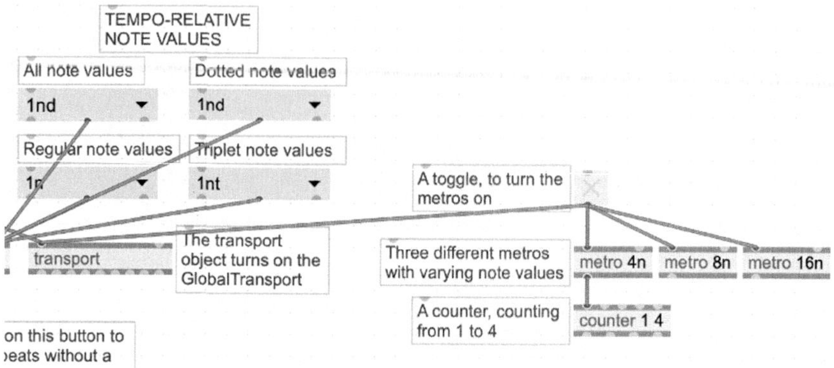

Figure 4.23 The new bit of code connects the second toggle to the transport, connecting the tempo-relative metros to the counter object.

arguments. With the arguments "1 2 3 4," a "1" input sends a bang out of the first outlet, a "4" input sends a bang out of the fourth outlet, etc.

- Connect the outlet of the "metro 4n" to the leftmost inlet of the select object.

Adding a kick:

- Make another new message object and double click into it to add some data, the number "36." In the General MIDI protocol, the pitch 36 should play a kick drum sample, but if you are building the patch in Max-for-Live with Ableton Live (and some other systems), it may be a different pitch. It may be best to go to the number object on the first beat maker we made and figure out what MIDI pitch corresponds to a kick drum sound by clicking in the number object and increasing or decreasing the number with the arrow buttons until you hear the right sound.
- Connect the select object's first outlet to the leftmost inlet of the message "36."
- Connect the outlet of the message object to the makenote's leftmost inlet.
- Turn on the toggle to see if this is working. If it is, you should hear a kick drum playing a downbeat on 1. If not, back up a few steps and check your work (Figure 4.24).

Adding a snare:

- Create a new message object and add the data point "38." In General MIDI, 38 is the pitch corresponding to a snare sound. Again, if you need to search for an appropriate GM pitch, do so and use whatever works best in your situation.

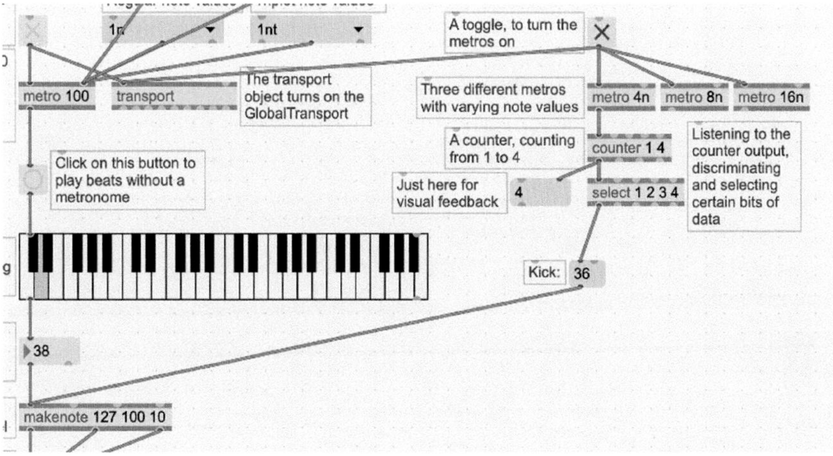

Figure 4.24 A new drum beat machine, with kick drum downbeat abilities.

- Connect the second outlet of the select object to the leftmost inlet of the message "38."
- You should now have a kick on 1 and a snare on 2.

Adding a closed hi-hat:

- Underneath the "metro 8n" create a new counter with the argument "1 8," meaning it will count from 1 up to 8. Connect the outlet of the "metro 8n" to the leftmost inlet of the new counter.
- Create a new select object with the argument "1 2 3 4 5 6 7 8." This will allow us to discriminate outputs from the counter and selectively send out bangs for our hi-hat. Connect the leftmost output of the "counter 1 8" to the leftmost inlet of the new select.
- Create a new message object below the select and add the data "44." In the GM protocol, 44 is the pitch of a closed hi-hat sound. Connect outlets 2, 3, 4, 6, 7 and 8 of the select object to the leftmost inlet of the message "44."
- Connect the outlet of the message "44" to the leftmost inlet of the makenote object.

Adding an open hi-hat:

- Create a new message object below the select object we used for the hi-hat and add the data "46." In the GM protocol, 46 is the pitch of an open hi-hat sound. Connect outlet 5 of the select object to the leftmost inlet of the message "46."
- Connect the outlet of the message "46" to the leftmost inlet of the makenote object (Figure 4.25).

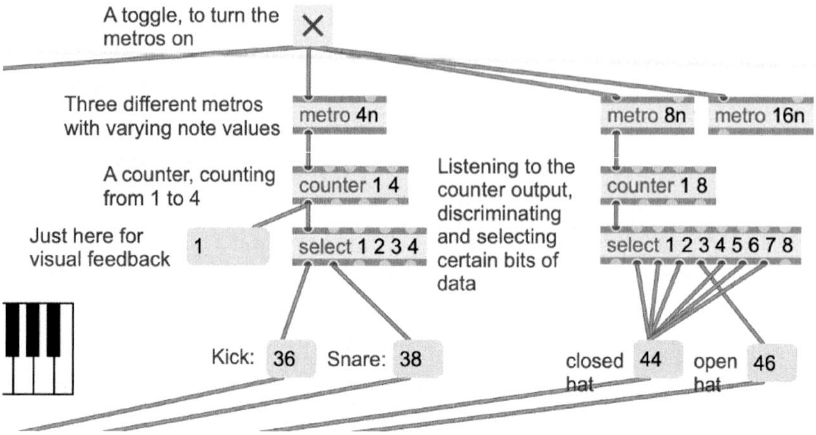

Figure 4.25 A new drum beat machine, with snare and hi-hat abilities.

- You may of course make different choices if you desire, but remember that human drummers don't usually play the hi-hat open and closed at the same time, and it would be good for us to model that behaviour with our machine.

Adding a pseudorandomised shaker:

- Create a new object under the "metro 16n" called "decide." The decide object is a simple random binary number generator which takes in a bang and decides randomly between 1 and 0. Connect the outlet of the "metro 16n" to the leftmost inlet of the "decide" object.
- Create another select object below the decide object and give it the arguments "0 1." Connect the outlet of the decide object to the inlet of the select object.
- Create a new message object below the select object and add the data "69." In the GM protocol, 69 is the pitch of a shaker sound. Connect outlet 5 of the select object to the leftmost inlet of the message "69."
- Connect the outlet of the message "69" to the leftmost inlet of the makenote object.
- Turning the toggle on to listen to the full kit, you will now hear randomised shaker beats on semiquavers. Since the decide object decides pseudorandomly between two numbers, the probability that it plays on any given semiquaver is 50% (Figure 4.26).

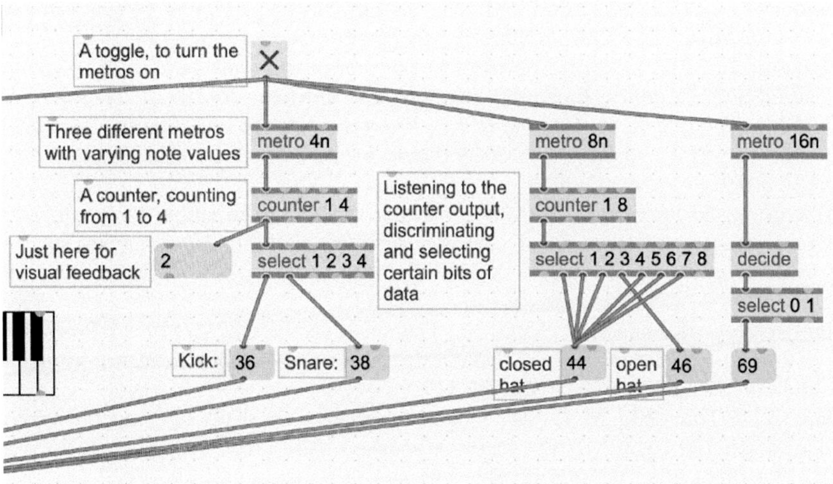

Figure 4.26 The full kit, complete with a randomised shaker.

Personalising your kit:

- Now that we have one drum machine, why not change the connections to your own specifications? Don't like the kicks merely on 1 and the snares merely on 2? Why not change it? Where else could you use the decide object?

Where Do We Go Now?

In this chapter we learned about some basic principles and terminology of the symbolic approach to AI. Understanding terms like abstract reasoning, problem solving, future planning, and symbolic thought is key to understanding this approach. We then spent some time experimenting with symbolic representation and then built our own system for beat making that is based in symbolic representations of the Core Auditory Parameters of music.

Now that we can make beats our ears can detect the audible sound, and our minds can predict what comes next. We hear these repeating beats and our minds begin counting, "1, 2, 3, 4," and then loop around again, "1, 2, 3, 4." We instantly begin matching the tempo with very little effort. Could a machine do the same? Importantly, can we build a machine that can listen to another musician and play along appropriately?

References

Atance, C. M., & Meltzoff, A. N. (2005). My future self: Young children's ability to anticipate and explain future states. *Cognitive Development, 20*(3), 341–361. https://doi.org/10.1016/j.cogdev.2005.05.001

Bandoim, L. (2023, September 13). The anatomy of the prefrontal cortex. *Verywell Health*. https://www.verywellhealth.com/prefrontal-cortex-5220699

Diamond, A. (2002). Normal development of prefrontal cortex from birth to young adulthood: Cognitive functions, anatomy, and biochemistry. In M. H. Johnson, Y. Munakata, & R. O. Gilmore (Eds.), *Brain development and cognition: A reader* (pp. 466–503). Oxford University Press. https://doi.org/10.1093/acprof:oso/9780195134971.003.0029

Friberg, A., & Sundström, A. (2002). Swing ratios and ensemble timing in jazz performance: Evidence for a common rhythmic pattern. *Music Perception: An Interdisciplinary Journal, 19*(3), 333–349. https://doi.org/10.1525/mp.2002.19.3.333

Hansen, N. C., Kragness, H., Vuust, P., Trainor, L., & Pearce, M. (2021). Predictive uncertainty underlies auditory boundary perception. *Psychological Science*. https://doi.org/10.1177/0956797621997349

Hare, B., & Tomasello, M. (2004). Chimpanzees are more skilful in competitive than in cooperative cognitive tasks. *Animal Behaviour, 68*(3), 571–581. https://doi.org/10.1016/j.anbehav.2003.11.011

Haugeland, J. (1989). *Artificial intelligence: The very idea*. Bradford Books.

Huron, D., & Margulis, E. H. (2010). Musical expectancy and thrills. In *Principles of frontal lobe function* (pp. 575–604). Oxford University Press. https://doi.org/10.1093/acprof:oso/9780199230143.003.0021

McCorduck, P., & Cfe, C. (2004). *Machines who think: A personal inquiry into the history and prospects of artificial intelligence* (2nd ed.). A. K. Peters.

Tomasello, M., Carpenter, M., Call, J., Behne, T., & Moll, H. (2005). Understanding and sharing intentions: The origins of cultural cognition. *Behavioural and Brain Sciences, 28*(6), 675–735. https://doi.org/10.1017/S0140525X05000129

Turing, A. M. (1950). Computing machinery and intelligence. *Mind, 59*(236), 433–460. https://www.jstor.org/stable/2251299

5 Symbolic AI, Part II

In the previous chapter we built a system for making some simple drumbeats. In this chapter we will build another patch that will eventually be able to analyse an input and respond to what it has heard. In a later chapter we will begin experimenting with symbolic representations of audio in Max. Perhaps it is obvious but it's relevant to say that audio is a completely different phenomenon from MIDI. MIDI is, at its root, a symbolic system that represents musical actions, events, and procedures relating to electronic music equipment. Like music notation, MIDI data is not music itself, but a way one could express musical ideas, codifying them for dissemination to other musicians (human or machine). This presents a host of complications so great that we will continue to focus mainly on MIDI for the time being.

Audio is the physical evidence of music itself, the real-world sound waves travelling through the air towards our ears as we enjoy a musical performance, live or in our AirPods. Our sensitive ears take in audible signals and parse the signal into the four Core Auditory Parameters (pitch, dynamics, duration, and timbre), and then our brains process the patterns of meaning in these signals using the five Core Perceptual Parameters (range, repetition, contrast, contour, and frame). This parsing process happening in the human brain implies that there is a deeply embedded biological system that turns musical phenomena into electrical impulses, which is itself a kind of symbolic representation (Patel, 2008). If we possessed a sufficiently advanced "dictionary" capable of decoding how the brain processes musical input, we could, in theory, transform an electroencephalogram (EEG) of someone listening to music back into audible sound. We could even transmit new music directly into a patient's brain without stopping first at the ears. As a side benefit, these abilities would also greatly assist us in the search for a musical artificial intelligence. For now, these things remain beyond the reach of current science (Pasley et al., 2012; Meng et al., 2025).

In the absence of a fully realised brain-computer interface (BCI), researchers have often turned to more accessible, albeit imperfect, methods such as audio-to-MIDI conversion. Despite its technical constraints, this approach has facilitated meaningful interactions between acoustic performers and digital music systems for decades—a practice shaped in large part by the innovative

DOI: 10.4324/9781003534211-7

work of the electronic music luminary George Lewis (Steinbeck, 2019). Later chapters include a lot more about audio and even tutorials on performing audio-to-MIDI conversion in Max. But for the time being, we begin with an appropriately Lewis-ian scenario, two improvisers meeting on a stage to improvise together without a prearranged plan.

Modelling Human Listening

Imagine that two human musicians (let's call them Chloe and Regan) are going to improvise together using electronic drum instruments. Chloe decides to begin playing first. Let us codify what the "opening moves" of the improvisation might be using pseudocode.

//Listening protocols

1. The improvisation *starts*
2. *REGAN* listens to *REGAN* (specifically her audible output) and *CHLOE*
3. *CHLOE* listens to *CHLOE* (specifically her audible output) and *REGAN*
4. *CHLOE* plays *notes* on a MIDI-enabled electronic *drum controller*
5. Notes are *analysed* by *REGAN*
    a. *Note*: Single note strikes are analysed by *REGAN* using a *melodic cataloguing* process (while drum sounds are only somewhat analogous to what we mean when we say "notes" in the traditional sense, in this context "notes" could also mean "instrumental sounds played" e.g., if Chloe plays a snare sound, that is marked by Regan as a distinct "note").
    b. *Chords*: Regan and Chloe both only have four limbs with which to play the drums, which means there is a distinct probability that sometimes multiple notes will be struck at the same time. Any occurrence of more than one note should be labelled as a *chord*. Multi-note strikes or notes struck at the same time are sent to a *harmonic cataloguing* process.
    c. The beginning of the note triggers a *clock* measuring the time until the *note ends;* add these clock measurements to a *timing catalogue*.
        i. After *a few* durations have been measured on the clock, *REGAN* extrapolates a *tempo (BPM)* and sets her internal *BPM* to match.

6. Once *N beats* from *CHLOE* have been *clocked* (measured) by *REGAN*, *REGAN* begins to trigger *generation* of *new beats* on a MIDI-enabled *electronic drum* controller

The reader may have noticed words in boldface. These words highlight the important variables the system will need to store and the necessary actions the system will need to carry out to achieve the desired output. Somewhere inside Regan's brain (or perhaps in her mind, in conjunction with her body, if you are a phenomenologist), some definition of these variables must be represented symbolically.

Here is an example of what Regan's behaviour might look like, expressed in pseudocode:

//Response protocols

7. Possible rules for generation of new beats:
   a. *Randomly* choose between the following options:
      i. NOTE CHOICE 1: choose from among *N notes* (struck pads on the MIDI controller, iterated one after another; chosen from the *melodic catalogue*)
      ii. NOTE CHOICE 2: Construct a *chord* (chosen notes from the *harmonic catalogue*)
      iii. DURATION CHOICE: for each new *note* or *chord* played, choose from among *4 durations* (chosen from the *timing catalogue*)
      iv. *After N new beats, randomly* choose *4–8* new *notes* or *chords* from *either catalogue.*
   b. *Choose 4–8 random durations* (the same number as chosen from the note catalogues) from the *timing catalogue*

The behaviour above is one of a multitude of such behaviours Regan may choose as a collaborative response to Chloe's opening. While Regan is performing this behaviour, Chloe is performing similar mental tasks, listening and cataloguing what Regan is playing. Similarly, Regan's ears and mind also continue to track Chloe's performance. There is little need to add a new protocol because this is essentially a repeat of the Listening Protocols from above.

Both players make special note of any time their partner introduces new elements or begins to manipulate a new Core Parameter, for instance:

c. *CHLOE* gradually increases *volume* over *N beats*

If Regan is going to respond, she must have some mental apparatus for detecting these changes and a method for performing similar actions, necessitating something like a *volume catalogue*. However, human musicians do not often play notes at exactly the same volume, though this is somewhat common in electronic music, where volume is often rendered as a static knob or setting, rather than something that must be continually physically produced (e.g., the volume of a trumpet is determined by the amount of air strenuously breathed into the instrument by the player). While the volume of a MIDI channel is a controllable setting, the MIDI protocol appropriates and controls the volume (strength) of a note using the *velocity* message. Velocity is not the same thing as volume, however. The connection between the speed of the key being pressed down (thus velocity) and the actual volume of a note being pressed on a MIDI controller is just the best compromise available (Patterson, 1974).

The topic of music dynamics is deep and complicated (Arnheim, 1984), but broadly speaking, humans approach dynamics as more-or-less static or homogeneous ranges. The MIDI system does not approach musical dynamics in relation to more-or-less homogenised dynamic levels, but instead it approaches dynamics based on each note. This is quite different from the way that human musicians approach this topic. Human musicians perform dynamics more improvisationally, generally sticking within a dynamic range and bringing some lines, or notes out dynamically in a smooth contour. The MIDI approach to dynamics is more scattershot, with every dynamic existing on its own with no context. This is a significant problem that continually makes MIDI instruments sound unhuman.

That said, it is imperative that any artificial musical system appropriates and controls dynamics in some form, but it is less important to model the actual dynamics performed by their partner, the human performer. To model our dynamics more upon human dynamic performance, let us model how Regan might listen and appropriate a dynamic range from her partner Chloe.

//Definitions

8. Note dynamics are evaluated within the range of comfortable human hearing, bounded on one end by perceptual *silence* and on the other by the perception of *pain*
    a. *Pain* = the level of dynamics at which a human listener will experience pain, either in the production of the musical event or in the hearing of same.
    b. *Silence* = since, as John Cage said, "there is no such thing as silence," silence is not a physical reality but more of a perceptual boundary (Cage, 1961; Palamara & Deal, 2020). There is a level of noise that is beneath notice, below which ambient noise is referred to as silence.

    //Assessment of overall dynamic

    a. *Single* note dynamics are continually sent to the *dynamic cataloguing* process
    c. The *velocity cataloguing* process does not store all dynamic levels, but constantly monitors the *peak* and *nadir* dynamic levels.
    d. Like a human performer, the dynamic level should also periodically *pause* and *remain static* for *N notes.*

With these definitions established, Regan is then free to generate new dynamics for the notes she plays. Let us assume Regan decides to play dynamics conservatively, rather than countermanding what Chloe has established.

//Generation of new dynamics for REGAN

b. *New beat dynamics* are generated from the current average of *N notes* stored in the *dynamic cataloguing* process, falling within the current *peak* and *nadir*

The reader may have noticed that this process could fit quite logically between steps 2 and 3 above, but in computer programming, the ordering of the steps need not be laid out from top to bottom in the written representation of the code.

Thus far, this section has been a largely theoretical exploration of how humans listen. Let us try our hand at turning this pseudocode into a functioning Max patch, using the patch we made last chapter as a starting point.

Turn the Beat Around

Building a Virtual Improviser (Chloe)

Since Chloe was the improviser who began the improvisation. Since her part of the improvisation is closest to what we did in Chapter 4, it is easiest to begin building her processes. Regan's part in the exercise was largely responsive. Let us ignore the actions relating to Regan for the moment, and the actions Chloe would take in response to Regan. Chloe begins by playing some notes, which, since they can either be singular or multiple notes in a chord, the impulse to play must be divided by some probability between the two choices. For this and other reasons, the patch we wrote in Chapter 4 will need to be modified to more accurately stand in as a substitute for a human.

As you did in Chapter 4, access Max, either the standalone or Max-for-Live via Ableton Live and open the patch you previously made for Chapter 4 (refer to Chapter 4 if you don't remember how to do any of this). At the top menu, click "File/Save as . . . " and give the patch a different name. Test it to make sure everything still works by turning on the toggle button either on the right side or the left side. Then continue to the instructions below.

In Max-for-Live OR Max Standalone:

- Unlock the patch.
- On the left side, we have a sort of "human beat machine" we used to learn some things about Max. We will return to this at the end of the chapter, but for now we will focus on the right side of the patch, which is where we built a "machine beat machine." Note that as you follow the signal all the way from the toggle down through the various metros to the message boxes (Kick/36, Snare/38, etc.), the output is 100% deterministic, except for the shaker sound (MIDI pitch 69), which passes through a decide object, thus ratioing the probability of a shaker sound playing to 50%. The human player (Chloe) is unlikely to play beats in the exact same way every time, so we will add some more randomisation to the output of the other sounds to make the beat sound a little more human.
- Firstly, disconnect the output of the select objects from the message objects for the Kick, Snare, Closed Hat, and Open Hat (leaving the select object attached to the shaker alone). (N.B.: In the pictures for this chapter a second makenote and noteout objects have been placed underneath the right side of the patch, for clarity. A second transport object has been added as well, negating the need to stretch wires from one side of the patch to the other. This has little effect on the patch's functionality, other than making it all a bit cleaner. Feel free to copy these steps or ignore them.) Since the

select objects were serving as the "inciting impulse" to play these sounds, it makes sense to add some probabilistic variation here (Figure 5.1).

A Probabilistic Kick Drum

- Above the "36" message box (the kick drum trigger), create a new object called "random" and give it the argument "100." This object is a random number generator. When it receives a bang message, this object will generate a random number in the range specified by the argument. Since the argument is 100, the random object will generate numbers from 0 to 99.
- Under the "random 100" object, create a new object called "<" which is the Max "less than" operator, comparing integers in the left inlet to integers in the right inlet and outputting the number if it meets the required condition. Connect the outlet of the "random 100" to the leftmost inlet of the "<" object.
- Above the "<," create a new object called "live.dial." This object gives us a useful GUI for controlling the probability of a certain number being chosen. However, the default argument of the live.dial object is 1–127 and we need it to be 1–100. Click on the object to select it and hit Command (CMD) + i (on a Mac, Control/CTL + i) to open the object inspector. In the inspector window that opens on the right side of the patch, look for a setting called "Range/Enum." Double-click on the range and type "1 100" to set the object correctly. Then look for a setting called "Unit Style" and change it to Percentage so the live.dial will display correctly with the

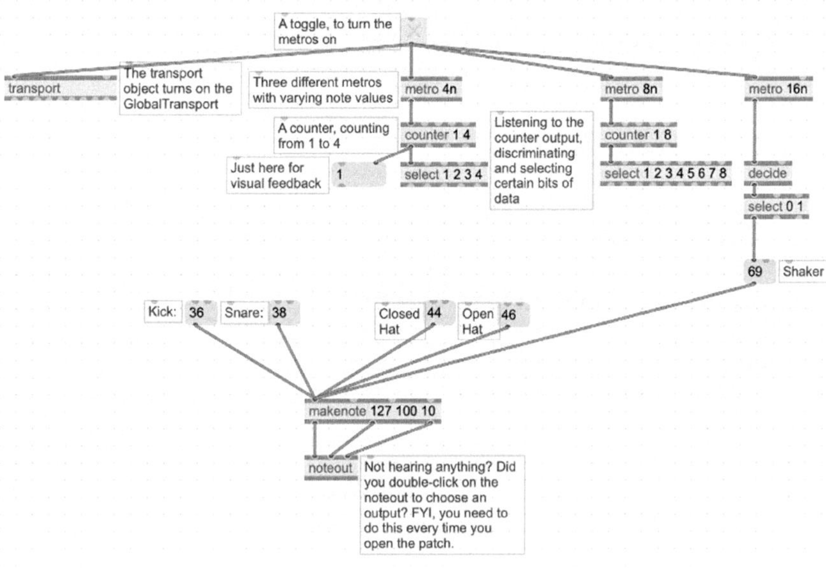

Figure 5.1 This patch will stand in for a human while we build the next patch.

% symbol. Lastly, look for a setting called "Short Name" and change it to "Kick prob." Once these things are done, close the inspector window. Connect the leftmost outlet of the live.dial object to the rightmost inlet of the "<" object.

- Under the "random 100" object, create a select object and give it the argument "1," meaning it will take in a stream of data and send out a bang message every time it encounters a one. Connect the outlet of the random object to the leftmost inlet of the "select 1" object.
- Remember how the kick drum in the Chapter 4 patch was connected to the 1 and 3 outlets of the "select 1 2 3 4" object? Instead of connecting these outlets to the Kick/36 message, connect them to the leftmost inlet of the "random 100." Lock the patch and drag the dial setting to either 100% or 1%. Test this patch by turning on the toggle at the top and you will find the kick now plays 100% of the time if the dial is set to 100% and plays only seldomly if the dial is set to 1% (Figure 5.2).
- If this has worked, congratulations, on making your first probabilistic music system.
- We probably want the default message of the live.dial to be 100%, so above the live.dial object, create a new object called "loadmess" and give it the argument "100." Connect the outlet of the "loadmess 100" to the leftmost inlet of the live.dial. This will ensure that when the patch is loaded, the live .dial object receives a default argument of 100%.

A Probabilistic Snare Drum

- Let us do a similar thing for the snare sound.
- Unlock the patch and select all the objects from the "loadmess 100" to the "select 1." Click CMD + D (on a Mac, or CTL + D on a PC) to duplicate them.
- Move these new objects to an empty spot in the patch, over the snare (38) message box.
- Connect the 2 and 4 outlets of the "select 1 2 3 4" to the leftmost inlet of the second "random 100."
- Connect the leftmost outlet of the second "select 1" to the leftmost inlet of the message carrying the snare sound pitch (38).
- In the inspector window, change the Short Name setting for the snare dial to "Snare prob."

Hi Logic

- (N.B.: If you are using a drum kit in Ableton Live, not only will these MIDI pitches be different, but your kit may not, in fact, operate this way, so take this section with a grain of salt if this does not pan out in your situation.) A physical hi-hat has two states, open and closed, depending on whether the

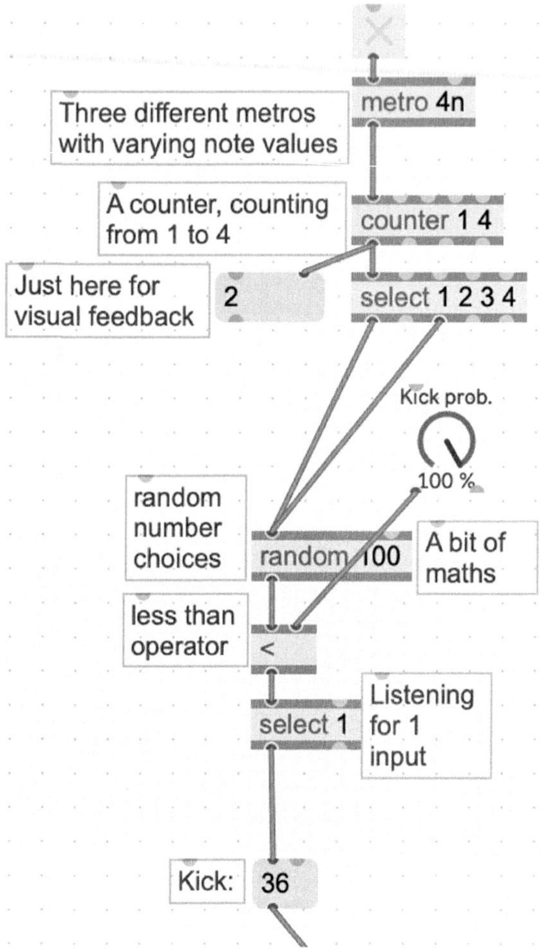

Figure 5.2 A probabilistic system that plays kick drums on 1 and 3 (a variable percentage of the time).

player is depressing a foot pedal. Electronic drum kits follow a similar logic, even though an electronic drum machine could in theory play both sounds at the same time. Furthermore, the General MIDI protocol sounds operate in such a way that MIDI pitch 46, on its own, plays the sound of a sustained open hi-hat. MIDI pitch 44, on the other hand, not only plays the sound of a closed hi-hat but also ends the sustaining sound of MIDI pitch 46. Good drummers, whether they are playing an electronic kit or an acoustic one, use this instrument in complex ways we should model, if possible.

Using Probability Another Way: A Probabilistic Right Hand

- Unlock the patch and select all the objects from the "loadmess 100" to the "select 1." Click CMD + D (on a Mac, or CTL + D on a PC) to duplicate them again.
- Lock the patch and turn the new live.dial object up to 100%.
- Unlock the patch. Below the "select 1," create a new object called "drunk" and give it the argument "4." The drunk object is another random number generator that creates what is called a ***drunken walk***, meaning the numbers stumble up and down, often repeating, and never straying very far in one step. This will be perfectly appropriate for drummer right hand behaviour (drummers usually play all cymbals with their right-handed stick). Since we have chosen 4 as the argument, the possible outputs are 0, 1, 2, and 3.
- Underneath the "drunk 4" object, create a new select object with the argument "0 1 2 3." Connect the outlet of the "drunk 4" object to the leftmost inlet of the "select 0 1 2 3."
- Connect the leftmost outlet of the "select 0 1 2 3" (the 0 outlet) to the leftmost inlet of the closed hi-hat (44) message object. Connect the second-from-the-left outlet to the open hi-hat (46) message box. Now create a new message box and type into it the message 49, which corresponds to a crash cymbal sound. Now create a new message box and type into it the message 53, which corresponds to a ride cymbal sound. Connect the outlet of both messages to the "makenote 127 100 10" object. Connect the third-from-the-left outlet of the "select 0 1 2 3" to the leftmost inlet of the "49" message and the fourth-from-the-left outlet to the "53" message.
- In the inspector window, change the Short Name setting for the cymbal dial to "Cymbal prob."
- Lock the patch and turn the toggle object on at the top and you should hear various cymbals playing on quavers. If you would prefer less cymbal action, decrease the cymbal probability.

Sync Troubleshooting

- Has your drummer gotten out of sync? Most likely you played the toggle at some point and then rewired something with the counter and now one counter is on 1 and the other is on something else. This doesn't happen with human drummers very often because their "inciting impulse" is all responding to the same internal clock. But our drummer has three different metronomes and two different counters. To fix this, let us create a new object between the "metro 4n" and the "metro 8n" called "t." Give the "t" object the argument "1." The t stands for trigger, which hints at its use, which is to send out its argument whenever it gets triggered. Connect the outlet of the toggle to the inlet of the "t 1" object. Then connect the outlet of the "t 1" object to the second from the left inlet of both of counter objects. Arguments into this inlet will reset the counters back to their

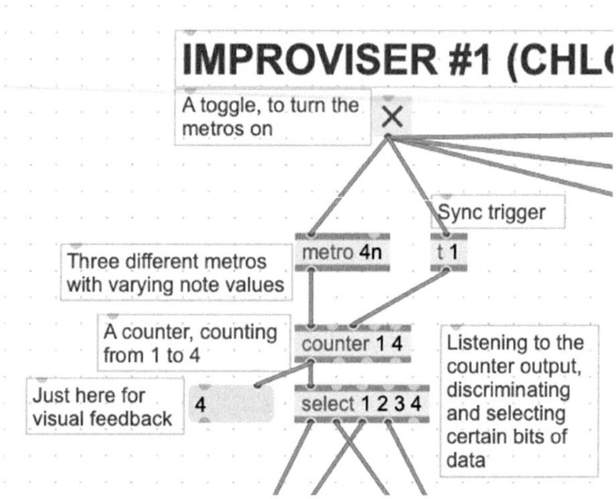

Figure 5.3 Resyncing the counters with a "t" object, argument "1."

starting point, which is why we are sending a "1" out of the "t" object whenever we start or stop the toggle. This should resync your counters so that they have the same definition of the downbeat (Figure 5.3).

Finishing Up

- Consider changing the arguments of some of the "loadmess" objects to provide more spicy defaults.
- Spend some time adding comments to the patch so you can remember what everything does later.
- Save the patch so you can find it in the future.
- N.B., if the focus of this book were learning Max and not Machine Musicians, now would be a good time to discuss making a proper interface for this Max patch. Interfaces are quite important, but much less relevant to a book about Machine Musicians. For more information and guided tutorials on how to properly finish up a professional looking Max patch or a Max-for-Live device, refer to Interactive Composition: Strategies using Ableton Live and Max-for-Live by V.J. Manzo and Will Kuhn, or Max/MSP/Jitter for Music by V.J. Manzo (Figure 5.4).

A Symbolic AI Stand-In for Improviser #1

Believe it or not, the patch you have just written is very close to early attempts at musical AI, which were built on symbolic representations of musical behaviours and structured rules guiding behaviour. This patch is far less complex or nuanced than something like the system that Lejaren Hiller and Leonard Isaacson used to generate the ILLIAC Suite, but it's in the same vein of work. Like the ILLIAC system, this patch has a probabilistic output governed by

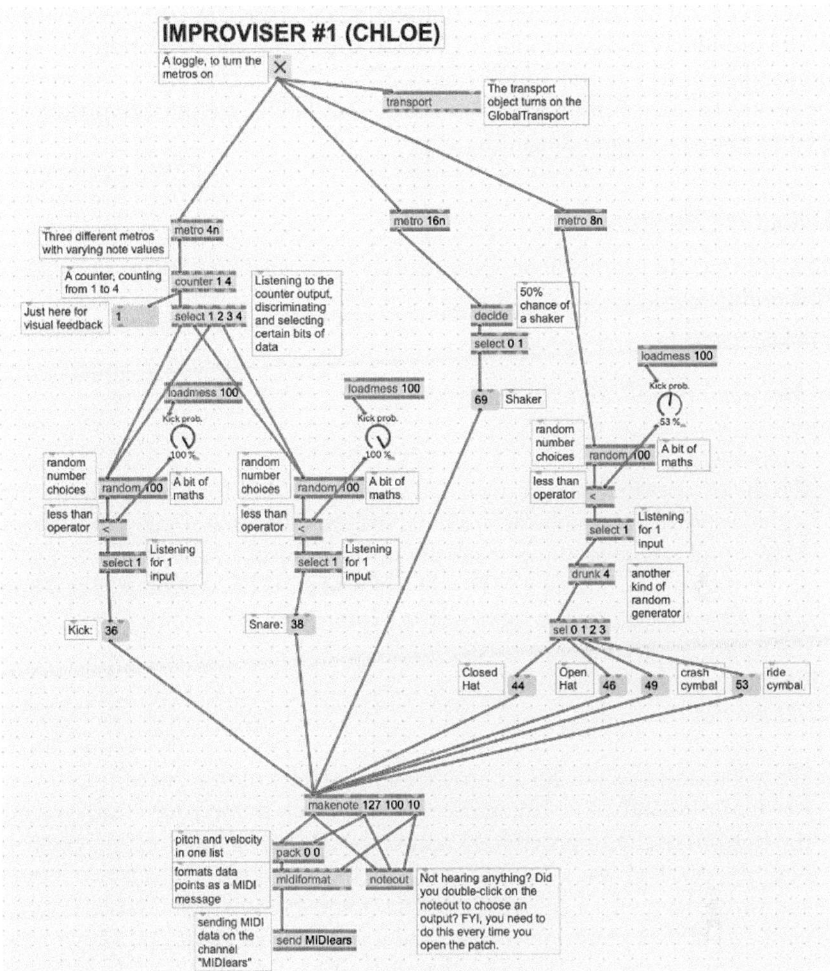

Figure 5.4 The full improviser #1 drum machine patch.

rules for rhythm and which determines what plays when. The outputs are modelled on standard human performance practices. There are similar processes underlying George Lewis's Voyager system, but that system has not only generative capacities but also the ability to listen and react appropriately, which we will focus on in the next section.

Hearing the Percussion (Building a Reactive Improvisation System)

We've now done our best to build a digital system approximating Chloe's human improvisational style. In this section we begin building a digital approximation of Regan's part. Since Regan's actions were largely responsive to Chloe, this last section of the chapter will focus on giving this patch the ability to hear what Improviser #1 is doing. One of the first things established by the pseudocode description of Chloe and Regan's improvisation was that "Regan listens to Chloe." In Chapter 6, we will begin building a system with the ability to learn from what it has heard. But before we go any further, we need to give our digital Regan some ears.

Sending and Receiving

Since this second patch will be driven purely by its analysis of what Improviser #1 is doing, let us first build a process for making beats that has no metronome driving it.

In Max-for-Live OR Max Standalone:

- Unlock the patch.
- On the extreme left side of the patch we have created for this chapter, there is still a sort of "human beat machine" we used to learn some things about Max. Duplicate everything from the button object to the noteout object at the bottom by hitting CMD + D (on a Mac, CTL + D on a PC). Drag these new objects to the right of the "Improviser #1 (Chloe)" section of the patch (Figure 5.5).

MIDI mouth:

- We will need some way for Improviser #2 to detect the output of Improviser #1. Unfortunately, our Improviser #2 sub-patch doesn't have ears yet. At the bottom of the Improviser #1 section to the left of the noteout, create a new object called "pack" and hit return. The pack object collects two inputs and turns them into a collection of data points called a "list." GOFAI deals with lists of data points quite a bit, and it is paramount that one knows how to manipulate them. The pack object has two inlets. Connect the leftmost outlet of the makenote object (the pitch outlet) to the leftmost inlet of the pack. Connect the middle outlet of the makenote (the velocity outlet) to the rightmost inlet of the pack object.
- Create a new object called "midiformat" and hit return. The midiformat object takes these disparate outputs and formats them as a coherent and properly formatted MIDI signal. Connect the outlet of the pack object to the leftmost inlet of the midiformat. Connect the rightmost outlet of the makenote object to the rightmost inlet of the midiformat object. This last step ensures that the MIDI channel message is sent along with the rest of the MIDI data.
- Finally, create a new object below the midiformat object called "send." The send object is a way to transport data from one area of the patch to another area within Max (or even to a completely different patch) without using patch cords. This object needs an argument that acts as a sort of "channel"

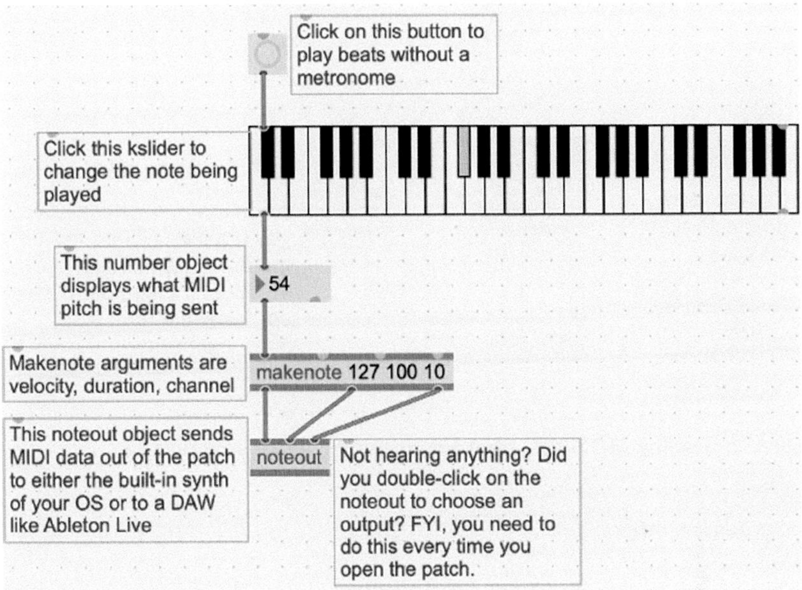

Figure 5.5 New objects to begin the Improviser #2 patch.

that other objects can listen on. Accordingly, give the send object the argument "MIDIears." Sending data in this way can get quite confusing if you are not careful, so stop here and make some comments so you know what is being sent through the "MIDIears" channel. Also, make sure you use the "send" object, not the similarly named "send~" object (Figure 5.6).

MIDI ears:

- In the Improviser #2 section of the patch on the right, create a new object called "receive" and give it the argument "MIDIears." The receive object receives data on channels sent by send objects. Make sure you use the "receive" object, not the similarly named "receive~" object.
- Underneath the "receive MIDIears" object, create a new object called "midiparse." The midiparse object is essentially the opposite of the midiformat object. Whereas midiformat puts MIDI messages together, midiparse breaks them apart again. Connect the outlet of the "receive MIDIears" object to the leftmost inlet of the midiparse object.
- To the right of the "receive MIDIears" object, create a new object called "midiin." The midiin object takes in MIDI from devices external to Max (like a physical MIDI controller, a DAW, or a notation program). Connect the outlet of the midiin object to the leftmost inlet of the midiparse object.

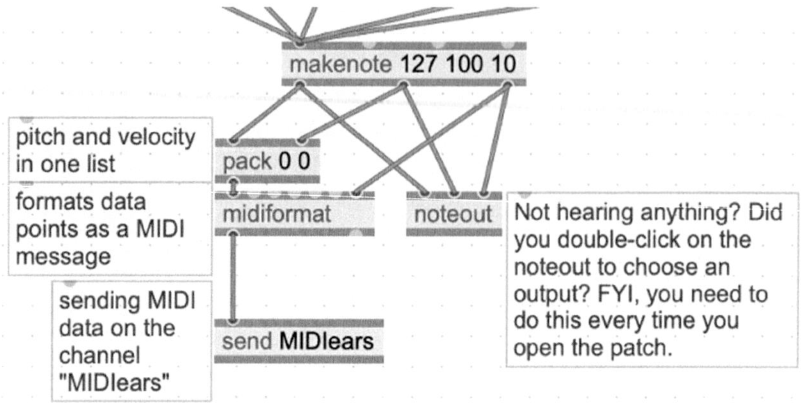

Figure 5.6 Sending MIDI data from Improviser #1 via the send object.

For standalone Max:

- Like the noteout object, midiin is one of those objects that connects to software and devices external to Max. To control what device midiin is listening to, lock the patch, double-click on the object, and click on your preferred input (like a connected MIDI controller or a signal from a DAW).

For Max-for-Live within Ableton Live:

- Like the noteout object, midiin is one of those objects that connects to software and devices that send a signal (in this case MIDI data) into Max-for-Live from the Ableton track where the device is located. This happens automatically, but if you don't have a MIDI controller connected and routed to this channel, this will not work. The track in Ableton must also be armed to record (by hitting the red arming button at the bottom of the track strip in Session View or on the extreme right side of the channel strip in Arrangement View) (Figure 5.7).

Towards the Continuation

While we have seen that it is quite easy in Max to pass signals (such as a starting and stopping impulse, maybe emanating from the toggle button that starts the Improviser #1 patch), in an attempt to keep this experiment as close to the physical reality of human improvisation as possible, this MIDI data is the only signal that will pass from Improviser #1 to Improviser #2. That means that, in true symbolic AI fashion, in Chapter 6 we will need to do some complex problem solving to make Improviser #2 respond appropriately.

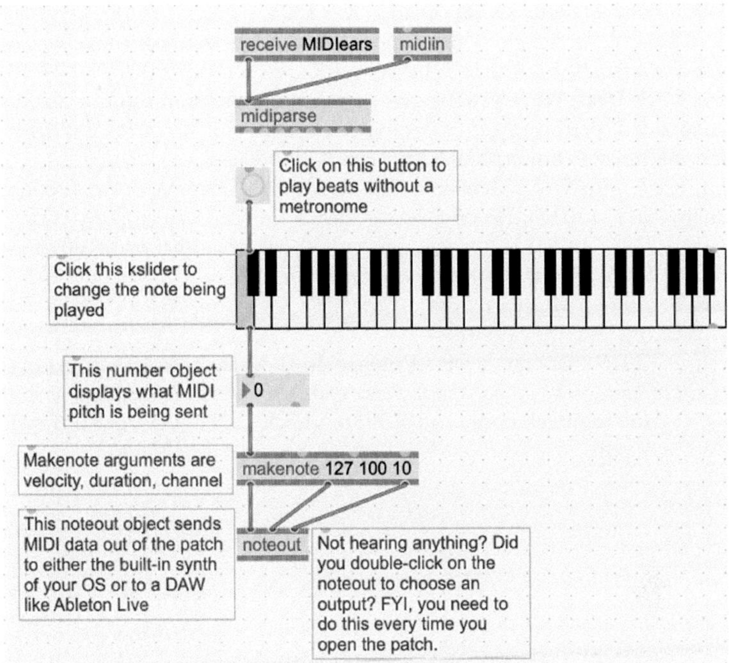

Figure 5.7 Receiving MIDI data from Improviser #1 via the receive object.

There are many problems associated with making a Machine Musician respond appropriately to a given context. At the very beginning of the improvisation (right under the comment "//Listening protocols"), the pseudocode begins by saying: "The improvisation *starts.*" How does Regan know the improvisation has started? A human improviser in this situation would be expecting a first note, followed by a series of other notes (something we might call a gesture). From these opening gestures, a human like Regan would assume the improvisation has begun the moment such a gesture is encountered. But this is just the beginning of the improvisation. Great improvisers have a sense of the time that has passed which informs them when things seem to have gone on "too long." Where does this self-awareness come from? To develop this in our patch, we will have to learn a little bit about machine decisions.

References

Arnheim, R. (1984). Perceptual dynamics in musical expression. *The Musical Quarterly*, *70*(3), 295–309. https://www.jstor.org/stable/742040

Cage, J. (1961). *Silence: Lectures and writings.* Wesleyan University Press.

Meng, Q., Tian, L., Liu, G., & Zhang, X. (2025, January 3). EEG-based cross-subject passive music pitch perception using deep learning models. *Cognitive Neurodynamics*, *19*(6), Article 6. https://doi.org/10.1007/s11571-024-10196-9

Palamara, J., & Deal, W. S. (2020). A dynamic representation solution for machine learning-aided performance technology. *Frontiers in Artificial Intelligence*, *3*, Article 29. https://doi.org/10.3389/frai.2020.00029

Pasley, B. N., David, S. V., Mesgarani, N., Flinker, A., Shamma, S. A., Crone, N. E., ... Chang, E. F. (2012). Reconstructing speech from human auditory cortex. *PLoS Biology*, *10*(1), e1001251. https://doi.org/10.1371/journal.pbio.1001251

Patel, A. D. (2008). *Music, language, and the brain*. Oxford University Press.

Patterson, B. (1974). Musical dynamics. *Scientific American*, *231*(5), 78–95. https://www.jstor.org/stable/24950218

Steinbeck, P. (2019). George Lewis's Voyager. In E. R. Lyon & A. T. McLean (Eds.), *The Oxford handbook of algorithmic music* (pp. 485–506). Oxford University Press. https://paulsteinbeck.com/Paul%20Steinbeck_2019_George%20Lewis%27s%20Voyager.pdf

6 Machine Decisions

Aymbolic AI, Part III

Chapter 5 ended with the problem of how a machine could know that a certain musical event had gone on "too long." Spend a moment thinking about the complicated logic underlying that question. The Humans often make claims like:

- This food is *too* salty.
- This music is *too* loud.
- This book is *too* hard to read.

What source could a machine reference to test whether these claims are accurate? Many times, human claims are made in the absence of a well-researched body of evidence. In this regard, humans can "shoot from the hip," or "eyeball it" in a way that machines find very difficult. Depending on the context, the definition of what is appropriate will vary greatly. This is not the same as our use of the letter "N" to stand in for an unknown variable, as in "Chloe plays *N* notes." Many scenarios leading to a definition of what is musically inappropriate have wildly disparate causes. Maybe the promoter of the event has determined that Chloe and Regan only have five minutes to perform before another act goes on. In this scenario, if Regan took four minutes to respond to Chloe's opening gesture, it would be highly inappropriate in this context. Perhaps the performers can sense that the audience is getting restless. In this scenario, perhaps the cause is that the volume is too quiet, or the tempo is too slow. Perhaps one performer simply gets bored easily and the other performer knows it's time to move on to another type of musical gesture. A machine musician that could respond to each of these scenarios would require some manner of sensor for this data and a process for analysing the data and coming up with the appropriate reaction.

A symbolic approach to this problem would be to first develop a way to sense the problem from the available data and then to develop a battery of appropriate options a system might choose under the circumstances. In this chapter, we will use the patch we built in Chapter 5 as a starting point to build an Improviser #2 system capable of responding appropriately to Improviser #1's actions. It would be good to save this file with a different name (by

DOI: 10.4324/9781003534211-8

clicking "File/Save as..." in Max), so you can refer to the earlier version that works well if you get into trouble.

Machine Interactivity

Since these two improvisers are playing percussion instruments, timing and duration would seem like a good place to start building the Improviser #2 system. In the pseudocode version of Chloe and Regan's improvisation, it states that "Once **N beats** from **CHLOE** have been **clocked** (measured) by **REGAN, REGAN** begins to trigger **generation** of **new beats**..." The pseudocode also mentions Regan would need some manner of memory bank (a *timing catalogue*) consisting of clock measurements and states that:

- After two or three durations have been measured on the clock, *REGAN* extrapolates a *tempo (BPM)* and sets her internal *BPM* to match.

Establishing how the system will handle time is also behind problems like "this musical event has gone on too long," which will start to crop up everywhere when you build a system like this. Let us begin by parsing the stream of MIDI data emanating from Improviser #1.

In Max-for-Live OR Max Standalone:

- Unlock the patch.
- Under the "midiparse" object, create a new object called "unpack." The unpack object breaks apart a list so you can deal with the data points in the list separately. Connect the leftmost outlet of the midiparse object to the inlet of the unpack object. This outlet of the midiparse parses the note on and off messages, which are a list consisting of first a pitch and then a velocity. Remember that velocities from 1 to 127 are considered note-on velocities, whereas velocity 0 is a note-off velocity. If we can time the occurrence of how fast these notes are streaming in from Improviser #1, we should be able to maths our way to figuring out the BPM.
- In this situation, we are more concerned with the beginning of the note and less concerned with when it ends. In audio terms, this would be called the *onset*. But the data stream we've parsed from Improviser #1 includes both onsets and the ends of each note. To parse this stream further, create another object below the unpack object called "stripnote." The stripnote object takes in a MIDI pitch and a velocity and ignores note-off messages, outputting only the onset. Connect the leftmost outlet of the unpack to the inlet of the stripnote, then connect the rightmost outlet of the unpack to the rightmost inlet of the stripnote object.
- Under the stripnote object create a trigger ("t") object and give it the argument "b," meaning that every time the object is triggered, it will output a bang message. Connect the leftmost outlet of the stripnote object to the leftmost inlet of the "t b" object.

- Create a new object under the "t b" called timer. The timer object is an object that times the time passed (in milliseconds) between bang messages. Connect the leftmost outlet of the stripnote object to BOTH the leftmost and the rightmost inlets of the timer.
- Finally, create a new "message" object under the timer object so we can see what the timer is reporting. Connect the leftmost outlet of the timer object to the rightmost inlet of the new message object. Go over to the Improviser #1 side of the patch, lock the patch, and turn on the toggle. Returning to the timer, you should see it reporting some time values like (assuming your GlobalTransport is set to 120 BPM) 0., 125., 250., 375., and 625 (Figure 6.1).
- These time values make some logical sense. 120 BPM equates to the following time values (Table 6.1):

Temporal anomalies:

- You may wonder why we are also getting periodic readings of 625. This reading or others like it are created because the beat generation system is not gridlocked to a time signature. 625 milliseconds equate to five semiquavers, which is not a standard note value we speak of regularly. Looking at duration in this way is often somewhat bewildering for humans, but this manner of symbolic representation is much easier for machines.

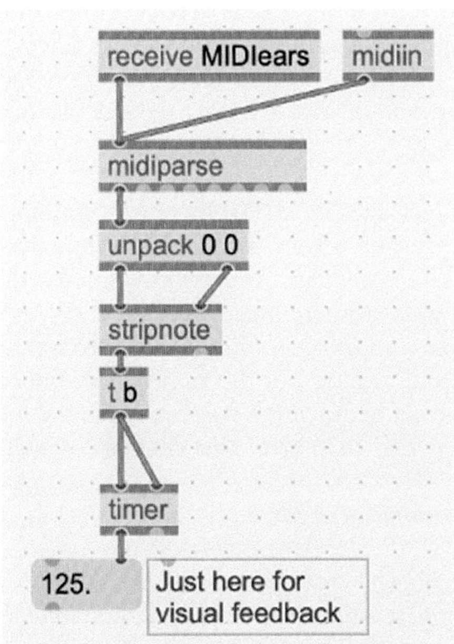

Figure 6.1 Timing the pitch onsets from the MIDIears channel.

Table 6.1 Millisecond timings for note values at 120 BPM

British name	*American name*	*Beats*	*Milliseconds*
Semibreve	Whole Note	4	2000
Dotted Minim	Dotted Half	3	1500
Minim	Half Note	2	1000
Dotted Crotchet	Dotted Quarter	1.5	750
Crotchet	Quarter Note	1	500
Dotted Quaver	Dotted Eighth	0.75	375
Quaver	Eighth Note	0.5	250
Dotted Semiquaver	Dotted Sixteenth	0.375	187.5
Semiquaver	Sixteenth Note	0.25	125
Dotted Demisemiquaver	Dotted 32nd	0.1875	93.75
Demisemiquaver	32nd Note	0.125	62.5
Dotted Hemidemisemiquaver	Dotted 64th	0.09375	46.875
Hemidemisemiquaver	64th Note	0.0625	31.25

- You may also wonder why we sometimes get a reading of 0 milliseconds. These readings are being caused by instances where more than one note happens at the same time. In these instances, the button is banging so quickly it appears to your eyes to be instantaneous, but the timer object is not fooled and records a duration of less than one millisecond and thence rounds it down to zero. If our goal is to collect these times in a timing catalogue, we probably don't want to include a zero since, if we want multiple notes to play on the Improviser #2 end, there's probably a better way to do it than making one of Max's timing devices play two notes, zero milliseconds apart.

Unlike the note-off messages in MIDI, there isn't a simple object (like stripnote) that can remove our zeroes. But luckily symbolic AI can provide an answer: an if/then/else statement. As previously discussed, symbolic AI models intelligence via a web of interconnected rules. If/then/else statements are a fundamental process computer programmers use to test or check the state of a variable. If we wanted to filter out the zeroes from Improviser #1, the symbolic AI approach would be to craft a statement like the following:

If the *number* is *greater* than *zero*, *then* allow it to pass, or *else* send it to a different place.

Conditional programming in Max:

- Under the timer object, create a new object called "if." The if object is probably the strangest object we've yet encountered. If you hit return / enter after creating, the object will "grey out" (change colour and become useless) because without a "then" argument, the term "if" is meaningless.

To the if object add the first argument, "$fl." The dollar sign ($) is used in many different computer programming environments, but it often means different things. In Max, the $ sign means essentially, "look for a new input." The next symbol "f" stands for float (a number with a decimal point), which describes the kind of input the if object should look for (this also happens to be the type of data the timer object is putting out). The number "1" indicates which inlet number to go to look for the input (because the if object can take more than one input from more than one inlet). Fully fleshed out, this argument means "the float input in your first inlet." This first argument will load the floats from the timer object into the if object.

- After the "$fl" object, create two more arguments "> 0." (make sure to include a decimal point after the zero and a space between the greater than sign and the zero). Fully fleshed out, the arguments so far mean, "if (the float input in your first inlet), is greater than 0...."
- Finally, we need to give this conditional argument something to do if the condition is met. After the "> 0," add two more arguments, "then $f0." The "then" argument defines the action telling the object what to do if the condition is met. The next argument, "$fl" means (as it did before) the float in the object's first inlet.
- The if object can also take yet another argument, "else," which defines what to do if the condition is not met, but that is not needed in this case. In this case, if the condition of being greater than zero is not met, the object will simply ignore it. Fully fleshed out, the entire conditional statement means, "if (the float input in your first inlet), is greater than 0. then (output the float input in your first inlet), else ignore the input."
- Connect the leftmost outlet of the timer to the leftmost inlet of the if object.
- Create a new message object and connect the leftmost outlet of the if object to the rightmost inlet of the message object. This will allow you to check to see if the if object is successfully weeding out the zeroes in the stream of data. If you see zeroes, check the previous few steps and troubleshoot (Figure 6.2).

Creating responses:

- Now that we have timed Improviser #1's outputs, we have a basis for some manner of musical response by the Improviser #2 system. Our next step will be to create a subsystem that randomly chooses from among four different drum sounds, playing in the tempo it is hearing from Improviser #1.
- Below the if object, create a new "metro" object. Connect the leftmost outlet of the if object to the rightmost inlet of the metro. This will pass the timer readings to a new metro, which we will use to drive Improviser #2's output response. Note that by using millisecond readings like "250.,"

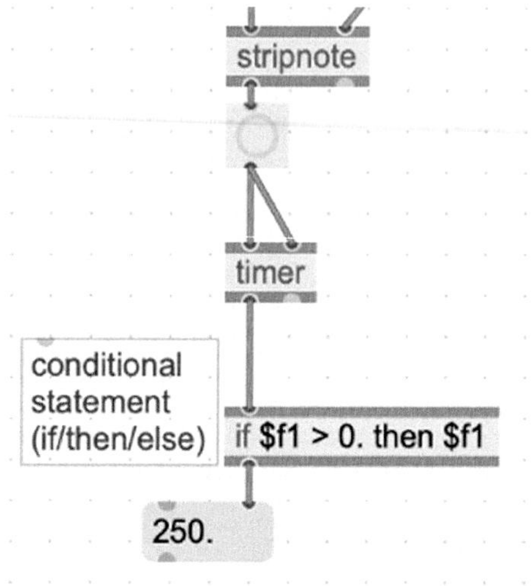

Figure 6.2 Defining the recency of Improviser #1's output.

we will be setting this metro without tying its internal clock to Max's GlobalTransport (as discussed in Chapter 4). This ensures we're following our design principle: using only the MIDI data stream—no outside signals—to drive the second system.

- Above the metro create a new "toggle" object and connect its outlet to the leftmost inlet of the metro.
- Underneath the metro object, create a new "random" object and give it the argument "3," meaning "generate random numbers between 0 and 3." Connect the outlet of the metro to the leftmost inlet of the "random 3" object.
- Underneath the "random 3," create a new "select" object and give it the arguments "0 1 2 3." Connect the outlet of the "random 3" object to the leftmost inlet of the "select 0 1 2 3" object.
- Underneath the "select 0 1 2 3" object, create four new message objects and type the following data into them (from left to right): 61, 60, 63, 64. Connect each of the first four outlets (from left to right) to each of the new message objects (leftmost inlets).
- Underneath the message objects, create a new "makenote" object and give it the arguments "127 100 10" (default velocity 127, default duration 100, and default channel 10). Connect the outlet of each of the message objects to the leftmost inlet of the makenote (the pitch inlet).
- Lastly, create a new "noteout" object. Connect the three outlets of the makenote to the three inlets of the noteout object.
- To test the system, lock the patch and start Improviser #1 (by clicking the toggle button). Then click the toggle button above the metro for Improviser #2. Does it play in an appropriate tempo? If so, congratulations

on making your first responsive symbolic AI system. If not, go back a few steps to troubleshoot. Or look at Figure 6.3 and compare it to your own patch.

- Take some moments to add some relevant comments to the patch (as I've done in Figure 6.3 above) and then save the patch.

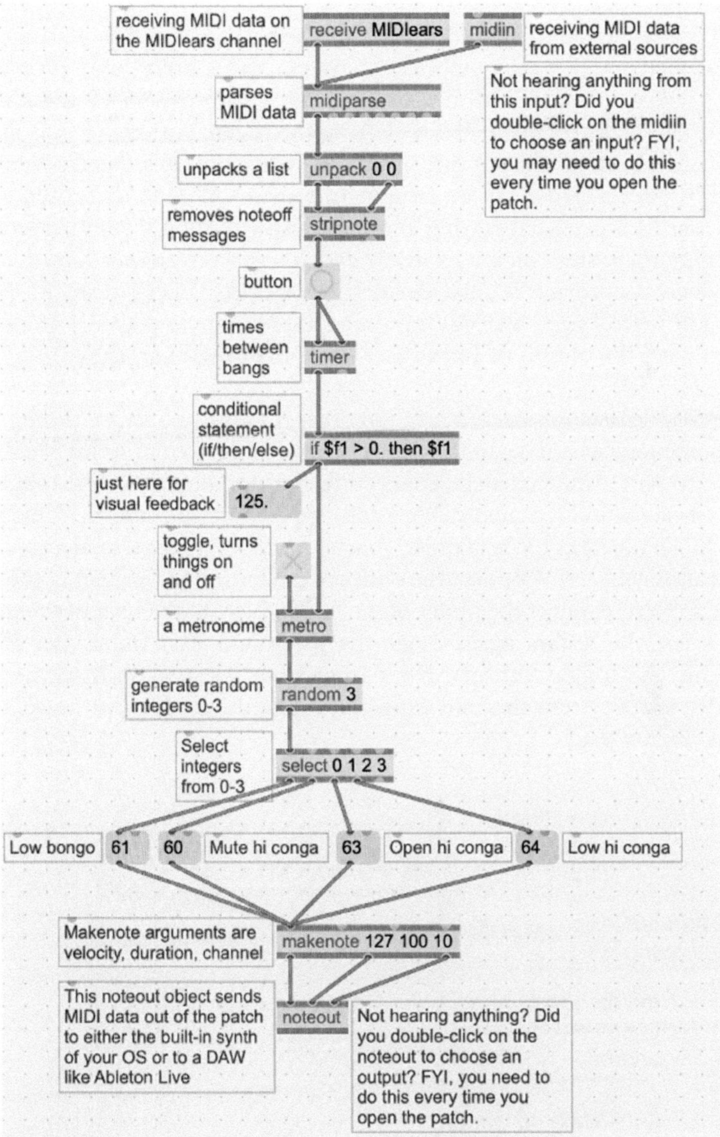

Figure 6.3 Improviser #2, a metrically responsive symbolic AI system.

- Want to see how responsive the patch is? Open the GlobalTransport (Max/Extras/GlobalTransport) and change the tempo up or down. Improviser #2 should change almost immediately (there will always be at least a one beat latency, since the system must listen to and analyse at least two beats before it knows a change to its metronome is appropriate).

On

As you can see, conditional programming is extremely useful in creating symbolic AI systems. But our symbolic AI system has another main problem in that it needs its own off button. Currently, both Improvisers #1 and #2 need to be turned on or off manually by clicking the toggle buttons. This is fine for Improviser #1 but breaks our rule of not receiving additional signals outside of the MIDI stream. How can we fashion Improviser #2 such that it recognises Improviser #1 has started playing and responds without human intervention?

Turning the system on is a relatively easy question to answer. This is a situation where Improviser #1 has decided to lead, so if Improviser #1 begins sending notes to Improviser #2, it must be appropriate to play. All we need to do is connect the output of Improviser #1 to the toggle somehow.

- The MIDI parsing process above the timer results in a button sending out a bang message whenever Improviser #1 plays a note, so that seems like a good place to start. Unfortunately, connecting a button directly to the toggle will turn it on and off repeatedly. We want it to turn on and stay on. Unlock the patch. To the right of the if object, create a new "t" (trigger) object and give it an argument "1." Connect the outlet of the button to the inlet of the "t 1" object. Next, connect the outlet of the "t 1" object to the inlet of the toggle.
- Let's test the system again. Lock the patch and start Improviser #1 (by clicking the toggle button). Does Improviser #2 start on its own? If so, you've got a system that not only plays responsively but also starts on its own (Figure 6.4).

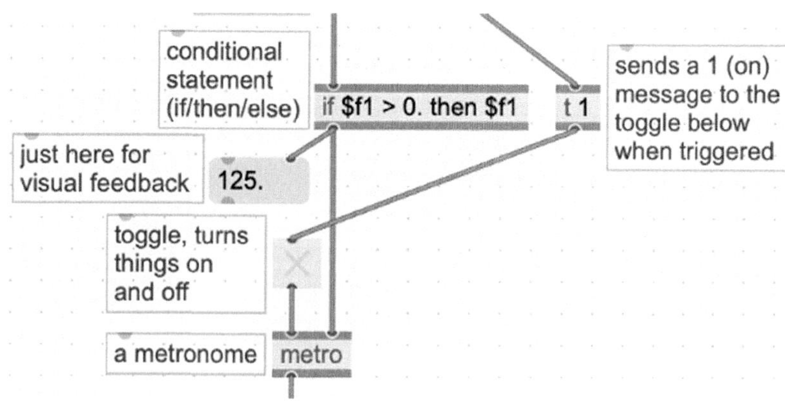

Figure 6.4 Improviser #2, with the ability to turn on its own metro.

Off

Turning the system off (ending the improvisation) will be somewhat trickier. Let us begin by describing a possible end to Chloe and Regan's improvisation in pseudocode.

//Ending

1. *Chloe* slows down her *tempo*, decreases *volume* gradually, and eventually *stops* playing
   a. *Regan*, detecting these changes, *plays* along in like fashion, but when *Chloe* stops, *Regan* detects this and *stops* playing as well.

While we haven't given Improviser #2 the ability to track and respond to dynamic or pitch changes, the Improviser #2 system is already responsive enough to follow Chloe's tempo slowdown. But how can we detect when Chloe has stopped? In one sense, Chloe stops playing all the time and we've already discussed these events, being defined as note-off messages or any pitch with a velocity of zero. Every time a note-off message is sent through the MIDIears channel, Chloe has stopped playing. What is truly meant by "eventually stops playing" is that Chloe "eventually stops playing (and does not start again)." Implied in the statement "and does not start again" is time, since (she is a professional musician) she may begin playing again someday, but maybe not anytime soon. What is implied in the use of such vague words like "may," "someday," and "not anytime soon," is what we might call "a range of appropriateness." For this situation, let us agree that the range of appropriateness for Regan to wait after Chloe has stopped playing to detect that Chloe has ended is between 1.5 and 4 seconds. This range is somewhat arbitrary but informed by the fact that the range between 1.5 and 4 seconds is the range between 3 quavers and two full measures in 120 BPM. What remains then, is to build a system that listens to the note-off messages from Improviser #1, times each of them, and sends out a stopping impulse when it encounters a timed stoppage within the range of appropriateness.

Building a Self-Directed Off Switch

- Through the following process we will build a system that detects note-off messages, then begins a counter counting down a variable amount of time (within the range of appropriateness) and sends out a "stop" message when the counter has counted all the way down. This process will be our most complicated bit of programming yet.
- We last left the topic of note-off messages with the "unpack 0 0" object that was connected to a "stripnote" object. To the right of the stripnote object, create a new "select" object and give it the argument "0" so that it is sending out a bang every time it encounters a zero. Connect the rightmost outlet of the "unpack 0 0" to the leftmost inlet of the "select 0."

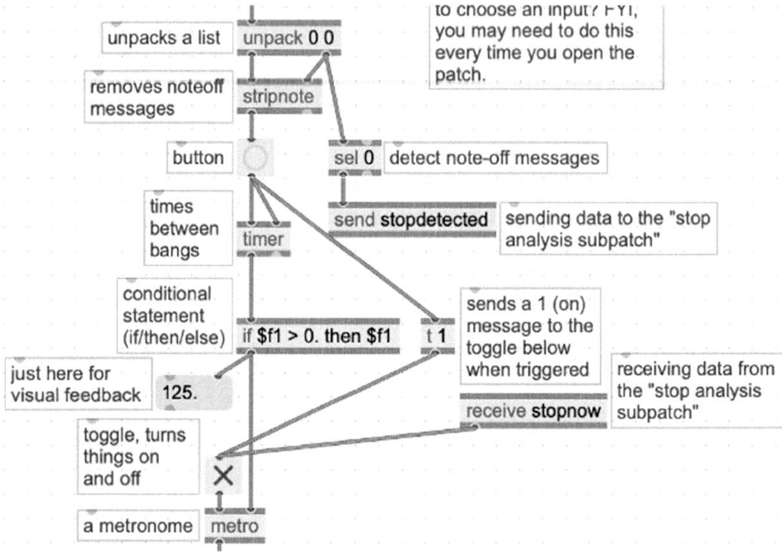

Figure 6.5 Making some room using send and receive objects.

- Since it's about to get a little crowded in this area, create a new "send" object with the argument "stopdetected." This creates a private channel via which we can send data. Connect the outlet of the "select 0" object to the inlet of the "send stopdetected" object.
- Next, above the "t 1" object, create a new "receive" object with the argument "stopnow." We will use these two data channels in a new subpatch to the right of the existing Improviser #2 system. Connect the outlet of the "receive stopnow" object to the inlet of the toggle object that drives the Improviser #2 metro. After we have built the timer, this will be the data channel through which we will send a stopping impulse to Improviser #2's toggle object (Figure 6.5).

Establishing a Range of Appropriateness

- The range of appropriateness is the amount of time that is appropriate for Improviser #2 to wait after Improviser #1 has sent out a note-off message. Since this amount of time is variable from situation to situation, it would be best if the system had the ability to somehow detect the appropriateness from its environment. Since this is all hypothetical, let us use a randomised process as a substitute for this variable.
- To the right of Improviser #2, create a new object called "loadbang." Like the loadmess object we previously used, "loadbang" sends out a bang whenever the patch is loaded. This object is often used to set new defaults in objects when the patch loads.

- Under the loadbang, create a new "random" object. We will use this random object in a different way than we have before. To the right of the word random type "@range" exactly (but without the quotation marks). Adding the "@" symbol adds assignable attributes to an object, which then requires a new argument. In this case the attribute we are assigning is the range. After the "@range" attribute, add the arguments "-1500" and "-4000." Fully fleshed out, this means that upon receiving a bang message, the random object will generate a new negative number between -1500 and -4000. The significance of these numbers will become apparent as we move on, but remember that the range of appropriateness is between 1.5 and 4 seconds (or 1500 and 4000 milliseconds).
- Under the "random @range -1500 -4000" object, create a new message object. Connect the outlet of the "random @range -1500 -4000" object to the rightmost inlet of the message object.
- Lock the patch and double-click the loadbang to trigger it. You should see a generated number in the range between -1500 and -4000, which we will use later.

The Final Countdown

- Below the, create a new "receive" object with the argument "stopdetected."
- Underneath the "receive stopdetected" object, create a new "t" (trigger) object and give it two arguments, "b 1" such that it sends out (from right to left) first the "1" and then a bang message. Since this object now has two arguments, you may notice that it has also grown a second outlet (some Max objects act this way, growing outlets or inlets as directed by their arguments). Connect the outlet of the "receive stopdetected" object to the inlet of the "t b 1" object. Connect the leftmost outlet (the "b" outlet) to the leftmost inlet of the message object (which will trigger the message, i.e., send its message to other objects down the patch).
- Under the "t b 1" object, create a new "toggle" object. Connect the rightmost outlet of the "t b 1" object (the outlet corresponding to the "1" trigger) to the inlet of this new toggle.
- Under the new toggle object, create a new "metro" object and give it the argument "1" so that it will send out a bang message every 1 millisecond. Connect the outlet of the toggle to the leftmost inlet of the "metro 1" object.
- Underneath the "metro 1" object, create a new "counter" object. Connect the outlet of the "metro 1" object to the leftmost inlet of the counter such that the counter object is counting bangs from the "metro 1." Connect the outlet of the message object to the second from right inlet of the counter object.

Explaining all of this is quite difficult. When a note-off message is received (via the "receive stopdetected" object), the "t b 1" object is triggered. Once triggered, it will first send out a "1" message (which turns on the toggle object and thence the "metro 1," which begins immediately sending out one bang message every millisecond). After the "1" message is triggered, the "t b 1" object sends a "bang" message out of its second outlet, which triggers the "range of appropriateness" definition being held by the message object. This definition of how long it is appropriate to wait is thus sent to the counter object, meaning "start at this number and count up to 0 every time you receive a bang."

Generating the Stopping Impulse

- Under the counter object, create a new "select" object and give it the argument "0" meaning it will send out a bang whenever it receives a 0.
- Underneath the "select 0" object, create a new "t" (trigger) object and give it the argument "0," so that it sends out a zero every time it receives a bang from the "select 0" object. Connect the leftmost outlet of the "select 0" object to the inlet of the "t 0" object. The "t 0" is the object that will generate a stopping impulse that shuts off Improviser #2's metro, shutting off playback. If the countdown is interrupted by a new note-on message, the counter will reset (after receiving the "appropriate wait time" message from the "t b 1" object) and begin counting down from the top again.
- We need to send this stopping impulse to Improviser #2's metro object. Create a new "send" object and give it the argument "stopnow." This will send the stopping impulse to the "receive stopnow" message we previously connected to Improviser #2's toggle.
- We need only one last step, which is to turn off the "metro 1" object, which is driving the counter object. Connect the output of the "t 0" object to the toggle controlling the "metro 1" object so that when the counter reaches 0, the metro is automatically turned off (Figure 6.6).
- Test whether this stopping impulse is functional by locking the patch and turning on the toggle for Improviser #1. Let Improviser #1 play a bit and then stop it by turning off the toggle. Improviser #2 should play along for an appropriate time and then stop on its own with no intervention. If this did not work, go back a few steps and check your work against the figures included in each section. If it did work, congratulations on building your first interactive symbolic AI system.
- Take a few moments to add comments to your patch and then save it.

Driverless Test Drive

While the controlled circumstances of the Improviser #1 patch have sufficed until now, it would be good to try out how this patch reacts to real-world situations. The procedure we have followed is quite useful when one is building

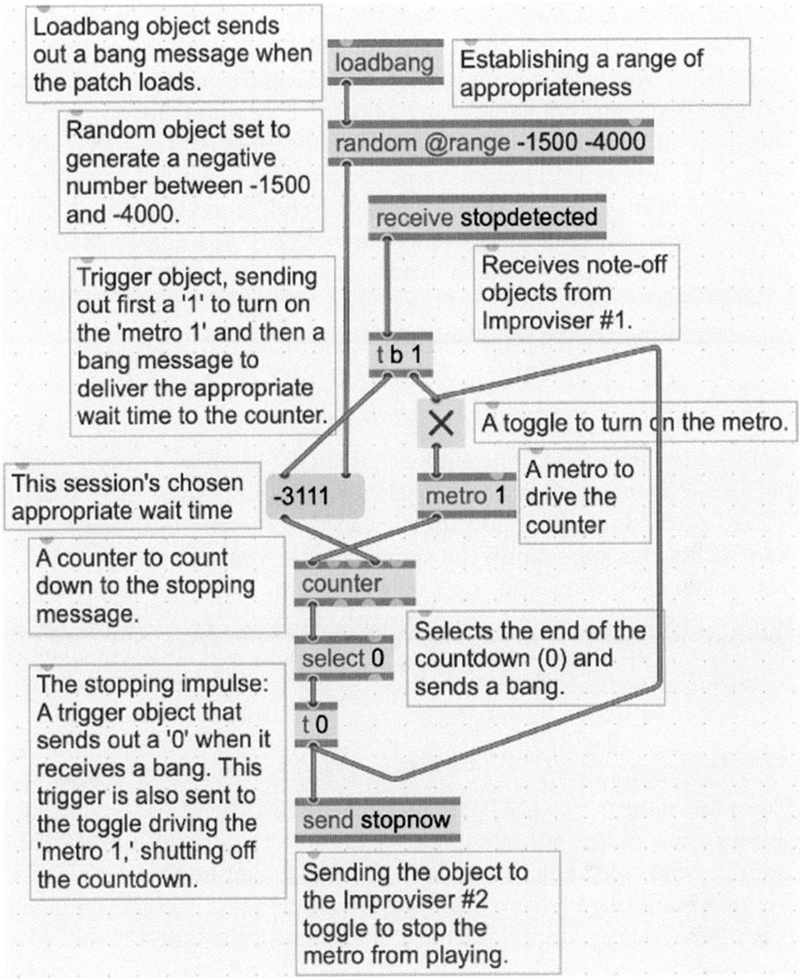

Figure 6.6 A subpatch that generates a stopping impulse for Improviser #2.

a complex interactive system: first build a model of the system it is interacting with so you can easily test at the click of a button, then build the interactive system. Later, if the first system (in this case Improviser #1) turns out to be less useful, it may be disregarded.

In Max Standalone or Max-for-Live via Ableton Live

- Remember the midiin object we added to Improviser #2? Connect a MIDI controller to your computer, lock the patch and double-click the midiin object, then select the MIDI controller you have just connected.

- You will need some way to hear your own performance. If you have some other sound generation you usually use with this MIDI device (such as a VST, or a DAW with a synth patch loaded) feel free to open it and use it in this experiment. For those using Max-for-Live with Ableton Live, drag and drop an instrument into the MIDI track in which your M4L device resides. If you do not have either of these options, you will currently not be able to hear your own performance. Currently, this patch has an output for Improviser #2's performance, and an input for the human's MIDI controller, but no output for the human's performance. We will need to do a bit more Max work to fix this. However, readers with different setups may choose to disregard the following section.

Readers with No DAW or Software VSTs Beyond Max

- Unlock the patch. Find some empty room in the patch we've been working on. In the Machine Musicians/Patches/Chapter 6 folder, there is a subfolder called "Snippets." Find the file called "general_MIDI_output.maxsnip." Drag this snippet into the empty space in your patch (Figure 6.7).
- This snippet will allow you this patch to take in MIDI data and output it to your operating system's built-in synth. Lock the patch and follow the directions in the comments about double-clicking and choosing a General MIDI sound with which to perform.

Improvisational Test Drive (For All Readers)

- Play a few notes on your MIDI controller. Improviser #2 should listen to you for a few notes and then join in. Continue to jam with Improviser #2 and then find an ending. Improviser #2 should stop shortly after you do.
- It is important that you don't skip this step. Don't just play a few notes and move on. Making music with a musical machine is the best way to discover its capabilities and detect any flaws. It's also a great way to come up with new ideas. Spend a good amount of time (much more than ten minutes) playing with the system. Aim for at least 30 minutes. What works? What doesn't it do? What should it do that it doesn't?

Customisation

- After you've played with the system you may notice a few things that you would do differently if you were starting over again. I've listed a few of these as customisation options and how you might go about changing the patch to affect these changes.
  - Wish Improviser #2 waited a bit longer before coming in? Add a "pipe" object between Improviser #2's stripnote and the "button" object connected to it. The pipe object requires an argument. Experiment with millisecond definitions or add tempo-relative note values.

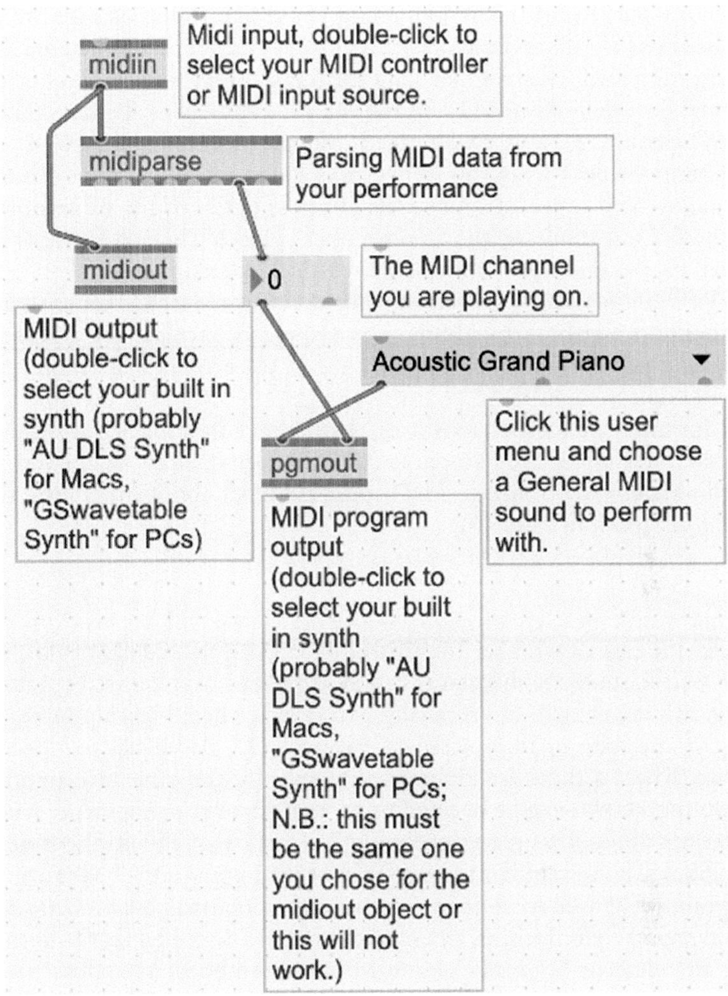

Figure 6.7 The "general_MIDI_output.maxsnip" snippet.

- Wish Improviser #2 could take an extended solo without dropping out? Adjust the range of appropriateness definition by changing the "random @range -1500 -4000" argument to choose a different range.
- Have you noticed that sometimes when responding to a human performance, Improviser #2 still plays super-fast notes? This is because humans sometimes play notes at extremely fast rates. Think of what your fingers do when you play a chord. Do all your fingers strike multiple notes at the exact same time as the Improviser #1 system does? Probably not. Improviser #1 measures these as minute beats of tens of milliseconds and then tries to play in a similar fashion. Fixing this is a complicated

endeavour, but if this is something you'd like to fix, change the argument of the "if" argument such that it says "if $f1 > $f2 then $f1." This argument will create a new inlet for the if object where it will take in a new float definition ($f2). In the Machine Musicians/Patches/Chapter 6 folder, there is a subfolder called "Snippets." Find the file called "time_filter.maxsnip." Drag this snippet to a space under the timer object and above the if object. Connect the leftmost outlet of the timer object to the rightmost inlet of the "p time_filter" object. Then open the time_filter snippet and try to understand what's happening here.

- Want Improviser #2 to play more or different notes? Consider changing the output settings to add more notes, maybe increase the argument of the "random 3" and the "select 0 1 2 3" to accommodate more/different choices.
- Improviser #2 focused mostly on rhythm and duration. How would you make this system responsive to MIDI velocity? How would you make this system responsive to MIDI pitches? What about other aspects of a musical performance?

Decision Trees

Consider the case of whether Improviser #1 has played recently or not. While at any specific moment this status can be expressed as a definitive state (like the logical statement "I am receiving MIDI data, therefore Improviser #1 is playing"), the state of Improviser #1 having NOT played has one necessary outcome, whereas there are different outcomes for the other two options. A problem such as this can be decided using an if/then else statement. But even after the condition "has played (recently)" is met, what should the system do next? Should the system continue to play or let Improviser #1 take a solo? A tactic commonly used to address these kinds of situations by symbolic AI is a decision tree. While decision trees are commonly discussed in the corporate world, the concept originally sprang from the symbolic AI approach of the 1960's (Quinlan, 1986). Decision trees in machine learning work in tandem with conditional programming to decide what choice is the best choice from a list of actions.

Decision trees are systems that include core elements called nodes, branches and leaves, arranged into a hierarchy. The function of each element is described below.

- Leaves: the decisions made by the deciding processes in various stages of the tree.
- Branches: possible choices (or outcomes) that might be decided by a decision process.
- Nodes: decisions that need to be made by the tree.
- Root node: a node from which other nodes may grow.

A simplified example of a decision tree could determine whether Improviser #2 should continue playing after Improviser #1 has stopped. The root node in this case represents the central question: "What should I play" This question branches into the first key decision point: "Has Improviser #1 played recently?" This decision has two potential answers, Yes or No. Here, the term "recently" is not fixed but represents a variable that can appropriate, perhaps depending on the time frame requested by the host or a number signifying audience restlessness. From this initial decision, additional branches could grow, leading to more refined questions or actions based on context (Figure 6.8).

Thus far, the predictable processes being enacted by the two improvisers have not involved the Improviser #2 system learning or changing, but instead these processes have been merely reacting to obvious states by triggering a variety of random or deterministic behaviours. But decision trees can be used in more interesting ways that would model how humans change their behaviours based on social contexts and the behaviour of other agents. To do this, our machine will need the ability to *learn*. Learning is the process by which an agent (e.g., a person, an animal, a process, or a machine) may acquire

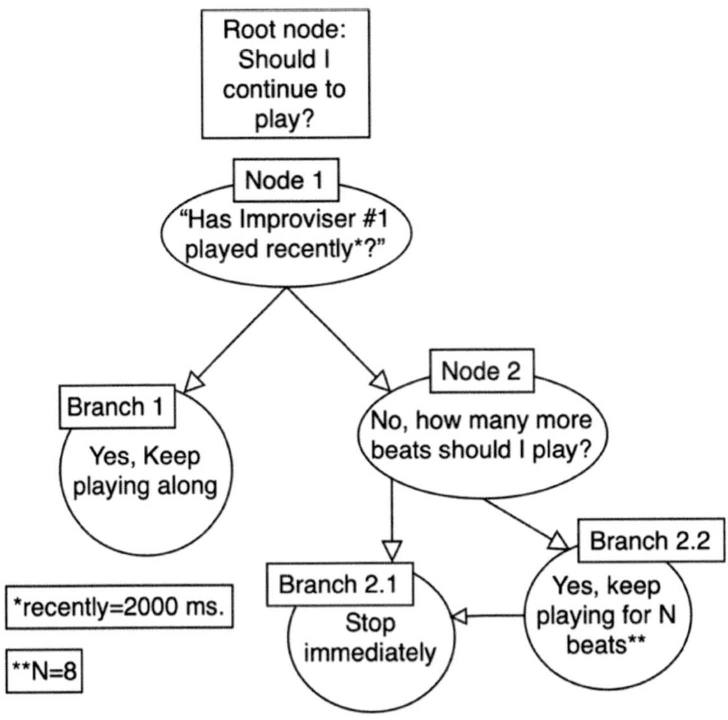

Figure 6.8 A simplified decision tree to determine whether Improviser #2 should continue playing.

knowledge, skills, or develop new context-appropriate behaviours from exposure to teaching or through experience.

The Limitations of a Symbolic Approach

In this chapter we built a system that can store data in encounters and can learn to associate certain inputs with certain outputs. This is an important step that should not be underestimated. While in the end, it may indeed be a fool's errand to try to quantify consciousness, scientist Ray Kurzweil and former director of Google Brain attempted this by introducing the *"Pattern Recognition Theory of Mind* (PRTM)," which argues that consciousness emerges from the brain's ability to recognise patterns and predict outcomes at multiple hierarchical levels (Kurzweil, 2012). Assuming this to be true, we have just taken our first step towards building an artificial mind. While many in the AI research field do not agree with this view, it is a good thing for us to sit back and appreciate the potential gravity of the work we are doing.

While the symbolic approach has proven effective and has produced at least this astounding result, there are some major drawbacks to this approach. Firstly, symbolic approaches must be developed on static rules, and symbolic representations that must be explicitly delineated beforehand. For instance, a harmonically interactive cousin to Improviser #1 would need to be supplied from the outset with definitions of what a chord is, which is a subject so complex that entire college courses (not to mention entire textbooks) are dedicated to it. Delineating every possible musical variable that may arise in a musical setting has proven beyond the limits of modern computer programmers. With every rule or decision tree, symbolic systems become increasingly large and rigid until the system overtaxes the computer system it is running on.

Additionally, symbolic systems encounter a great deal of difficulty handling data that is ambiguous, for instance a musical genre that doesn't fit their predetermined understanding of musical parameters. A symbolic system that was trained to analyse or interact appropriately with jazz would not respond appropriately to punk rock or rap. These systems lack the ability to grow or evolve without a time-consuming amount of coding by a human. Symbolic systems rely heavily on music theory, and music theories will always be biased towards the experience of the music theorist's own experience and culture. Unlike science, music is not so much built on fixed laws that are discoverable and falsifiable through experiment. Thus far, music has been generated by humans out of their personal experiences, cultures, and predilections. A symbolic system coded by an engineer from a Japanese background would not have the ability to appropriately interact with a Congolese Rumba group. The results might be interesting at first, but ultimately, a symbolic system would not change or evolve to be more appropriate over time without serious effort and some manner of cultural understanding being imparted to the Japanese engineer.

The objections above do not negate the fact that symbolic systems can create beautiful and astoundingly sophisticated musical material. But if one listens to a symbolic system long enough, they will undoubtedly have the reaction that Igor Stravinsky did upon listening to the music of Pierre Boulez, finding it, "either monotonously pretty or pretty monotonous" (Stravinsky, quoted in Slonimsky, 1965). That said, before we leave symbolic AI behind, we must address potentially the most useful tool in the symbolic toolkit: the Markov chain.

References

Kurzweil, R. (2012). *How to create a mind: The secret of human thought revealed.* Viking Press.

Quinlan, J. R. (1986). Induction of decision trees. *Machine Learning*, *1*(1), 81–106. https://doi.org/10.1007/BF00116251

Slonimsky, N. (1965). *Lexicon of musical invective: Critical assaults on composers since Beethoven's time* (Rev. ed.). W. W. Norton & Company.

7 Markov Models

Russian mathematician Andrey Markov was the first to write about a novel way of determining patterns in data (Markov, 1906). Markov, who had been studying probability theory and stochastic processes, developed a method for predicting the future state of a data signal by mapping instances of that data signal as it changes value. This process became quite useful for predicting all manner of processes in the sciences (particularly physics) and in economics (Seneta, 2006). By the dawn of the Dartmouth Summer Workshop, Markov chains were a well-known strategy for discerning patterns in data. Very quickly, the computerised implementation of this process became an integral part of the burgeoning AI field. Since then, Markov chains have become so ubiquitous in so many fields and are so widely known and accepted, that many in common parlance question whether Markov chains constitute "real" machine learning (a great example of the "moving goalpost" aspect of AI research, where the definition of AI is "whatever a machine can't do already"). Markov chains provide an excellent introduction to machine learning models.

Probably the best example of true AI musical work involving Markov chains and HMMs is David Cope's work with projects like *Experiment in Musical Intelligence* (EMI), and the generative computer program he named *Emily Howell* (Cope, 1991). As Cope famously said of this type of work, "When you had the database figured out it was really a one-stroke deal: you pushed the button and out came hundreds and thousands of sonatas or whatever." (Adams, 2010). Cope published extensively about this work, and to this day his many books and papers on his work are seminal reading for anyone interested in musical AI. Cope used a symbolic approach primarily based on making Markov models of various composers' work. Cope released many albums based on EMI's models of famous composers like W.A. Mozart, J.S. Bach, and Sergei Rachmaninoff (Edwards, 2011). In more recent times, data scientist and music enthusiast Uzo Ikwuakor has used Markov chains to create lyrical models of MF DOOM and other rappers (Ikwuakor, 2022). Modern software projects like *Riffusion* and *MuseNet* can generate intelligible chord sequences using Markov chains and HMMs (Xue et al., 2024; Sexton, 2023).

DOI: 10.4324/9781003534211-9

In this chapter, we will start learning about the precepts of machine learning in interest and have our first experience using machine learning to generate new music in real time.

Machine Learning Terms and Principles

The term machine learning is broad and covers all algorithms that allow a human-created artificially constructed *agent* to acquire knowledge, skills, or develop new context-appropriate behaviours from exposure to teaching or through experience. Many machine learning algorithms and methods are based on observations of human (and other biological systems) learning processes, but machine learning need not be limited to copying biological learning methods. While connectionist systems (which will be covered in subsequent chapters) are capable of many impressive feats of learning, symbolic ML systems learn patterns from streams of data that have been pre-identified (labelled) by the designer of an AI system.

Data

In computer science, *data* are points of information that can be analysed and/or processed. There are many types of data, some of which we have already encountered. For musicians, the most common types of data are:

- Integers: numbers without a decimal point.
- Floats: numbers with decimal points
- Symbols: generally, a representation of data that could include words, letters (Figure 7.1).

...but symbols could also include numerical data like integers and floats. Floats and integers are kinds of symbols, but the reverse is not true (Figure 7.2).

Ranges of data where the range is known and knowable are referred to as *discrete data*. There are 128 MIDI pitches and no more. If you are playing a MIDI pitch on a MIDI controller, it is one of these pitches. Almost all MIDI data is easily explainable as a set of discrete numbers from 0 to 127, e.g., there are 128 MIDI notes, the lowest of which is note 0 (C0, the C two octaves

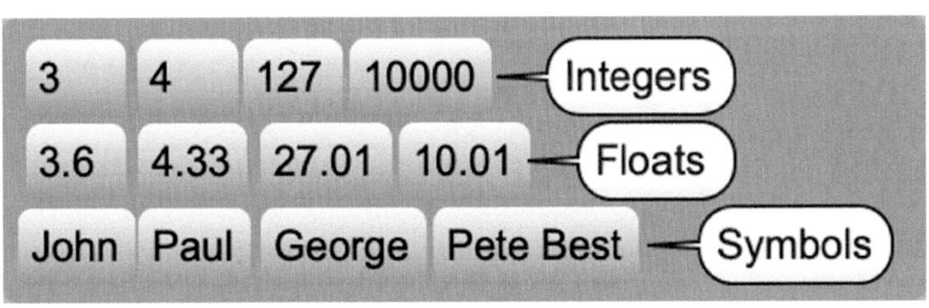

Figure 7.1 Three types of data.

Figure 7.2 Three types of symbols in four examples.

below the lowest A key on the piano) and the highest of which is note 127 (G10). It is quite easy to incorporate these data with machine learning algorithms because they are logically organised by the MIDI protocol by an internationally standardised source (the MIDI Manufacturers Association). MIDI data is (with rare exception) expressible by *integers* from 0 to 127. By contrast, digital audio is expressed in *continuous data*, using *floats*. As discussed in previous chapters, a *list* is a grouping of data points (pitch, velocity and channel, for instance).

In a MIDI system, all the data is of a known quality; notes are categorised as note data (note-on messages and note-off messages, depending on corresponding velocity data). Dynamic data is labelled as MIDI velocity, pitch bend, aftertouch, and many other MIDI data categories are formatted properly to MIDI standards, and thus this data comes pre-labelled, making it easy to perform ML algorithms using MIDI. Data that is this structured and known before it is processed by a machine learning process is often referred to as *labelled data*.

Machine learning algorithms operate by analysing large amounts of data. As such, these collections of data have a special name: *dataset*, which is a collection of data that can be evaluated, tested, or analysed for patterns by a machine learning algorithm. Datasets can also be described as labelled or unlabelled, depending on the level of preparation or organisation involved in their preparation.

Machine learning researchers think a lot about their datasets. Dataset development is a distinct (and often ignored) sub-field of AI research with its own conferences, journals, and theoretical frameworks. The word dataset is sometimes used synonymously with the word *corpus*, but corpus technically refers to unstructured data (natural data), whereas the word dataset most accurately describes data that has been formatted or sorted into a structure. A collection of MIDI files (which conform to a standard format) would make a fine dataset, whereas a collection of unedited audio files would more accurately be described as a corpus.

In the previous chapters, we have created patches which generate musical structures and even react to inputs, but without the machine learning any patterns from the data. In machine learning, a *model* (or a *machine learning model*) is a mathematical representation of patterns in data. A machine learning model provides a framework for a machine to understand patterns in data. The term machine learning model also refers to the stored pattern itself, after it has been learned. As human pedagogues know, for a human to learn, the human needs a learning style (visual, auditory, kinaesthetic, etc.). Machines quite similarly learn using different modes or styles, as represented by the various algorithms you may hear about (Markov chains, HMMs, GANs, CNNs, RNNs, etc.).

The concepts discussed in this book up to this point have all been feasible using standard objects that come "pre-loaded" in Max. However, Max is a general-purpose, object-oriented programming language, and not naturally optimised with all the algorithmic resources one would need to pursue machine learning and AI. Max has given users and third-party developers the ability to develop their own objects and devices that solve specific niche needs like DMX control of lights, communicating with Roli Blocks, or any other niche use one might be interested in via a third-party package manager. For any user of Max or Max-for-Live, packages found in the package manager are free of charge and easy to install.

Downloading the ml. Package*

In 2019, musician developer Benjamin Day Smith released the first machine learning-focused package of objects for Max under the name *ml.** (a.k.a. *ml .star*, Smith & Garnett, 2012). This package gives Max musicians the ability to utilise many machine learning algorithms quite easily. To run any of the patches in the sections below, the reader should follow these instructions to download and install the ml.star package from the package manager.

- Open Max (or alternatively, Max-for-Live, within Ableton Live).
- Click on File and then click "Show Package Manager" (Figure 7.3).
- You should see the package manager. In the upper right-hand corner, click on "search online" and then type "machine learning" (Figure 7.4).
- Several machine learning packages will pop up in the search window. We will eventually discuss all of them in this text, but as for right now click on *ml.star* (Figure 7.5).
- On the ml.star package page, click "Install" (Figure 7.6).
- Once the package is installed, feel free to click "Launch" to check out the various machine learning algorithms and tools you are now supplied with (Figures 7.7 and 7.8).

The object we will use extensively in this chapter is the *ml.markov* object. But feel free to click on any of these objects and take some time to explore the concepts this package gives you access to.

Markov Chains

How do we get a computer to recognise a pattern? A Markov chain is a mathematical model describing how states transition to other states in a system over time. A *state* is just a point of data. States could be pitches, velocities,

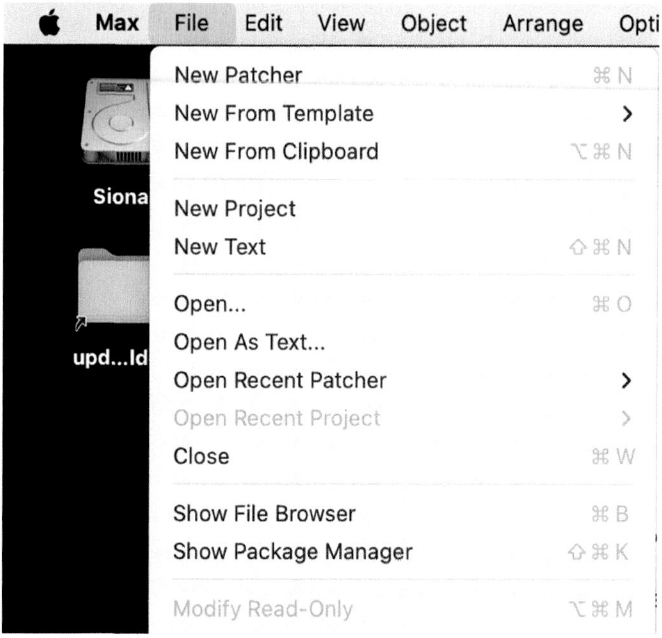

Figure 7.3 How to find Max's package manager.

controller numbers, or any other MIDI category of data. *State transitions* could also be used to describe the answer to a question like "is Improviser #1 still playing?" Or you could expand the problem beyond the binary stopped/playing to include finer gradations as in Figure 7.9.

However, analysing state transitions in music can get complicated quickly. Let us start with an extremely simple musical score (Figure 7.10):

This single crotchet in the time signature of 1/4 simply requires the performer to play once the pitch C5 and then stop. By one definition, there are two pitch states in this piece, playing a C and stopping. We can call the movement between playing the C and stopping a transition, the only one in the piece. Since the C only plays once and only transitions to the end of the piece, we can map out the entire life cycle of notes in this piece using a table like this, often referred to as a *state transition matrix* (Table 7.1).

In this state transition matrix, the numerator is the number of occurrences of a given state transition, and the denominator is the number of transitions from state to state. To further expound upon this, we know by counting the spaces between transitions that there is only one transition in the piece, from C to the end. Given a state (the note C) how many times does C transition to itself (the only note in the piece)? 0 out of 1 time, hence the 0/1 score in the matrix; how many times does C transition to the end? 1 out of 1 time, hence the 1/1 score in the matrix. The states listed on the left side of the matrix are

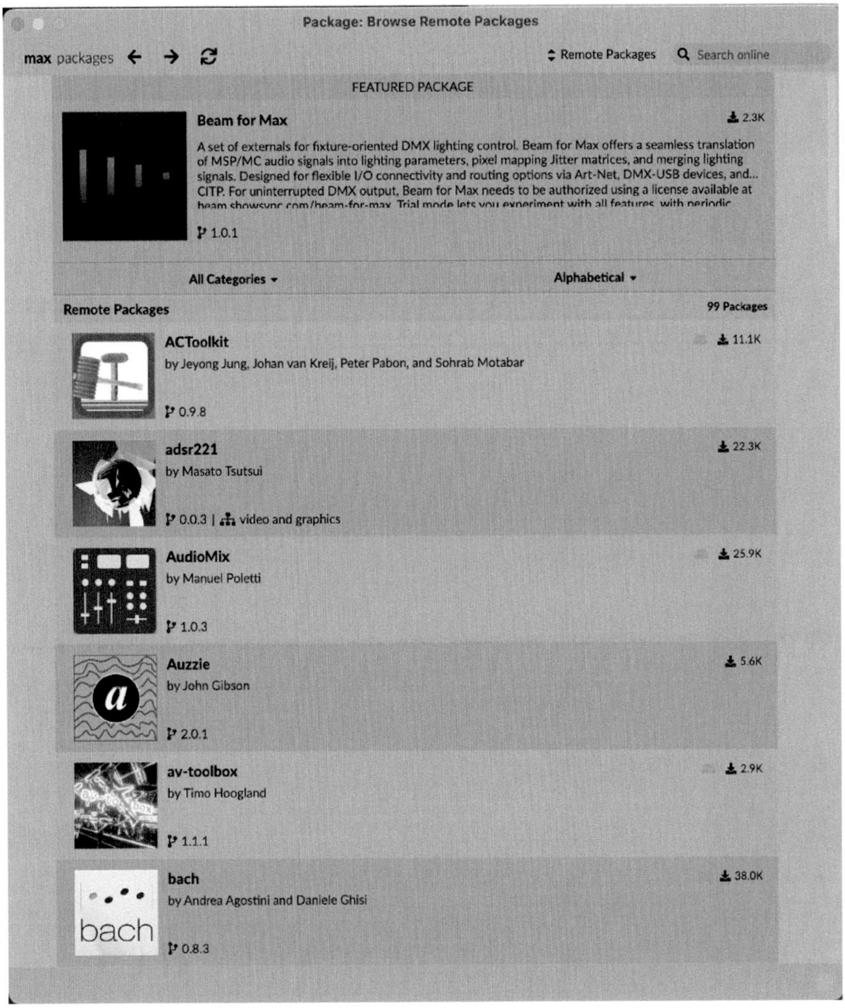

Figure 7.4 Max's package manager for third-party objects.

always the starting point for the counted instances to the right. Also, note that only played pitch states will be featured on the left of a state transition matrix, since to say that a "stop" event would transition to itself would be nonsensical.

Let us try this with an incrementally more complicated score (Figure 7.11):

In this score, there are three pitch states, C5, D5, and stop (do not play a pitch). There are two transitions, from the C to the D and from the D to stop (Table 7.2).

To give us a bit more practice with this, let us attempt an example with four pitch states (including three pitches and the stopped state) (Figure 7.12):

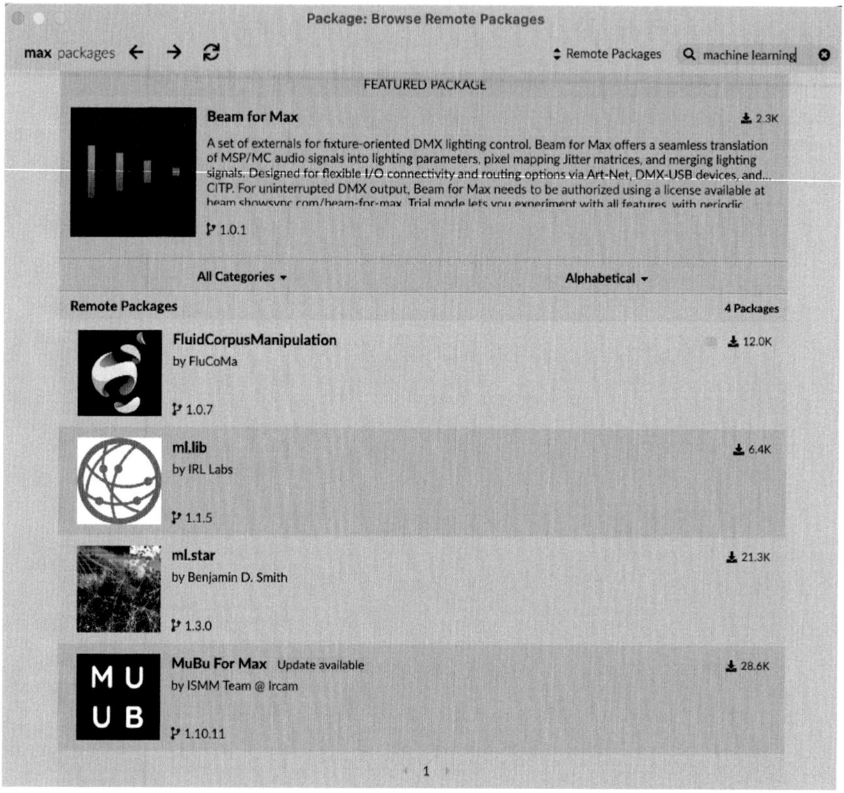

Figure 7.5 Machine learning-related packages.

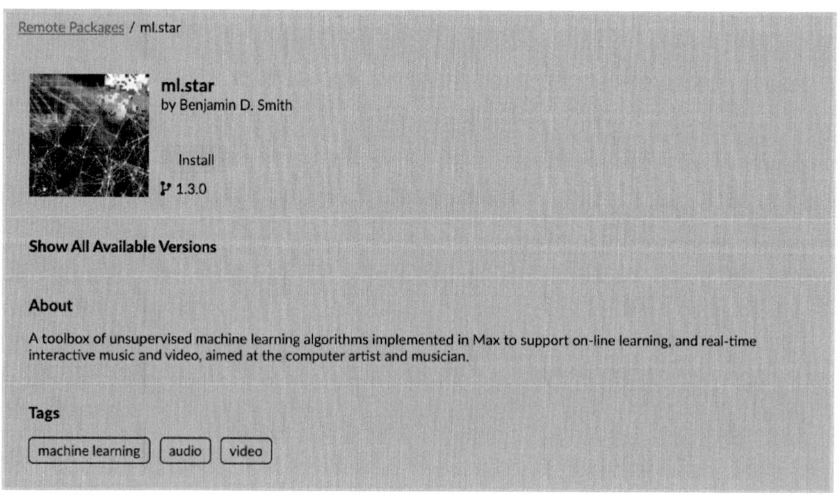

Figure 7.6 Benjamin D. Smith's ml.star package.

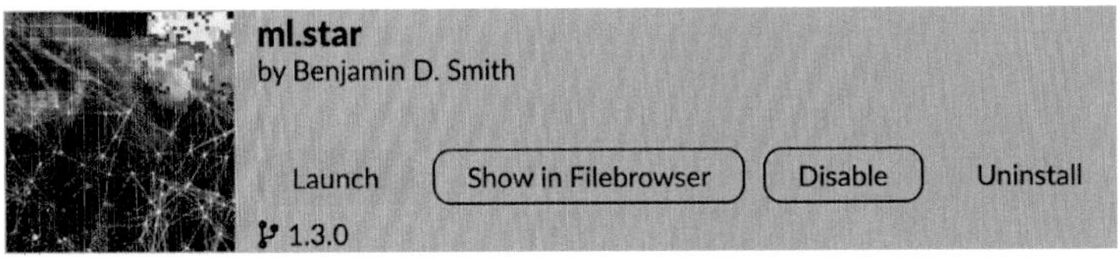

Figure 7.7 The ml.star package controls.

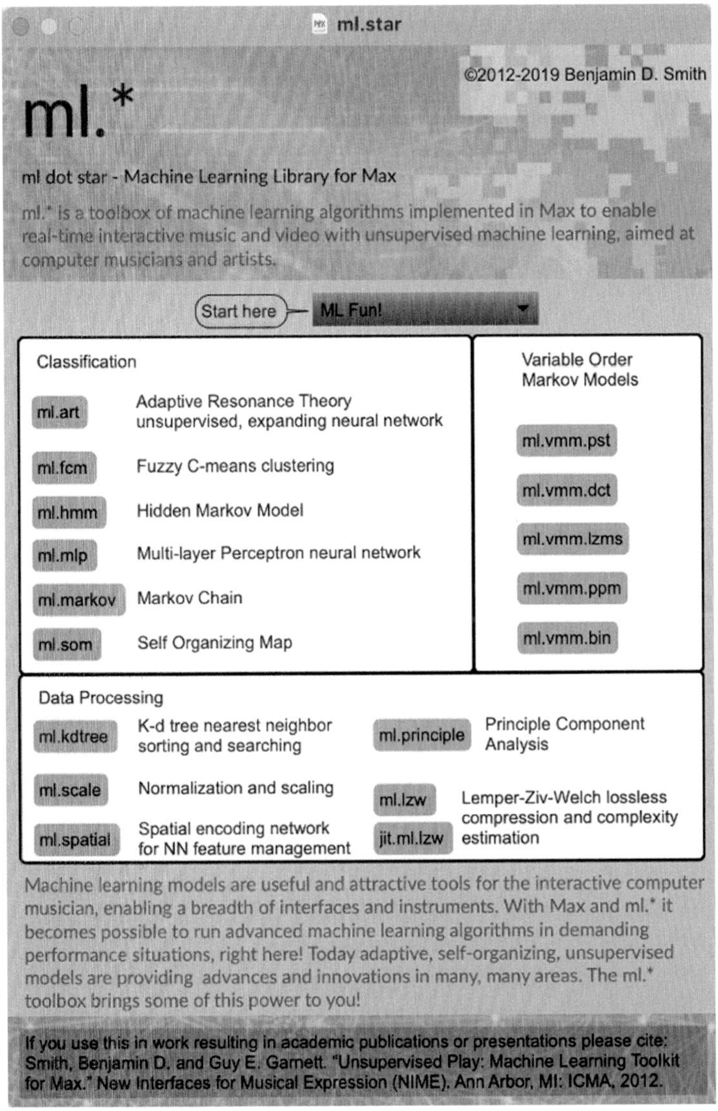

Figure 7.8 The ml.star overview page.

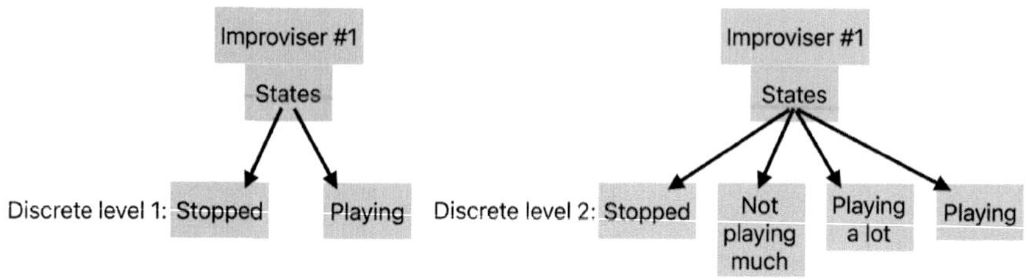

Figure 7.9 Varying levels of descriptions of whether Improviser #1 is playing or not.

Figure 7.10 An extremely simple musical score.

Table 7.1 A simple state transition matrix

States	*C*	*Stop*
C	0/1	1/1

Figure 7.11 A more complicated score.

Table 7.2 A more complicated state transition matrix for a passage with three pitch states

From > to	*C*	*D*	*Stop*
C	0/2	1/2	0/2
D	0/2	0/2	1/2

Figure 7.12 A more complicated score.

Table 7.3 A more complicated state transition matrix for a passage with four pitch states

From > to	*C*	*D*	*G*	*Stop*
C	0/3	1/3	0/3	0/3
D	0/3	0/3	1/3	0/3
G	0/3	0/3	0/3	1/3

Figure 7.13 The first measure of the Prélude to J.S. Bach's Cello Suite No. 1 in G major (BWV 1007) (transposed up an octave and in treble clef for ease of reading).

The four pitch states in this example are C5, D5, G5, and stop (the indication to not play a pitch). The corresponding state transition matrix would look like this (Table 7.3):

Now that we have a grasp of this process, let us try it with an excerpt of real music (Figure 7.13):

Analysing Bach's Prélude

In the passage above (Figure 7.13), we have the four pitch states G4, D5, B5, A5, and a stop. But unlike the previous examples, this passage includes some repetitions of each pitch state. By counting the spaces between pitch states, we can see there are 17 state transitions in the passage.

Each state transition in the analysis is referred to as an *observation*. In the example above, there are 17 total observations.

Generating New States

Now we will learn how to turn the machine learning above into new music. It would be a very simple thing to code a machine that played in the manner of

Table 7.4 A state transition matrix for the first measure of J.S. Bach's Cello Suite No. 1 in G major (BWV 1007)

From > to	*G*	*D*	*B*	*A*	*Stop*
G	0/17	2/17	0/17	0/17	0/17
D	1/17	0/17	4/17	0/17	1/17
B	0/17	4/17	0/17	2/17	0/17
A	0/17	0/17	2/17	0/17	0/17

Figure 7.10, since it only plays one note and then stops. If we wanted to do the same for the passage above, we might start by doing the kind of analysis shown in Table 7.4, and through that process taking notice of the way that 1 time in 17, a D triggers that the player should stop, but 1 time in 17 a D should trigger the next event should be a G.

Fractions like those in the state transition matrix above are ungainly to work with in a programming environment, so it would be better to work with a data type that is commonly accepted by Max objects: floats. What mathematicians would do at this next step is to *normalise* the fractions above into percentages, so the G-G transition (0/17) is normalised as a 0% probability (0., expressed as a float), whereas the B-D transition (4/17) is normalised as a 23.5% probability (0.2353, expressed as a float). Here is the same state transition matrix, but with our observations normalised as float-percentages (Table 7.5):

Table 7.5 A normalised state transition matrix for the first measure of J.S. Bach's Cello Suite No. 1 in G major (BWV 1007)

From → *To*	*G*	*D*	*B*	*A*	*Stop*
G	0	0.1176	0	0	0
D	0.0588	0	0.2353	0	0.0588
B	0	0.2353	0	0.1176	0
A	0	0	0.1176	0	0

Each of the values above represents the probability of one pitch state transitioning to another. To compose a new section of music using this model, we would need two components: a starting state and a method to calculate the likelihood of the next pitch state based on that starting point. Interestingly, if we sum up the probabilities of all state transitions in the matrix, they total 0.941 rather than 1. This discrepancy arises because one critical transition is missing: the transition from "no pitch" (before the piece begins) to the first pitch played, G. This transition, known as the *initial probability* or *starting state probability*, defines the probability of the system beginning with a particular state. The starting state probability assigns 100% likelihood to G, as it is the first pitch in the example. But this does not always need to be the case.

We could easily code a probabilistic solution to generating Bach-like music from these observations. But it would be a significantly more difficult process, and the complexity of the issue would only increase as we mapped further measures of Bach's *Prélude*. One could easily spend the rest of one's life doing these kinds of analytical operations on the rest of Bach's oeuvre. And this would only cover one aspect of Bach's music, that of horizontal movement from single pitches to single pitches. Luckily, this level of complexity is one *ml .star's* ml.markov object was designed to handle.

Understanding Markov Chains

The ml.markov object's leftmost inlet takes in discrete data and does exactly the kind of analysis we have been doing with the examples above. For each integer it receives, the object calculates a running matrix of state transitions that can be expanded continually in real time. Open the patch called "Understanding markov chains 1.maxpat" (to be found in the Machine Musicians/Patches/ Chapter 7 folder) (Figure 7.14).

Make sure the patch is locked. Click on the message object containing an integer, then click the "build" message. By doing this, we have given the ml .markov one point of data and built a state transition matrix, akin to Table 7.1. Next, click the "dump" message, then double-click on the print markov object; a popup window (the Max Console, which is helpful for debugging and checking your code in Max) should appear, showing you the following:

The messages indexed with the label "markov" are what have been received from the ml.markov object. Interestingly, the object reports that it has counted

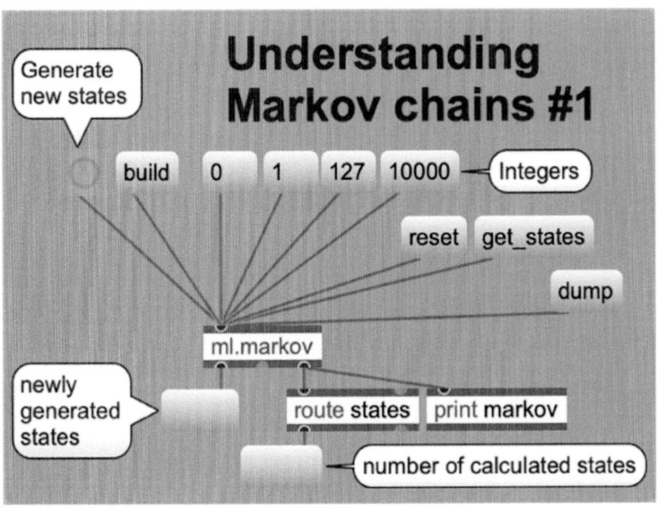

Figure 7.14 The "Understanding Markov chains 1" patch.

two states, even though we have only given the object one data point (the integer 0). It's kind of meaningless to have a state transition matrix with only one state. The second state included is the initial probability, mentioned in the previous section. To continue this discussion, we should click the "reset" message to "zero out" the object and make it forget its previous state transition matrix.

Now let's try giving the ml.markov object some more integers and see what it does. Since we're making a new state transition matrix, click "reset." Next, click the 0, 1, and 127, then the "build" message (in *exactly* this order); the object will make a state transition matrix based on these three numbers that looks much like the state transition matrix shown in Figure 7.15, but one that has four states instead of two. Now if we hit the "get_states" message, it reports it has counted 128 states. From this, we can glean that ml.markov is counting states numerically up from zero. This will be good to know for the future as for every state this object encounters, it will have to calculate state transitions from and to every single state, thus adding greatly to the computational load handled by this one object. Unfortunately, while Markovian operations can be used on floats and symbols (continuous data), ml.markov only operates on integers (discrete data). Floats and symbols will cause error messages, and the ml.markov object will need to be reset.

Once a markov model is built, you can send the ml.markov object a bang message to generate new states. Try this out for yourself:

- Click reset.
- Click integer messages 0, 1, 127, 10000, 0, 1, 127, 10000.
- Click build.
- Click the button below the comment "Generate new states."

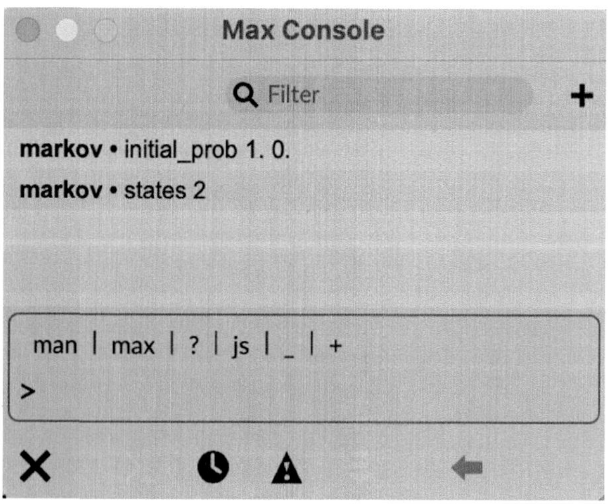

Figure 7.15 Max's Console window, useful for debugging messages.

After the matrix is built, click the button to generate new states. The states generated will go in the same order that you clicked the messages, 0, 1, 127, 10000, etc. However, the ml.markov will not stop generating new states. Ben Smith has wisely designed this object to continue generating even when it has reached the end of its state transition matrix. However, this will become an issue later if we need to remember what notes the final notes in a piece of music in order are so our improvising machine can model when it is appropriate to stop playing.

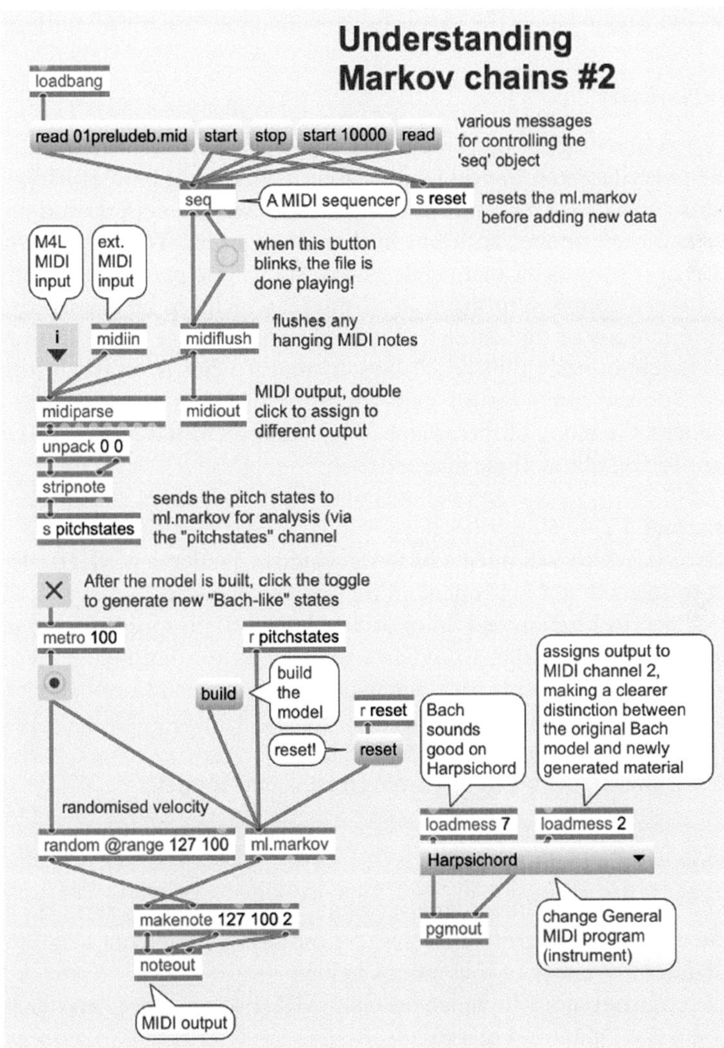

Figure 7.16 The "Understanding markov chains #2" patch.

Since MIDI pitches are easily defined as integers, it is a relatively easy task to use MIDI pitches from Bach's *Prélude* in the ml.markov. All we need to do is funnel MIDI pitches (note on messages only) into the ml.markov and then tell it to build a model. To experiment with this, open the patch called "Understanding markov chains 2.maxpat," (found in the Chapter 7 folder) (Figure 7.16).

To try out the patch, begin by hitting "start." The MIDI file will play through the sequencer, the process that starts with the midiparse object will funnel the pitch states into the ml.markov object. Once the *Prélude* is done playing, click "build" above the ml.markov object to build the model, then click on the toggle above the metro to generate new "Bach-ish" music.

Dataset Problems

If you know the original quite well, you might discern that these results have not fallen very far from the original dataset. This sounds kind of like a mish-mashed version of Bach's music where phrases have been cut up and put in a blender and then poured back out in the wrong order. You may like how it sounds, but it's doubtful that cellist Yo-yo Ma will be performing it anytime soon. This is a common problem in AI music, which can be blamed squarely on the limitations of our dataset. With only one piece of music in the dataset, our machine has only learned how to repeat what Bach did in this one instance. You can run as many files as you want into the ml.markov. Each new file broadens the scope of the model. If you happen to have some MIDI files you want to try, follow these instructions:

- Click reset.
- Click read, which will open a browser window. Find a new MIDI file, click on it to select it and hit "open" in the browser window.
- Click start (to listen in real time) or "start 10000" to speed run the file.
- When the button flashes to indicate the sequence is finished, either move on or repeat the process with a new file (don't hit build until all files have been loaded into the ml.markov).
- When all files have been played, click "build."
- Turn on the toggle button to listen to your new model.

Connecting to a Large Dataset

As stated previously, dataset management is a burgeoning sub-field of AI research. If you are interested in this, try inputting some data from a much larger dataset like either of the options below:

https://github.com/bytedance/GiantMIDI-Piano/tree/master/midis_for_evaluation/giantmidi-piano

https://kunstderfuge.com

Why Use Old Music?

The websites referenced above provide MIDI transcriptions in public domain works—compositions by musicians long since expired. While many websites exist providing transcriptions of more recent, copyrighted music, utilising such material for generative purposes raises ethical concerns and often runs afoul of legal boundaries. Consequently, the discussion of running files into the ml .markov object remains anchored in historical musical styles. Accordingly, the subsequent section focuses on interactive modelling techniques that derive their training data directly from the user, enabling the system to adapt in real time, rather than creating a model on someone else.

Machine Learning in Action

In this section we will begin modifying the interacting Improviser #2 patch you created in Chapter 6. However, it would be advantageous to save an incremental copy (so you can always go back to the working older version if you get in trouble down the line), so click on "Max/File/Save as..." and give this file a new name. Let us call this new patch Improvising Machine Patch #3, or "Imp3."

Starting with Improviser #2 as a base means a lot of the work is already done for us. In this exercise, Improviser #1 will be less useful to us, so we will start by deleting it.

In Max-for-Live OR Max Standalone:

- Unlock the patch.
- Select the objects to the right of Improviser #1 (CHLOE) and delete them.
- Next, select Improviser #1 (CHLOE) and delete them as well.
- Zoom out a bit until you can see the entire patch, select everything that is left (from Improviser #2 (REGAN) to everything to the right of it) and move it all over to the left.
- In the folder Machine Musicians/Chapter 7/Snippets, find the file called Simple_sequencer.maxsnip, and drag it into the patch, to the left of Improviser #2 (REGAN) (Figure 7.17).
- This sequencer can play MIDI files easily, which will stand in for our Improvisation partner in this exercise.
- Lock the patch and double-click on the "loadbang" object (since we copied this snippet into the patch, rather than loading it, the loadbang has not performed its function and double-clicking will make that happen). This will load the file "01prelude.mid" into the "seq" (sequencer) object.
- Remember that Improviser #2 was listening to MIDI data sent on the "MIDIears" channel, so we need to make sure the sequencer object is sending data on that channel as well. Unlock the patch and create a new "send" object, then give it the argument "MIDIears." Connect the outlet of the "midiflush" object to the inlet of the "send MIDIears" object.

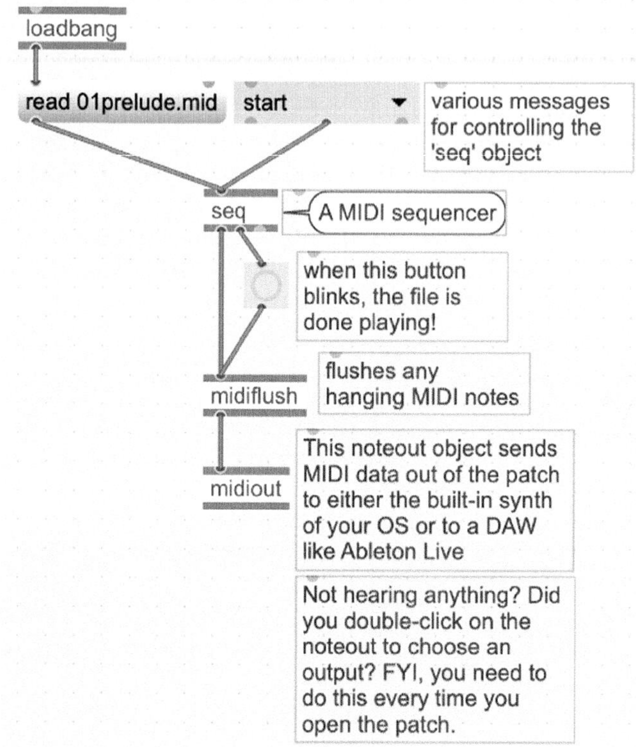

Figure 7.17 The "Simple_sequencer" Max snippet.

- Lock the patch. On the menu object, click "start" and check to see if the file plays, and that Improviser #2 is responding and playing along. If not, go back a few steps and troubleshoot.

Imp3

- Unlock the patch. Double-click the comment that says, "Improviser #2 (REGAN)" and change the name to "Imp3." This will help us keep track of the different systems we are building.
- Select everything below the "metro" object but not the "makenote 127 100 10" object and not the "noteout" object, nor any comments you may have created previously for these two objects. Delete the selected objects (Figure 7.18).
- Thinking about the "makenote 127 100 10" object, it would be good to pass the duration going into the metro (which controls the beginning of the notes) to the makenote object (which controls the ending of the note). This was less an issue with percussion sounds but will be more an issue with

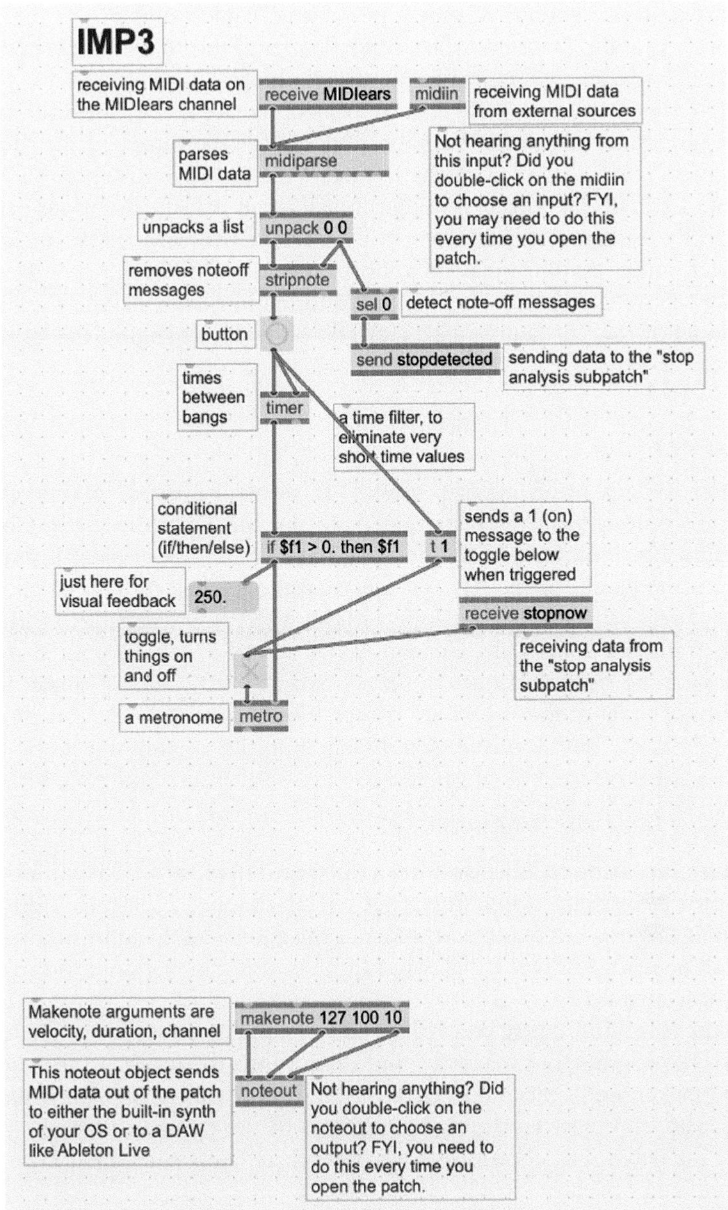

Figure 7.18 Making some room for new objects in Imp3.

non-percussion sounds. Create a new "send" object and give it the argument "duration." Connect the leftmost outlet of the "if $f1 > $f2 then $f1" object to the inlet of the "send duration" object.
- Above the "makenote 127 100 10" object, create a new "receive" object and give it the argument "duration." Connect the outlet of the "receive duration" to the third-from-the-left inlet (the duration inlet) of the "makenote 127 100 10" object. Doing this will mean that the durations decided upon by the timer object above will be fully performed by the makenote object, rather than just playing a short note lasting 100 milliseconds.
- Since we want Imp3 to play pitched information, let's change the default channel of the "makenote 127 100 10" object by changing the last argument "10" to "2."

Max Standalone

- When we get Imp3 making sounds, it would be good to differentiate Imp3's output from the tester patch. In the Machine Musicians/Chapter 7/Snippets, look for a file called "MIDI_program_out.maxsnip" and drag it into the patch, to the right of the "makenote" object. This snippet will allow users using Max standalone without a DAW or a separate synth output to choose a different General MIDI sound for the output of Imp3. Connect the rightmost outlet of the "makenote 127 100 2" object to the rightmost inlet of the "pgmout" object. Next, lock the patch, and choose a sound other than "Acoustic Grand Piano" on the umenu object.

Readers Not Using Max Standalone

- Users outputting to Ableton Live, a different DAW, or a VST synth should (if possible) create a new input on MIDI channel 2 playing a different sound. If this is not feasible or difficult, the patch should still work, though it will be more difficult to tell what Imp3 is doing in response to the tester sequence patch.
- In the Machine Musicians/Chapter 7/Snippets, look for a file called "MIDI_program_out.maxsnip" and drag it into the patch, to the right of the "makenote" object. Connect the rightmost outlet of the "makenote 127 100 2" object to the rightmost inlet of the "pgmout" object. Next, lock the patch, and choose a sound other than "Acoustic Grand Piano" on the umenu object.

In Max Standalone or Max-for-Live via Ableton Live

- The Improviser #2 patch outputted percussive sounds by banging message objects with MIDI pitches. Imp3 will use a ml.markov object, which will do a lot of the analysis, but also will generate new pitch states. Create a new "ml.markov" object and give it the attribute "@dynamic 1." Unlike the previous examples involving ml.markov, Imp3 will need to accept pitch states and build its model continually. This attribute will allow our ML model to grow as we add more pitch states.

- Where will we get the pitch states from? In this instance, we will need to use note-on messages, rather than the twice-duplicated note-on/note-off combination, so find the "stripnote" object above the timer. Because this patch is getting relatively complicated and we could use some space, create a new "send" object and give it the argument "pitchstates." Connect the leftmost outlet of the "stripnote" object to the inlet of the "send pitchstates" object.
- Create a new "receive" object and give it the argument "pitchstates" so it is receiving the pitch states played by the tester patch. Connect the outlet of the "receive pitchstates" object to the inlet of the "ml.markov @dynamic 1" object.
- Once the ml.markov object receives a few notes, it will be ready to make a model and generate new pitch states, but we don't want to send the bang message from the metro object to the ml.markov object until it has had a chance to listen to some pitch states. Create a new object called "gate" below the metro object. The gate object will allow data to pass through it when opened but deny that data when it is closed. The gate object is controlled by a toggle object or the messages 0 (which closes the gate) and 1 (which opens the gate). Connect the outlet of the metro object to the rightmost inlet of the gate object so that the gate is gating the bangs which will generate new pitch states. Connect the outlet of the gate object to the "ml.markov @dynamic 1" object (Figure 7.19).

Controlling the Gate

- The gate will load in a closed state when the patch loads, so the first few bangs from the metro object will always be ignored, but now we need to create a way to turn it on. Create a new "counter" object and give it the arguments "0 7" so that it will count from 0 to 7. Connect the outlet of the metro object to the leftmost inlet of the "counter 0 7" object.
- The counter object's rightmost outlet sends out a bang every time the maximum of the argument is reached (the "carry count"). This will be useful because we want to wait the 8 beats (an arbitrary amount) before we send a "build" message to the ml.markov object. Below the counter object, create a new message object and in it, type the word "build." Connect the outlet of this message object to the ml.markov object. Doing this will ensure that every 8 beats, the ml.markov will build its model. Connect the rightmost outlet of the "counter 0 7" object to the leftmost inlet of the "build" message object. The "build" message only really needs to be sent once to the ml.markov object, but doing it more times won't cause any problems.
- We want to control the gate with a 1 or a 0, and we want it to vacillate between these two messages back and forth. This will be a tricky bit of patching. Below the "counter 0 7," create a new counter and give it the

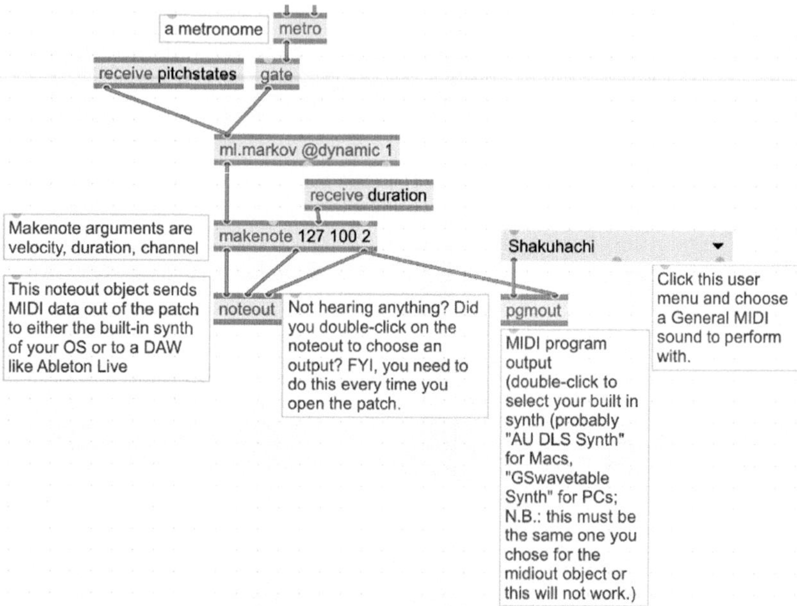

Figure 7.19 A gate and an ml.markov for Imp3.

argument "2." This second counter will count from 0 to 1 and repeat with every bang. Connect the rightmost outlet (the carry count outlet) of the "counter 0 7" to the leftmost inlet of the "counter 2" object.

- Below the "counter 2" object, create a "toggle" object. Connect the leftmost inlet of the "counter 2" object to the inlet of the toggle. Connect the outlet of the toggle object to the leftmost inlet of the gate. Thus, the first counter will count 8 bangs from the metro, send out a carry count update, and every second cycle will open the gate, passing bangs from the metro to the ml.markov, thus generating new pitch states (Figure 7.20).

Machine Forgetfulness

- One last thing remains. Resetting the ml.markov when the patch decides that it is appropriate to stop. Without this, the ml.markov object would continue to build a matrix of pitches forever. This might seem like a good thing, but human music tends to operate in smaller chunks of material, and we want our patch to be responsive to changes in the style between sessions. We already have a process that decides when it is appropriate to stop playing; all we need to do is connect the "stopnow" data channel to a "reset" message so that the ml.markov is wiped clean after each session. Underneath the "receive stopnow" object, create a new "t" (trigger) object and give it the arguments "b 0" such that every time it is triggered, it will

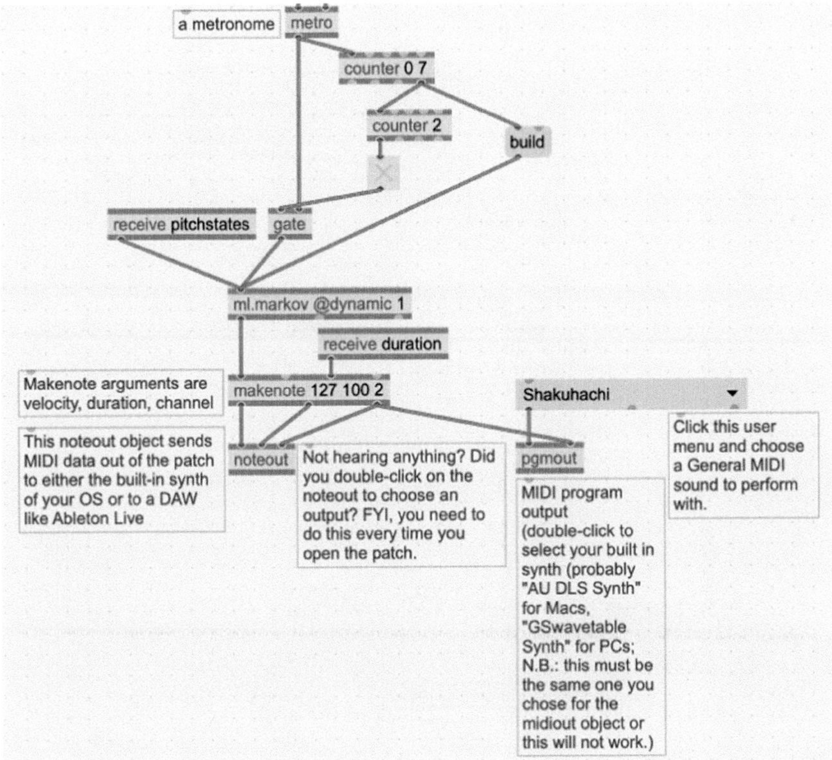

Figure 7.20 Controlling the gate for Imp3.

send out first a zero (to shut the gate) and then send out a bang message. Connect the outlet of the "receive stopnow" object to the inlet of the "t b 0" object.

- Below the "t b 0" object, create a new message object and type the word "reset" into it. Connect the leftmost outlet of the "t b 0" object (the bang outlet) to the leftmost inlet of the "reset" message. Connect the outlet of the "reset" message object to the inlet of the "ml.markov @dynamic 1."
- Connect the rightmost outlet of the "t b 0" object to the toggle above the gate (Figure 7.21).

Test Drive

- Save the patch.
- To test whether this works, lock the patch and click the "start" message in the umenu on the tester subpatch. Imp3 should wait for a while and then start jamming with the Bach Prelude, and it should sound like it (kind of) knows what it is doing. If this doesn't work, try working backwards from the last few steps until you find an issue and the problem is fixed.

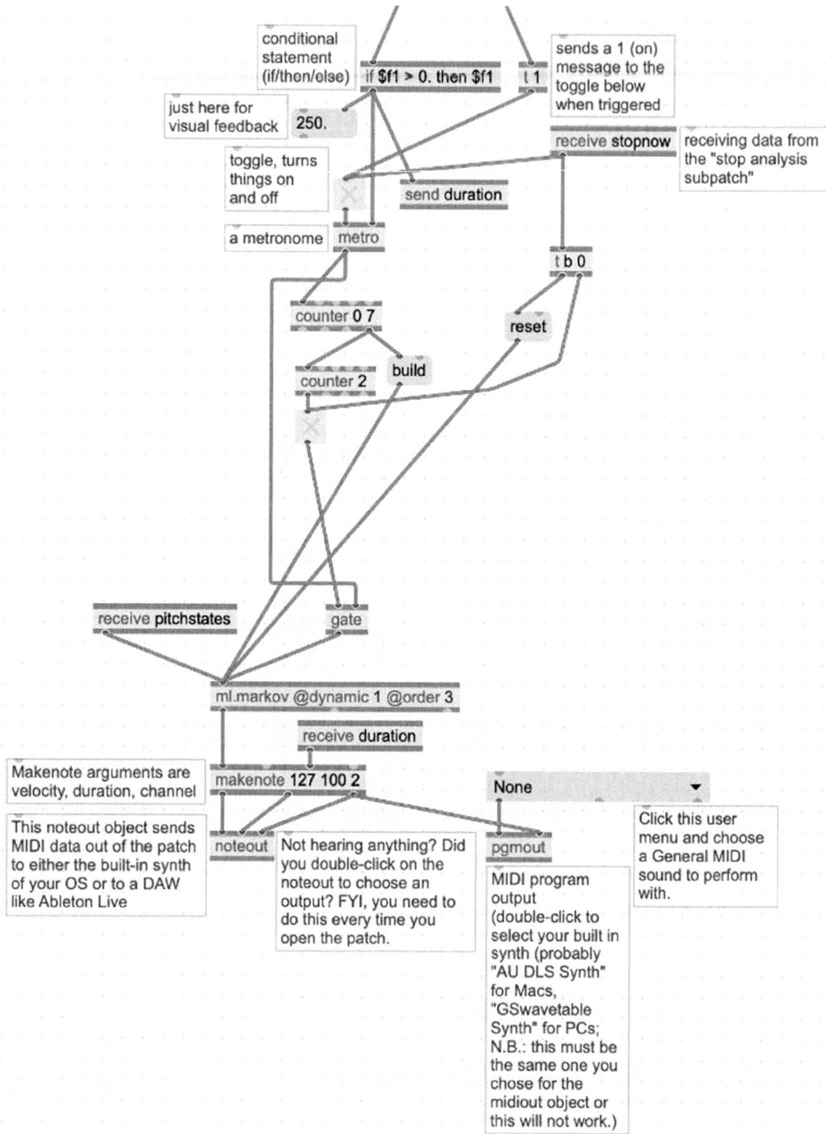

Figure 7.21 Resetting the ml.markov object between sessions and closing the gate.

Order

This kind of Markov chain, where only one memory input is analysed, is referred to as a *first order Markov chain*, where the future state depends only on the immediate previous state. As more memory is added, the chain evolves into a higher order Markov process, where the future state depends on multiple

Figure 7.22 An ml.markov object, adapted to create a third-order Markov chain.

Table 7.6 A second order state transition matrix for the first two measures of Bach's Prélude

From → To	*G*	*D*	*B*	*A*	*Stop*
G, D	0	0	1	0	0
D, B	0	0.333	0	0.667	0
B, A	0	0	1	0	0
A, B	0	1	0	0	0
B, D	0.25	0.25	0.5	0	0
D, G	0	1	0	0	0
B, D	0	0	0	0	1

previous states, allowing for more complex dependencies to be modelled. The ml.markov object handles this easily using the added argument "@order" and an integer indicating the amount of memory places to remember, as shown in Figure 7.22. The argument @order 2 would indicate a second order Markov chain, @order 3 would indicate a third order Markov chain, etc.

The first order Markov chain we have been using in this patch does not remember previous states, but changing the order to two means a radical change to our state transition matrix paradigm. Going back to Table 7.5, which mapped the transitions of one note to another in Bach's *Prélude*, rather than mapping the state transitions from one state to another, in Table 7.6, we are mapping state transitions from two positions to a third.

-Thus, given that the first two pitches are a G, followed by a D, there is a 100% chance (1.0) of the next chance being a B. This has a couple of practical effects. Firstly, this music will tend to sound even more Bach-ish than previous attempts, simply because you are modelling more complete sections of Bach's original music. Taken to an extreme extent, since there are 17 choices in most measures of Bach's *Prélude* (the piece is rhythmically monodurational, all semiquavers, plus the final transition to the next measure), a 17th-order Markov chain would most likely produce an exact replica of the original piece with no variation. This is referred to as *overfitting*, when AI technologies match a source or dataset too closely without enough variation. Overfitting is a bad thing, but it would be good for our patch to match the dataset a bit more than it does at present.

Changing the Order

- Unlock the patch and add the "@order 2" attribute to the "ml.markov @ dynamic 1."
- Test the patch again and see how it has changed. Unlock the patch again and change the order to 3 or 4 and test it again. You will start to notice this overfitting issue with fourth-order Markov chains and higher, especially if your dataset is small.
- When you are satisfied with the order you've chosen, try the test again with a MIDI controller, so you can get a feel for how the machine responds to live input.

Two Brains Are Better than One

- Believe it or not, one of the best things about human beings is our ability to multitask. Automaticity allows us to perform some very complicated tasks like driving a car while also carrying on a deep conversation. Our patch does a lot of stopping and waiting while it receives some new pitch states. What if it could listen and play at the same time as humans can?
- Unlock the patch and select the "receive pitchstates," the "gate," the "toggle" and the "ml.markov @dynamic 1 @order 3" (or whatever order you ended up liking most). Duplicate these four objects by hitting CMD+D (on a Mac, or CTL+D on a PC). Drag the new objects to the right of the originals.
- Connect the leftmost outlet of the second "ml.markov @dynamic 1 @order 3" to the leftmost inlet of the "makenote 127 100 2."
- Connect the outlet of the metro object to the rightmost inlet of the new gate object.
- Connect the rightmost outlet of the "t b 0" object (the 0 outlet) to the inlet of the second toggle object.
- Select the "connect 0 7" object and the "build" message and duplicate them as well, dragging the new objects to the other new objects you have duplicated.
- Connect the outlet of the metro to the leftmost inlet of the second "counter 0 7."
- Connect the second "build" message to the leftmost inlet of the second "ml.markov..." object.

Corpus Callosum

- Our patch needs a way to switch one on and one off so the two ml.mark ov objects don't try to play while the other is playing or listen while the other is also listening. The two hemispheres of the human brain have a connection point called the *corpus callosum* that allows for inter-hemisphere communication. Under the first toggle object, create a new "select" object and give it the arguments "0 1." Connect the outlet of the toggle object to the leftmost inlet of the "select 0 1" object.

- Under the "select 0 1" object, create two new message objects. In the left message object, type "1" and in the right, type "0." Connect the leftmost outlet of the "select 0 1" to the "1" message object and the middle outlet to the leftmost inlet of the "0" message. Connect the outlets of both message objects to the inlet of the second toggle, so that when the left toggle is turned on, it will turn off the right toggle. When the left toggle is turned off, the right toggle should turn on.
- Lastly, connect the rightmost outlet of the "t b 0" to the leftmost inlet of the second gate, so that when the "stopnow" message is received, both gates are closed automatically (Figure 7.23).

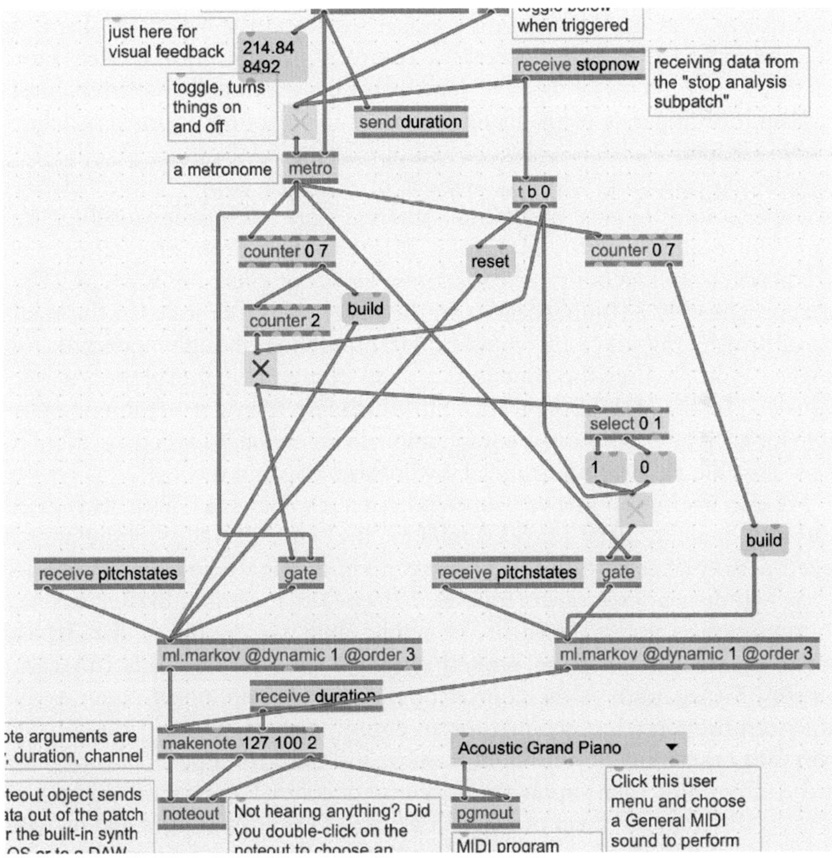

Figure 7.23 Using two ml.markov objects in tandem.

Clean Up and Alpha Test

- This chapter has featured an intense amount of patching. It would be a very good time to stop, save the patch, and add some comments.
- Test the patch to see if everything is working and troubleshoot as needed.
- If you are satisfied that the patch works, try making some real music by improvising with it for 30 minutes. What works? What doesn't it do? What should it do that it doesn't?

The Complexity Problem

The so-called *complexity problem* is one that continues to dog AI researchers to the present day. This problem was first addressed in early chess-playing systems of the 1950s and '60s that used rule-based pruning to reduce the preponderance of choices available to a player during much of the game (Russell & Norvig, 2009). Until now we have been utilising what has been referred to historically as the "divide-and-conquer" or modular approach (Laird & Rosenbloom, 1992), which breaks a complex problem into smaller, more manageable problems (as we have done by breaking a complex stream of musical data into disparate elements like the nine core musical parameters delineated in Chapter 2).

Musically speaking, the vast number of data points in a musical dataset (whether sounds or symbols) complicates real-time machine learning applications. For example, with 128 possible MIDI pitches—from no pitches to all 128 played simultaneously—the total number of combinations is 21,282,128, or approximately 340 undecillions in the American short scale (in the traditional British long scale, this would be 340 quintillion, though modern British English typically uses the short scale). This combinatorial explosion is only worsened by the MIDI 2.0 protocol, in which fine-tuning gradations are possible for each pitch, making it computationally infeasible to assign a symbol to every possible pitch combination. How infeasible would this be?

My own institution's newest supercomputer, the Indiana University BigRed 200, was built in 2019 for $9.6 million. BigRed 200 has a computational speed performance of 6 petaflops (quadrillion floating-point operations) per second (Indianapolis Business Journal, 2019). Data regarding BigRed's power consumption is not available to the public, but it is estimated that typical power consumption for the BigRed system is 1 to 5 megawatts (for comparison, 5 megawatts is the equivalent power consumption of about 4,150 American households combined for an entire year). If we could run a patch with 300 ml.markov objects all modelling 300 different aspects of musicality at the same time, then supply the system with a very large dataset comprised of many different examples of different genres of music, we might end up with a very sophisticated machine, capable of generating beautifully sophisticated music. Presumably the reader does not have access to these kinds of resources. But lest the reader despair, it would also be good to note that the human brain is capable of 10–20 petaflops of calculation a second and does it all while only consuming 20 watts of power (Herculano-Houzel, 2009). The simplicity with which the human brain calculates has a lot to do with its biological nature, which is beyond the scope of this text to address, but this should highlight the need for better modelling efficiency by our autonomous music system.

As a result of this complexity problem, most current technologies for generating music via machine learning operate too slowly to be viable in improvised performance contexts. Systems such as Magenta (Hawthorne et al., 2018), and Aiva (Gobet & Sala, 2019) are better suited to generating pre-composed music rather than real-time improvisation (Dolan et al., 2018). Until code efficiency improves significantly, or computational hardware becomes vastly more powerful, real-time generative music technologies must straddle this line between symbolic AI and newer, more powerful ML algorithms.

Going Further with ml.star

The *ml.star* package goes deeper into other types of Markov models, which approach the basic concept of a Markov chain in varying ways. Many of these objects make use of an algorithm called *context tree weighting* that predicts the next symbol in a sequence by evaluating the most recent context (Willems et al., 1995). The *ml.vmm.pst* object involves what is called a *probabilistic suffix tree Markov model* (Begleiter et al., 2004). The *ml.vmm.dct* object features a variable order Markov model that can perform general-purpose sequence prediction. The *ml.vmm.lzms* object provides a kind of lossless data compression via a *Lempel-Ziv 78 variable order Markov model* (Jacquet & Szpankowski, 2020). The *ml.vmm.ppm* object makes predictions of sequences by finding matches for sub-sequences in the training data, even if those matches are only partial (Cleary & Witten, 1984). The *ml.vmm.bin* makes use of a binary alphabet to make predictions.

The reader is also encouraged to investigate George Meikle's gtm.markov package, also found in the Max package manage (Meikle, 2024). This package, while containing a much smaller number of objects, focuses on second-order Markov chains, and (rather importantly) deals not only in discrete data but in continuous data (specifically with the gtm.markov~ object). Another major benefit of this package is the included RNBO~ open-source code, which will allow future innovators to make VST and AU plugins, and many other projects using the embedded gtm.markov object.

References

Adams, T. (2010, July 11). David Cope: 'You pushed the button and out came hundreds and thousands of sonatas.' *The Guardian*. https://www.theguardian.com/technology/2010/jul/11/david-cope-computer-composer

Begleiter, R., El-Yaniv, R., & Yona, G. (2004). On prediction using variable order Markov models. *Journal of Artificial Intelligence Research, 22,* 385–421. https://doi.org/10.1613/jair.991

Cleary, J. G., & Witten, I. H. (1984). Data compression using adaptive coding and partial string matching. *IEEE Transactions on Communications, 32*(4), 396–402. https://doi.org/10.1109/TCOM.1984.1096090

Cope, D. (1991). *Computers and musical style.* A-R Editions.

Dolan, D., Jensen, H. J., Mediano, P. A. M., Molina-Solana, M., Rajpal, H., Rosas, F., & Sloboda, J. A. (2018). The improvisational state of mind: A multidisciplinary approach to classical music repertoire performance. *Frontiers in Psychology, 9,* 1341. https://doi.org/10.3389/fpsyg.2018.01341

Edwards, M. (2011). Algorithmic composition: Computational thinking in music. *Communications of the ACM, 54*(7), 58–67. https://doi.org/10.1145/1965724.1965742

Gobet, F., & Sala, G. (2019). How artificial intelligence can help us understand human creativity. *Frontiers in Psychology, 10,* 1401. https://doi.org/10.3389/fpsyg.2019.01401

Hawthorne, C., Elsen, E., Song, J., Roberts, A., Simon, I., Raffel, C., Engle, J., Oore, S., & Eck, D. (2018). Onsets and frames: Dual-objective piano transcription. In *Proceedings of the 19th international society for music Information Retrieval Conference (ISMIR 2018).* Paris, France.

Herculano-Houzel, S. (2009). The human brain in numbers: A linearly scaled-up primate brain. *Frontiers in Human Neuroscience, 3,* 31. https://doi.org/10.3389/neuro.09.031.2009

Indianapolis Business Journal. (2019, May 10). IU upgrades research power with nation's fastest university-owned supercomputer. https://www.ibj.com/articles/74098-iu-upgrades-research-power-with-nations-fastest-university-owned-supercomputer

Ikwuakor, U. (2022, February 16). The making of a rapbot: A rundown on how I taught a machine to rap like MF DOOM using Markov chains. *Medium.* Retrieved from https://medium.com/@uzo.ikwuakor/the-making-of-a-rapbot-b6032813eb82

Jacquet, P., & Szpankowski, W. (2020). *Analysis of Lempel-Ziv'78 for Markov sources.* Proceedings of the 31st International Conference on Probabilistic, Combinatorial and Asymptotic Methods for the Analysis of Algorithms (AofA 2020), pp. 15:1–15:19.

Laird, J. E., & Rosenbloom, P. S. (1992). In pursuit of mind ...: The research of Allen Newell. *AI Magazine, 13*(4), 17–45. https://doi.org/10.1609/aimag.v13i4.1019

Markov, A. A. (1906). Extension of the law of large numbers to dependent quantities (in Russian). *Izvestiia Fiziko-Matematicheskogo Obshchestva Kazanskogo Universiteta, 15*(2nd Ser.), 135–156. [Also, 37, 339–361].

Meikle, G. (2024, June 19). gtm.markov (Max package) [Software]. *GitHub.* https://github.com/ge0rgeme1kle/gtm.markov

Russell, S., & Norvig, P. (2009). *Artificial Intelligence: A modern approach* (3rd ed.). Pearson.

Seneta, E. (2006). Markov and the creation of Markov chains. In A. N. Langville & W. J. Stewart (Eds.), *MAM2006: Markov anniversary meeting* (pp. 1–20). Raleigh, NC: Boson Books.

Sexton, T. (2023). Electronic resources review: MuseNet. *Music Reference Services Quarterly, 26*(3–4), 151–153. https://doi.org/10.1080/10588167.2023.2247289

Smith, B. D., & Garnett, G. E. (2012). Unsupervised play: Machine learning toolkit for Max. In *Proceedings of the international conference on new interfaces for musical expression (NIME)* (pp. 1–4). International Computer Music Association.

Willems, F. M. J., Shtarkov, Y. M., & Tjalkens, T. J. (1995). The context-tree weighting method: Basic properties. *IEEE Transactions on Information Theory, 41*(3), 653–664. https://doi.org/10.1109/18.382013

Xue, J., Deng, Y., Gao, Y., & Li, Y. (2024). Auffusion: Leveraging the power of diffusion and large language models for text-to-audio generation. *ArXiv*. https://arxiv.org/abs/2401.01044

8 Music and Language

As stated in Chapter 2, the most intelligent creatures in nature use some sort of language. Many creatures use a kind of language to disseminate thoughts and knowledge to other members of their species (Jurafsky & Martin, 2020), thus passing these important ideas to other members of the species. Humans are the most intelligent creatures of which we know, and humans use language more widely and deeply than any other creatures, so it stands to reason there must be a connection between the two phenomena, language, and intelligence (Weizenbaum, 1966). Accordingly, Alan Turing's famous "Imitation Game" (a.k.a., the Turing Test) focuses on language as the greatest measure of human-level intelligence (Turing, 1950).

The question of music's candidacy as a language is widely debated and beyond the scope of this text. It suffices to say that music shares some characteristics of language, but it also acts differently from language in other ways. Like language, music is used to convey emotional meanings (Meyer, 1956; Elliott, 1995; Bunt, 2010) and at least partially shares with language a syntactical structure (Lerdahl & Jackendoff, 1983; Huron, 2006). Music, like language, is often ordered according to rules determining the order of elements. In many kinds of music, smaller elements (like motifs) must precede other small elements to create a kind of grammar (like the "back beat" of Ringo Starr's drumming patterns, or the way a blues turnaround inevitably falls into the tonic). However, unlike language, the reversing of a rule does not negate an example's validity as music. Quite bafflingly, music that does not adhere to strict linguistic structures (for instance, free jazz, or noise rock) can still legitimately be categorised as music due to its manipulation of the Core Auditory and Perceptual Parameters. In this sense, musical grammar isn't about correct or incorrect *syntax* but about creating expectation and release—structuring elements so that our ears lean forward in anticipation and then sigh in recognition (Huron, 2006).

Music theorists have often relied on linguistic structures to describe melodic development in terms like "sentence" and "phrase." Music is even processed by the same parts of the brain as language (Patel, 2008). However, despite these similarities, in many respects music does not act like a language and may even be a distinct and unique form of symbolic communication (Nattiez,

DOI: 10.4324/9781003534211-10

1990). Ultimately, music is close enough to a language that AI music researchers have found linguistic research to be quite relevant to the study of musical AI. In this chapter, we will conclude our discussion about the symbolic approach by introducing some deeper topics within the science of linguistics. The chapter includes an interactive system that can parse incoming MIDI data into higher-level patterns symbolising musical phenomena, involving a new machine learning algorithm called a Hidden Markov Model.

NLP and Symbolic AI

How can linguistic ideas interact in a musical space? In Chapter 7, we created an autonomous music system (Imp3) that models pitch using a one-dimensional Markov chain and added reactive responses for duration and an arbitrary static argument for dynamics (velocity 127). The inclusion of these other parameters creates what is called *cohesion* by linguists. Cohesion is like a glue that binds disparate elements together into a unified experience (Halliday & Hasan, 1976). Think of what raw pitches would sound like without any dynamic or rhythmic variation. A patch generating these disparate elements would lack cohesion.

Conversely, musicians often find ways to "bring out" certain notes, rhythms, phrases, etc. by giving them more dynamic prominence over another event (Schoenberg, 1967; Forte, 1973), creating what linguists researchers call *salience* (Lerdahl & Jackendoff, 1983; Sloboda, 1985; Huron, 2006). Salience is the "spotlight" given to elements that are cognitively "activated" (Grosz et al., 1995). To pull off this effect, composers use many different tricks and tools. Composers sometimes change the range of one instrument so it stands out; improvising musicians will often decrease their dynamics instinctively when another player is taking a solo. Guitarists sometimes change their strumming patterns to be more prominent at a particular point; drummers tend to play a beat slightly differently to cue the end of a section. Examples of this are ubiquitous in all genres of music.

But what if an element is poorly matched to a musical context, sticking out like a sore thumb? How well elements match or "gel" with each other creates what linguists call *coherence*. Coherence describes the logical connectedness of one element in a collection to another (Barzilay & Lapata, 2008). Traditional Congolese Rumba usually involves a singer, guitars, drums, hand percussion, keyboards, and a horn section. It would violate a sense of coherence for a Rumba musician to show up to a rehearsal with bagpipes. It may seem like these concepts should be feasible to control in a rule-based system. However, due to the complexity problem (mentioned in the last chapter), we can assume that even though Markov chains can adequately model the patterns underlying many musical phenomena, rule-based systems eventually become too complex for modern computing devices to be effective at handling the complex interaction between musical parameters. To manage this complex interplay of parameters, we must delve deeper into linguistic concepts.

Natural Language?

Many early pioneers of symbolic AI came not from the study of informatics, but from the field of linguistics. Incidentally, the subfield of *Natural Language Processing* (NLP, the science of building systems that can analyse, recognise, and generate language) has been an integral part of the AI field from the beginning. In one sense, a "natural" language is language that is used commonly by human beings for communication (as distinct from human-developed computer languages, like Python, C+, HTML, etc.) as it exists without any strict rules governing grammatical correctness. Natural language is what you speak when you order food at a restaurant, when you answer a phone call from a telemarketer, or text your sister. Natural language can generally be spoken, written, or signed (e.g., British Sign Language; Chomsky, 2006). A computer system built with the ability to decipher and generate natural language would have the ability to interact with humans in the real world, without preparation or translation. *Natural music* (a riff on natural language) similarly refers to music that is unprepared and unlabelled beforehand. Natural music is any music you may encounter in the real world.

The ability to understand and manipulate language requires a vast amount of data, the ability to generalise (make assumptions), and the ability to represent symbols and concepts abstractly (without a prompt or clue involving other sensory inputs; Boden, 2006). After the foundational work by researchers like Turing and Weizenbaum, NLP systems built in the '80s and '90s could process vast datasets of natural language like the Statistical Machine Translation system at IBM's T.J. Watson Research Center (Brown et al., 1990). In the 2000s and beyond, the study of NLP moved on to use deep learning algorithms and neural networks, which have led to major breakthroughs like the development of Transformers. The development of Transformers has allowed for even more advanced language models like the Bidirectional Encoder Representations from Transformers (BERT) algorithm developed by Google (Devlin et al., 2018). Modern chatbot systems like ChatGPT, Claude, and Microsoft Copilot are developed using modern NLP techniques and incredibly massive datasets.

NLP Terms and Principles

Semantics are meanings conveyed primarily by words, but also by extension, phrases, and sentences. The word *drum* stands in for the concept of a musical instrument, generally a membranophone covered by a natural or a synthetic membrane, often beaten by various beaters (sticks, mallets, hammers, etc.) or by hands. Other words are often used to create short phrases in order to further discriminate some potential meanings of words from others. For instance, the phrase *snare drum* eliminates the potential that we are discussing a drum that might be struck with a hammer.

According to the subject-verb order (a syntactical rule governing the English language), the following is a correct sentence:

Drew (subject) plays (verb) drums (object).

And the following is an incorrectly ordered sentence:

Plays drums Drew.

This somewhat simple schematic for sentence structure allows for generalisation. Human children begin to learn the advanced rules of natural language syntax between 24 and 30 months of age (Snow, 2010). If we were building a machine to understand sentence structure, a basic understanding of English syntax would help the machine understand the sentence above to mean that:

Drew (subject, a particular human named Drew) plays (verb, a musical word) drums (object, a particular musical instrument).

And not this:

Drew (the past tense of draw) plays (acting frivolously) drums (a large container for shipping).

Words and phrases can at times have multiple meanings, creating what NLP researchers refer to as *ambiguity*. The meaning of ambiguous words and phrases depends on the context in which they are used. For instance, this sentence below would make sense in some contexts but the ambiguity inherent in these words might lead some to glean a different meaning from the sentence:

Drew was so busy playing around with those big drums, he didn't get any of his boxes shipped.

Ambiguous Songs

There are many musical examples of this interplay between ambiguity and pragmatism. The rhythm of the piano intro to Radiohead's "Pyramid Song" (from *Amnesiac*, 2001) seems to inexplicably vacillate between a shaky 3/8 and 4/8 for nearly two minutes, until the drum entrance removes the ambiguity by playing a swung 4/4 beat (Bennett, 2019). Examples of this reliance on ambiguity are ubiquitous in every genre of music. The preponderance of examples shows that ambiguity in music is not merely a quirk, but a deliberate compositional device that teases the listener's perception, inviting active interpretation. In each case, the eventual clarification—the pragmatic side—depends on how the tension of the preceding uncertainty is resolved or withheld, and on how it aligns (or misaligns) with the listener's internalised sense of musical syntax.

Musical Syntax?

If the reader has taken a beginning music theory course, it is possible they may have been introduced to what some theorists believe to be the underlying structure of music by popular music theory texts like Kostka and Payne's *Tonal Harmony* (originally published in 1989, current edition, 2020). Kostka & Payne's approach, steeped in the work of linguistics-influenced music theorists like Lerdahl and Jackendoff, promoted a deep vein of syntax governing tonal music (Schenker, 1979; Lerdahl & Jackendoff, 1983; Kostka & Payne, 2020).

Kostka and Payne's syntactical arguments have been used to analyse non-Western musics as well in the writings of Kofi Agawu, Michael Tenzer, and Bruno Nettl (Agawu, 2003; Nettl, 2005; Tenzer, 2006).

Analysing musical structure syntactically involves focusing on what is referred to as "functional" harmony. In Kostka and Payne's work, chords are defined as fulfilling roles in a key. Thus, in the Kostka and Payne understanding of tonal harmony, there are three classes of chords in a major key: tonics (I, iii, and vi), subdominants (IV and ii), and dominants (V and vii). Each of these chord classes in a major key includes a prototypical chord (I, IV, and V) and two substitutes (iii and vi are tonic substitutes, ii is a subdominant substitute, etc.). The prototypical chords exemplify the characteristics of their class the strongest, whereas the substitutes exemplify these characteristics but weakly. In general, the function of tonic chords is to act as a sort of home base, stasis points (akin to punctuation marks) from which to transition. The function of the dominant chords is to act as a strongly dissonant force that pulls toward the tonic, and the subdominant acts as a mid-point between the two.

Building NLP Principles into an Autonomous Music System

Schemas are what NLP researchers call the mental structures humans use to predict musical events from a given context. Schemas act like grooves humans can "lock in" to, which limit the vast array of musical choices to a small set of context-appropriate choices. For instance, human performers often think of their range in terms of octaves, which represent a repeating schema for understanding the entire range of human hearing. A tuning system is another kind of schema: it is not a physical fact, but more a grid that works particularly well with the human ability to hear distinct changes in pitch.

Once a musician knows a particular schema, they can play appropriately to a given context. But a schema like this is rather difficult for a computer to instantiate because of the complexity problem such a solution might create. Coding a recognition protocol for this and every other key possibility would take an inordinately long time and be a major drain on computing resources. Luckily, this is a problem perfectly suited for a special kind of Markov model.

Hidden Markov Models (HMMs)

The algorithm referred to as a *Hidden Markov Model (HMM)* was introduced by Leonard E. Baum in his foundational paper "An Inequality and Associated Maximization Technique in Statistical Estimation for Probabilistic Functions of Markov Processes," (Baum, 1966). Hidden Markov Models operate using many of the same concepts as discussed with Markov models in Chapter 7. HMMs still make observations about states by doing calculations on state transitions and still may operate using an order argument (1st, 2nd, etc.). However, HMMs may also be used to make estimates about other states extant in training data but which later do not appear in an input. A classic example of this ability involves predicting the mood of a friend (let's call him Liam) by observing the current state of the weather.

Here is a more musical adaptation of the classic example: Liam (the drummer in your band) often plays slower when the rehearsal studio is a few degrees too hot. You observe this behaviour over many rehearsals; when the room is too cold, Liam plays faster; when it is warmer, he slows down. One day you were sick and the band rehearsed without you. So you wouldn't be out of the loop, they recorded a video of their rehearsal of a song you know very well. You notice that Liam's playing is a little fast in the recording. With no other information, you assume that the recording studio was a tad colder than usual that day. Just as a Markov model allows you to predict a future state from a previous state, a Hidden Markov Model allows you to predict an *unobserved state* from observed data. Since there is a connection between the speed of Liam's performance and the temperature of the room, these states are referred to as *paired states.* Including the ability to infer an unobserved state from observable data could allow our autonomous music system to generalise when only partial data is heard.

A Schema Machine

Have you ever collaborated with a musician who "just knew" what you were thinking artistically? A drummer who knew the exact drum beat that your song needed, or a bass player who knew the best bass line to add to what you're playing on the guitar? Imagine an autonomous music system possessed of the ability to listen to a combination of notes and "jam" along appropriately. This would probably involve a bit of error given a limited set of data (consider that Mixolydian and Aeolian only diverge from each other by two intervals). The following tutorial will focus on taking in some pitch data and triggering a drum pattern, rather than jamming along in the same key or recognising a scale. But this ability will bring us much closer to our end goal … and even great musicians might guess incorrectly sometimes. As with the previous tutorials on Markov models, this will not be feasible without adding a package of special objects to Max's retinue.

Downloading the MuBu for Max Package

The *MuBu* package was developed by IRCAM's *Interaction Son Musique Mouvement* team (ISMM; formerly *Interactions Musicales Temps Réel*) to more easily connect Max to gestural data from sensors and vice-versa. As a side benefit, this package gives Max musicians the ability to utilise some machine learning methods not otherwise feasible in Max. To create any of the patches in the sections below, you will need to follow these instructions to download and install the MuBu package from the package manager as you did with the ml.star package.

In all versions of Max:

- Open Max (or alternatively, Max-for-Live, within Ableton Live)
- Click on File and then click "Show Package Manager"
- You should see the package manager. In the upper right-hand corner, click on "search online" and then type "machine learning."
- Click on *MuBu for Max* (not the related package *CataRT-MuBu*, which was also developed by the ISMM team).
- On the *MuBu for Max* package page, click "Install" and then click "Launch" to see the MuBu overview page (Figure 8.1).

We will use several *MuBu* objects in the tutorial below. The *MuBu* overview page refers to *MuBu* as a "multimodal toolbox for analysis of sound and

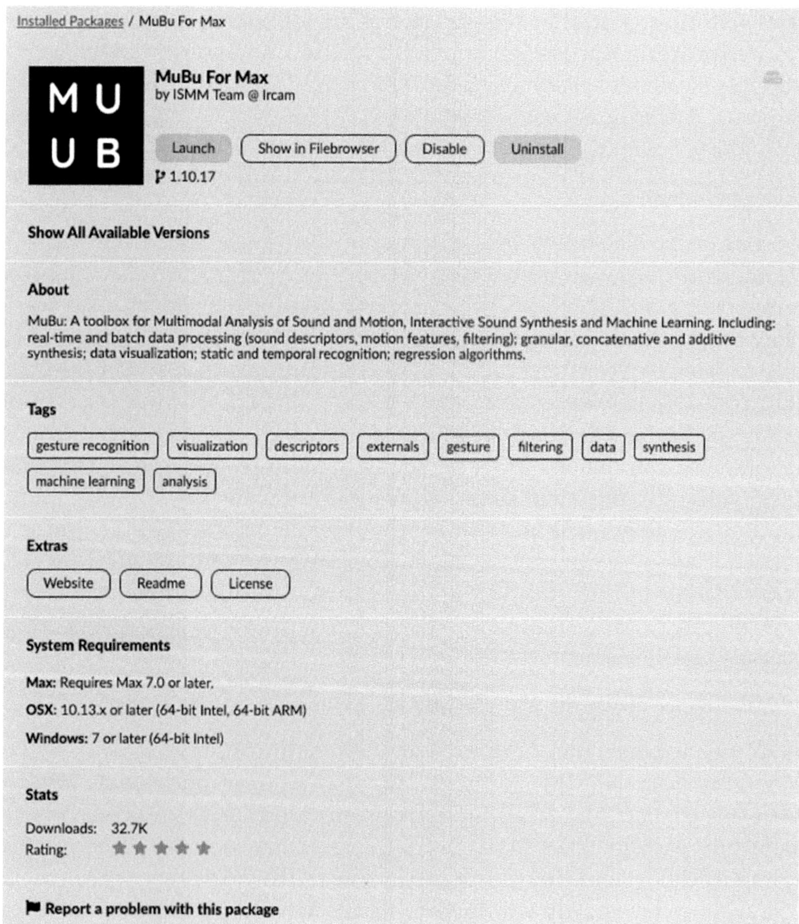

Figure 8.1 The MuBu for Max package landing page.

motion, interactive sound synthesis and machine learning" (ISMM, IRCAM, n.d.). There's an intense learning curve to understanding this package, so the tutorial below will stay firmly in the shallow end of the *MuBu* discussion. Broadly, this package is centred around a special container for holding data called a *buffer*. While buffers that hold data are commonly used in electronic music, the type of buffer *MuBu* uses is specialised such that it contains multiple buffers (hence the name).

Imp4

The system we will build will take in MIDI data from a MIDI controller and respond to it in real time, and after some training, will be able to detect different musical ideas and respond to them however you wish. We will call this system Imp4, adding it to our growing ensemble of autonomous musical agents.

In all versions of Max:

- The system we will build will need to take in a MIDI signal from your controller and send its own MIDI out to a sound-making MIDI-capable synth of some kind. By now you should be skilled at creating a Max patch in your version of Max, and in sending MIDI signals out of the device so that you can hear it played by a synth. If you need a refresher, refer to the tutorials in previous chapters.
- In the patch, create a new object called "mubu." This object is a multi-buffer or container that can hold many kinds of data including audio, MIDI, or gestural data from a sensor. So that other mubu objects can operate on the data in this mubu, you will need to give it a name, so give this mubu the argument "imp4."
- Above the "mubu imp4" object, create a loadmess object and give it the message "numbuffers 4." We will use this message to preload the mubu with four internal buffers to hold data. Connect the outlet of the loadmess object to the inlet of the "mubu imp4" object. Since this object wasn't in the patch when we loaded it, lock the patch and double-click the loadmess object to send its message into the mubu, then unlock the patch for the next step.
- The process of recording training data into a mubu is somewhat labour-intensive and it would be nice if the model we create for one session would be there in the next session. Click on the mubu object and then type Command (CMD) + I (on a Mac, Control + I on a PC) to open the mubu's inspector window. Find the attribute called "Save content with patcher" and set the attribute to "yes." Now when you record some data in your mubu, it will be waiting if you close and then return to the patch.
- Under the mubu, create a new object called imubu. The imubu object is a powerful GUI for viewing the data in the multiple buffers of the mubu. Like the send and receive objects, the mubu objects do not need to be wired together but can instead be connected to each other by the name of

the mubu container. As such, we will need to create a message object above the imubu and type into it the name of our buffer, "imp4." Connect the outlet of the message object to the inlet of the imubu, lock the patch, click the message box, and then unlock the patch again before the next step. At the bottom of your imubu, you should see numbers from 1–4, which are like tabs, allowing you to view the buffers independently.

- It will also be useful down the line for us to be able to clear the data out of the mubu. Above the mubu, create a message object and type into it the message "clear." Connect the outlet of this object to the inlet of the mubu.
- The mubu buffers need some "track" definitions before it can accept data. A mubu track is like a predefined matrix or grid the data can be filed into as it comes in. To provide this, create a new object called "mubu.track" and give it the argument "imp4" to connect it to the mubu. After "imp4," type the number 1 (indicating that you want to create 1 track) and then type the word "somedata" to give the track a name. Next, we need to give the mubu.track some attributes including "@predef yes" (which means we are predefining the track's structure, as you can also use mubu without predetermining their structure), "@timetagged 1" (which means that the data we will be inputting should be catalogued by the buffer according to millisecond time stamps), "@matrixcols 1" (meaning create 1 column in the matrix, other than the time stamp), "@matrixcolnames pitch" (meaning this column should be named pitch, since this is the only data we will be inputting), and "@maxsize 10000" (which will resize the track to handle 10,000 entries. The default size of the mubu.track is 256 entries which will not be enough for the present experiment). After hitting enter, you may notice that the imubu looks different, responding to the way the mubu.tra ck object has changed the buffer structure (Figure 8.2).

Recording data into a mubu:

- Create a fourth object called "mubu.record." This object will allow us to record data into the mubu, but first we will need to connect it to the mubu with the argument "imp4" and the track structure we'll be recording into with the argument "somedata." After the word "mubu.record," type "imp4 1 somedata."
- We will need a control mechanism to tell the mubu.record what buffer we want to record into. Create a new object called "prepend" above the mubu .record and give it the argument "bufferindex." The prepend object will add the message bufferindex to the beginning of any input. Connect the outlet of the prepend object to the inlet of the mubu.record.
- Next, create four new message objects and type into them the numbers 1, 2, 3, and 4, then connect the outlet of each of them to the inlet of the "prepend bufferindex" object. Now we can click on each of these messages to alert the mubu.record what buffer we want to record into.

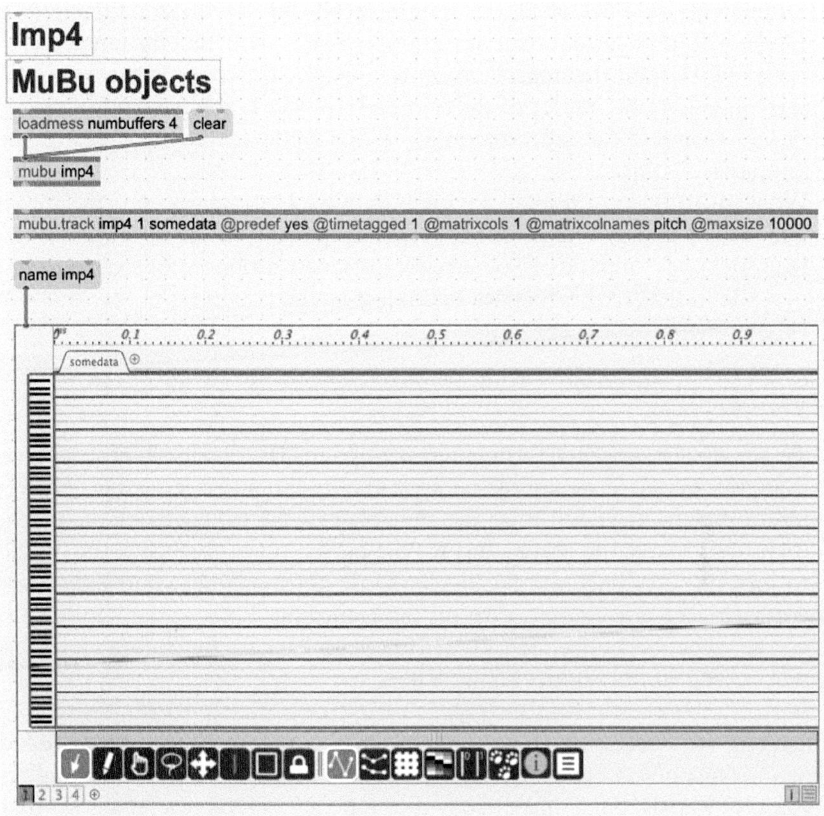

Figure 8.2 Our properly structured mubu objects.

- We will also need a way to tell the mubu.record to start recording. Create another prepend object and give it the argument "record." Connect the outlet of the "prepend record" object to the inlet of the mubu.record. Then create a toggle object above the "prepend record" object and connect its outlet to the inlet of the "prepend record." Now we will be able to click on the toggle to turn on and off the recording function of the mubu .record object.
- Next, we will need to supply some data to the mubu.record object. Create a midiin object, and then a midiout, so we can hear what we're playing. Connect the midiin to the midiout.
- To the right of the midiout, create a midiparse object and connect the outlet of the midiin to the inlet of the midiparse. Remember that midiparse is the object we use to break apart the very complex MIDI signal into its constituent data.

- Ultimately, we'd like to fill our mubu.record object with some pitch data. Under the midiparse, create an unpack object with the argument "i i," meaning we want the unpack object to unpack a list consisting of two integers. The leftmost outlet of the midiparse object is the pitch and velocity outlet. Connect the leftmost outlet of the midiparse to the inlet of the "unpack i i" object.
- We want to make sure that the pitch data we're inputting into the mubu .record is just the note-on messages, and ignoring the note-off messages, so under the "unpack i i" object, create a new stripnote object and connect the outlets of the "unpack i i" object to the two inlets of the stripnote (Figure 8.3).

1st Test—Recording

- To see what this does, let's do a test with your MIDI controller (remember that you may need to double-click on the midiin and select your controller for data to be passed from the controller to the patch). Lock the patch, click the 1 above the prepend to set the buffer index, then click the toggle to turn on recording, and finally play some notes on your controller. After you've played a few notes, turn off the recording. Look at the imubu...do you see what looks like pitch data? If not, go back to the beginning of this section and troubleshoot (Figure 8.4).

If the test was successful, the mubu side of this system is mostly assembled except for one object. The objects in the MuBu Package are useful for analysis of complex signals, but along the way they have also added several objects that instantiate machine learning algorithms in real time. We will be using an object

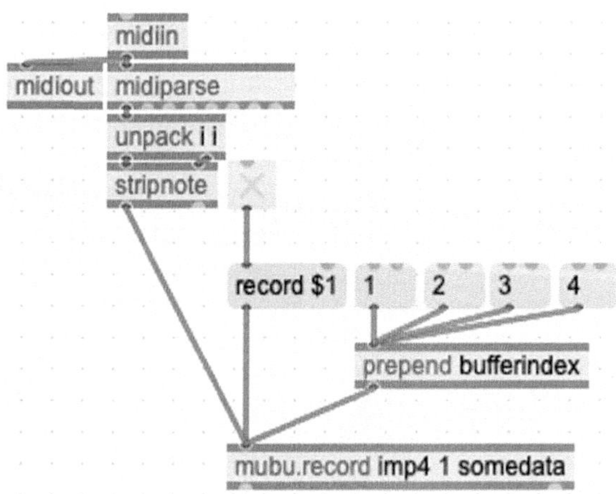

Figure 8.3 Connecting controls and MIDI data to the mubu.record object.

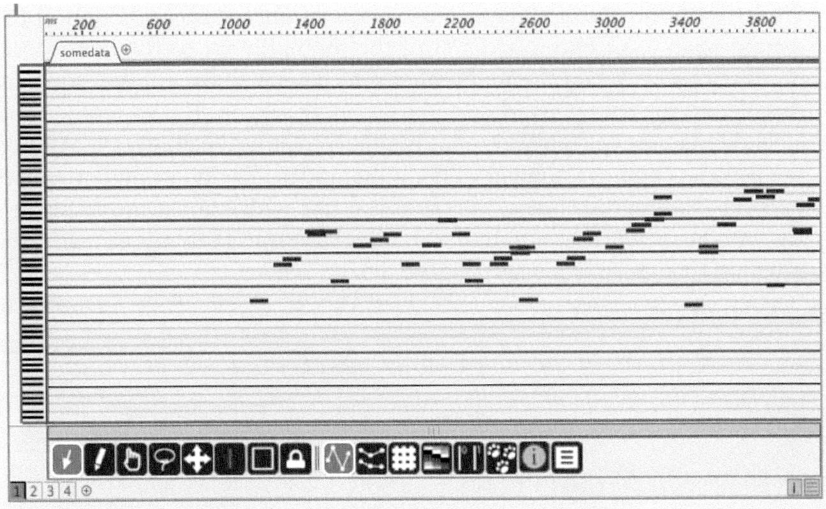

Figure 8.4 The imubu with some pitch data recorded in buffer #1.

called mubu.hhmm, which looks at a mubu container and creates a Hidden Markov Model based on the data in the buffers. The extra "h" in mubu.hh mm stands for "hierarchical," but the distinction between an HHMM and an HMM is not going to mean much to the present enterprise.

mubu.hhmm

- Unlock the patch. To the right of the mubu objects and below the strip-note, create a new object called "mubu.hhmm" and give it the arguments and attribute "imp4 somedata @play 1." The first two arguments should be self-explanatory at this point. The "@play 1" attribute will allow the mubu .hhmm object to play along, sending out its analytical data as it receives new data in real-time.
- Above the "mubu.hhmm imp4 somedata @play 1" object, create a new message object and type into it the message "train." We will use this command to train the mubu.hhmm after we put some data in the container. Connect the outlet of the "train" message to the inlet of the mubu.hhmm.
- Next, create a loadbang object above the "train" message. Assuming you recorded some data Imp4's mubu, you want to be able to use the mubu .hhmm immediately upon loading after you close the patch. Connect the loadbang to the "train" message.
- Next, we need to provide the mubu.hhmm with some data to respond to in real time. Since we already have a midiin object and a midiout, we don't need another. In fact, we can take the data right out of the stripnote object's (leftmost) pitch outlet and connect it directly to the mubu.hhmm.

- Underneath the mubu.hhmm, create a new "number" object. Connect the second from the rightmost outlet of the mubu.hhmm to the inlet of the number object. When the mubu.hhmm receives new data, it will compare this data to the data it listened to in its training session. If it matches, it will label this data using its buffer index number, creating a paired state between the new data and the number of the buffer index. The mubu.hhmm object calls this pairing "likeliness," because just like with human musicians, it's always a guess when you're trying to infer someone's intentions merely by listening to a musical passage (Figure 8.5).

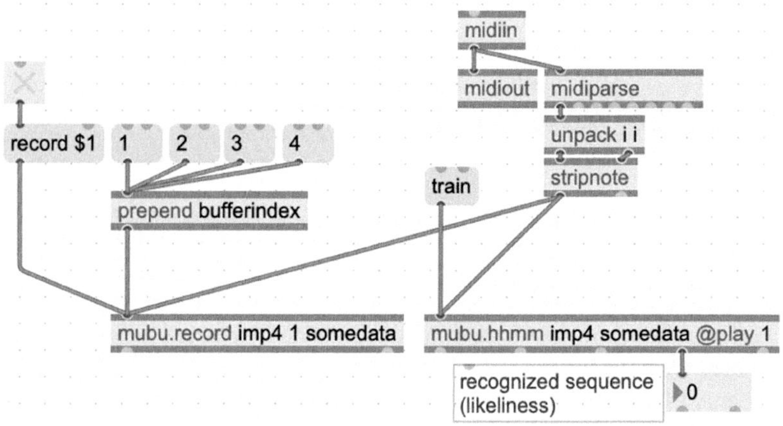

Figure 8.5 Incorporating the mubu.hhmm object.

2nd Test—Creating an HHMM

- Lock the patch and click the "clear" message above the mubu to delete the data from our previous recording. After you do this, the imubu should look empty.
- You will need to record four buffers' worth of MIDI data that is different in a way that the mubu.hhmm can recognise. Remember that we are only feeding these objects monophonic pitch data, so it needs to look different from that perspective. I would suggest playing some notes in four different octaves. For each recording, follow this procedure:
  a. Click the number of the appropriate buffer (1–4).
  b. Click the toggle to start recording.
  c. Play some MIDI pitches in one of four octave ranges.
  d. Click the toggle to stop the recording.
  e. Continue to the next buffer and start over again.
  f. You can click on the buffer tabs at the bottom of the imubu to see the data you've recorded in each buffer.

- When you have finished recording data in each of the four buffers, click the "train" message above the mubu.hhmm (it's a bit anticlimactic, because nothing happens when you do this, but in that time the object has constructed a Hierarchical Hidden Markov Model of the data in the mubu container). Next, play the same notes on your controller in the same octaves you played for the different tests. If you see the number object underneath the mubu.hhmm shifting between 1–4, congratulations, your HMM has recognised a connection between your performance and something it has encountered before. If not, go back to the beginning of this section and troubleshoot.

Live.step

- We've already built a rudimentary drum machine in Chapter 5 and—were this a book solely dedicated to learning Max—the next step would be building one with an editable sequencer like the live.step object. Since building complex sequencers is beyond the scope of this text, a Max snippet containing a drum machine and four basic sequences is supplied in the Machine Musicians/Patches/Chapter 8 folder called "drumbeats_for_mubu.maxsnip." Find this file and drag it directly into the patch (Figure 8.6).
- The live.step object is so complex and powerful that Greg Taylor's book *Step by Step* (aside from being a great tutorial on sequencing in general) is primarily a treatise on how to use it (Taylor, 2018). By clicking on the button above the "random 4" object, you can switch between four precomposed drumbeats. Clicking the toggle at the top left will turn the sequencer on and off. The live.step is set up such that each instrument (kick, snare, hats, etc.) is accessible by clicking on the umenu object in the middle. To edit the different modes, like pitch, velocity, and duration, click in the "attrui" (attribute user interface) object labelled "mode." If you come up with a sequence you like, click the store buttons to save it to the appropriate sequence (1–4). To save the patterns with the patch, click the "save" message (and then don't forget to save the patch as well). This snippet uses an object called "pattrstorage" to load four preset drumbeats into the live.step. This is done automatically by sending a bang to the "read mubudrumbeats.json" message object upon loading. Since this loadbang wasn't there when the patch loaded, lock the patch and double click the loadbang. Once you have done this, click on the toggle object to start the sequence and click the button above the "random 4" to cycle through the different beats. This snippet comes complete with its own MIDI output, but you may need to double-click the noteout object at the bottom to send the data to the correct synth.

Appropriateness

- Remember the system we built for Imp3 to determine a range of appropriateness for stopping? It would be good to use the same thing here, so open

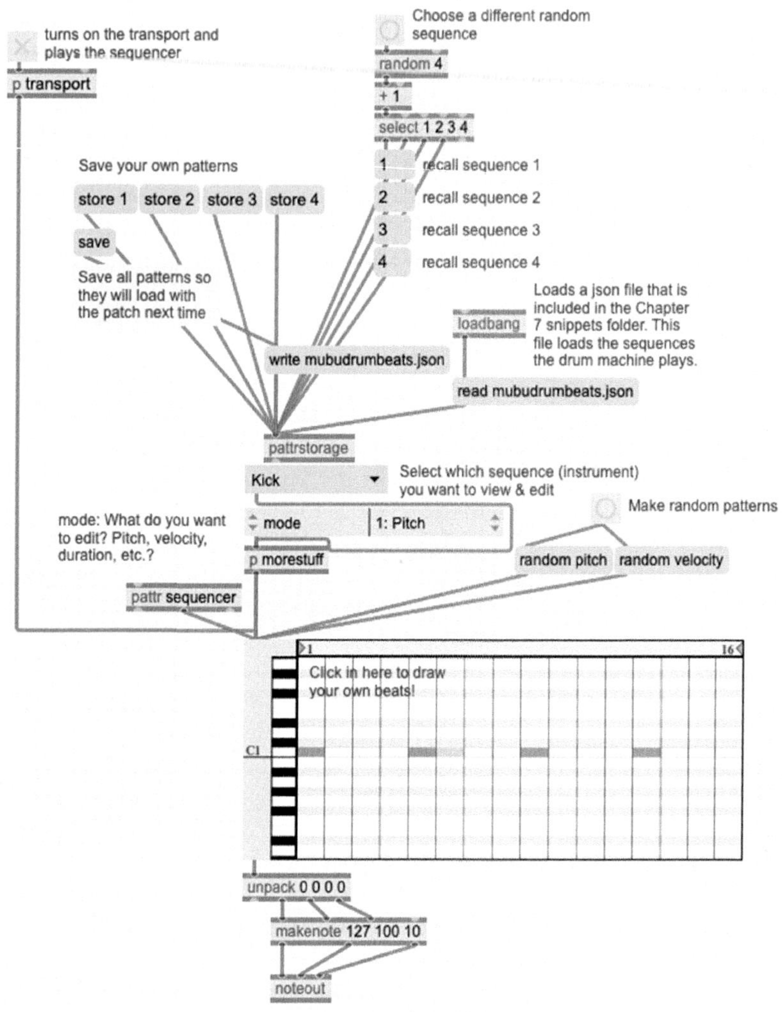

Figure 8.6 The "drumbeats_for_mubu" snippet file.

Imp3 and copy the system for establishing a range of appropriateness (it began with a loadbang object and ended with a send object sending on a channel called "stopnow"). If you will need the MIDI program changer for built-in MIDI output or the ASCII key to MIDI data sections of the patch, copy them over as well.

- As stated previously, send and receive objects can pass from one patch to another, so it would be good to isolate the messages from Imp3 and Imp4, so they aren't sending erroneous messages to each other willy-nilly. Change the "receive stopdetected" object by adding a 2 at the end (without a space) so that the object will now receive on a channel called "stopdetected2." Similarly, the "send stopnow" object at the bottom of this section should be changed to send on a channel called "stopnow2."

- This small subpatch took in MIDI note-off messages and then counted down from a randomly selected wait time and then sent a message to stop metro playback. We will need to supply this patch with some note-off messages to make this work. To the right of the "unpack i i," create a new "select 0" object. We will use this object to filter the MIDI velocity messages for note-off velocities. Connect the rightmost outlet of the "unpack i i" object to the leftmost inlet of the "select 0."
- Under the "select 0" create a new send object and set it to send on the "stopdetected2" channel. Connect the leftmost outlet of the "select 0" to the inlet of the "send stopdetected2" object. This section of the patch will now take in MIDI data and send out a stopping message when a randomised range of appropriateness has been reached.
- For reasons that will become clear in the following section, we will also need to send this appropriateness definition elsewhere in the patch, so under the "random @range -1500 -4000" object, create a new send object that will send on a channel called "appropriateness."
- Since the loadbang object that drives this process wasn't in the patch when we loaded it, lock the patch and double-click it to create a new random appropriateness definition. Then unlock the patch (Figure 8.7).

Tempo Generation

- Being a drum machine, we will need to establish an appropriate tempo and it would be great if it didn't always default to 120 BPM. Above the "p transport" object, create a new float object (the object is called "flonum") and connect its outlet to the rightmost inlet of the "p transport." This inlet takes an argument establishing a new tempo (BPM), which will set the Global Transport.
- Above the float object for BPM, create a new "random @range 60. 150." object. This object will generate a new tempo between 60 and 150 BPM whenever it receives a bang. Connect the outlet of the random object to the inlet of the float. N.B.: feel free to choose your own tempo definitions. Unlike Ableton Live, which has hard limits between 20. and 999. BPM, Max can perform any tempo above 0.0 BPM, the only upper limit being the performance of your CPU.
- Above the random object, create a new object called "delay." As you might imagine, the delay object delays a bang when it receives one. Give this object an argument "1000" such that it will delay the bang for 1000 ms. (1 second). Connect the outlet of the "delay 1000" to the random object.
- Above the delay object, create a loadbang object and connect it to the delay. This will cause a new tempo to be generated when the patch is loaded.

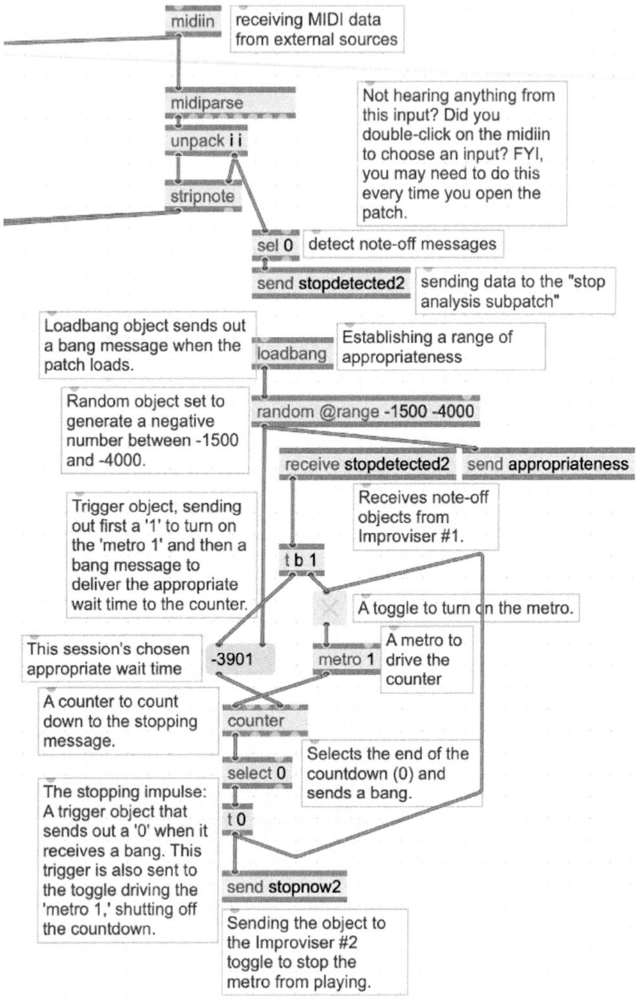

Figure 8.7 Imp4's newly modified system for defining a range of appropriateness.

Since this loadbang didn't load with the patch, lock it and double-click the object to create a new tempo (Figure 8.8).

A Mubu-Triggered Behaviour Changer

- Since the mubu.hhmm object can recognise four paired states from your MIDI performance, the "likeliness" output we've already connected to a number object could be connected to as-is to the "select 1 2 3 4" object above the live.step drum machine. However, in my experience, the output

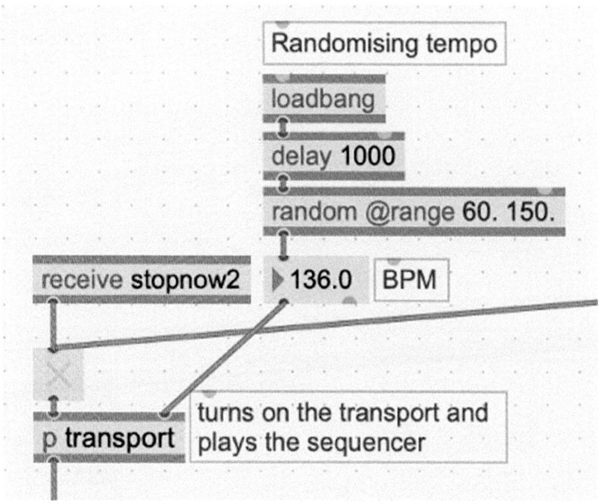

Figure 8.8 Imp4's randomised tempo generator.

of the mubu.hhmm changes so rapidly that it would result in a rather glitchy performance by the drum machine. To fix this, create a "speedlim" object under the number object connected to the mubu.hhmm. The speedlim object gates inputs faster than its argument (either in milliseconds or time values like 4n, 8n, etc.), so we can use it to limit signals that are too fast. Since the transport will be running, give the speedlim object an argument "1n," such that it will only send out a message to change the drum beat once every measure in whatever tempo is chosen by the patch. Connect the outlet of the number box to the leftmost inlet of the "speedlim 1n" object.

- The speedlim object will slow the message outputs from the mubu.hhmm, but we will still have "false-positive" messages when a certain behaviour is chosen but hasn't changed. This will regularly reset the live.step sequencer when no behaviour change is called for. To fix this, create a new object called "change," under the "speedlim 1n" object. This object takes in a number and only sends it out if it has changed. Connect the outlet of the "speedlim 1n" to the change object and then connect the leftmost outlet of the change object to the leftmost inlet of the "select 1 2 3 4" object (Figure 8.9).

3rd Test—Performance and Appropriate Behaviour

- Lock the patch and turn on the toggle that drives the drum machine. Play some of the gestures you previously recorded into the four buffers of the mubu. Does the drum machine change its beat? If not, go back to the beginning of the last section and troubleshoot.

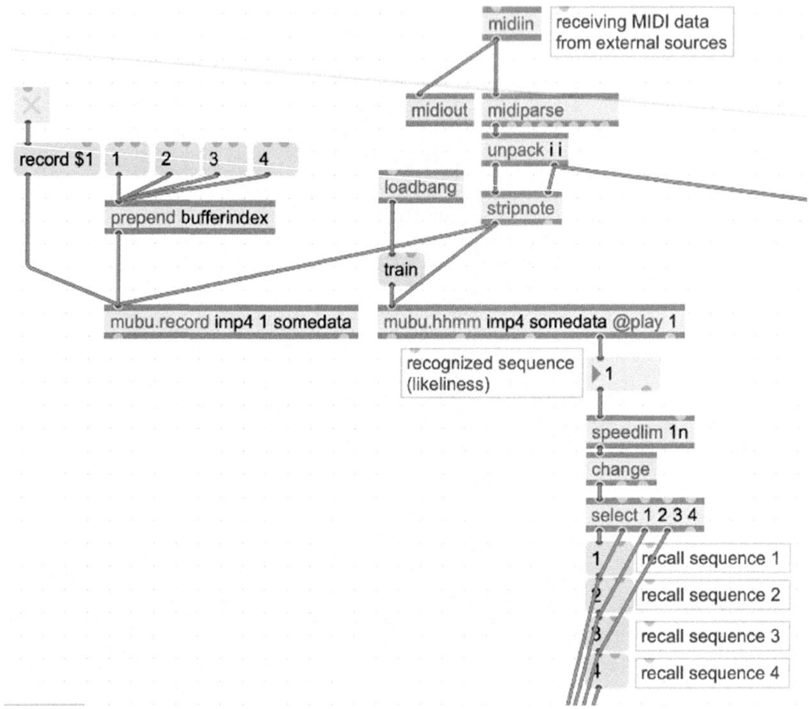

Figure 8.9 Connecting the mubu.hhmm to the Imp4 drum machine.

A Proactive Machine Musician?

- The systems we have built thus far have been reactive. What if Imp4 was a leader, rather than a follower? This should be relatively easy to pull off given that the patch already does several things when the patch loads using the objects loadbang and loadmess. But we probably don't want the drum machine to start immediately upon loading…that could be kind of alarming, and at least one of these procedures is delayed by a second. Above the toggle that starts the drum machine playing, create a new "receive appropriateness" object to receive the definition of appropriateness when the patch loads.
- Since this process was designed to generate a negative number, we will need to multiply it by a negative number to use it as a delay. Also, history has taught me that when a patch loads, it's always good to allow plenty of time before anything plays audibly. Let's multiply the definition of appropriateness by -2. by creating a "* -2." object below the "receive appropriateness" object. Connect the outlet of the "receive appropriateness" object to the leftmost inlet of the "* -2." Since the range of the random object generating the definition is between 1.5 and 4 seconds, the appropriateness definition

for the starting impulse beginning system playback will be between 3 and 8 seconds.

- Beneath the "* -2." object, create a pipe object, which is much like a delay object in that it delays a signal, the difference being that it delays any signal, not just bang messages. Give this pipe object an argument "0." so it will accept floats. Above the "pipe 0." create a new "t" (trigger) object and give it the argument "1" so it will send out the message "1" whenever it is triggered. Connect the outlet of the "t 1" to the leftmost inlet of the pipe object and connect the outlet of the "* -2." to the pipe's rightmost inlet. Next, connect the outlet of the "* -2." to the inlet of the "t 1" object, so that when a definition of appropriateness is generated, this message also sets the pipe to wait an appropriate amount of time and then also sends a "1" message through the pipe that will (eventually) start the toggle.
- Experience has also taught me that it is a good idea to have a way to "defuse" these kinds of processes. It is not always advantageous for your drummer to start the show the moment he shows up, a fact that could be sensed by human drummers, but which will be unknown to an AI drummer with no ability to read the room. To the left of the "receive appropriateness" object, create a "key" object. We will use the escape key (ASCII #27) to act as an emergency defuse button for the automatic process.
- Under the key object, create a new "select 27" object. Connect the leftmost outlet of the key object to the inlet of the "select 27."
- Under the "select 27," create a new "t stop" object that will send out a "stop message when triggered. Connect the leftmost outlet of the "select 27" to the inlet of the "t stop" object. Connect the outlet of the "t stop" object to the inlet of the pipe. If allowing the drum machine to start automatically is inappropriate for reasons your AI drummer could not perceive, hit the ESC/escape button immediately when the patch loads (Figure 8.10).

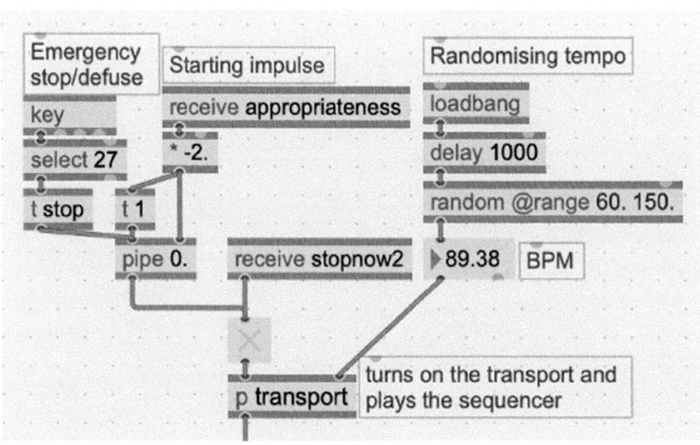

Figure 8.10 Imp4's starting impulse generator.

4th Test—Partial Test Drive

- Since this patch is proactive, let's do a test run of the procedure with all the parts in place. This assumes that you recorded data into all four buffers of the mubu.
- Open the patch, wait for the drums to start playing.
- Jam along with the drums using gestures you recorded into the mubu.
- The drum patterns should change appropriately with your performance
- If the drum patterns do not change, go back to the beginning of the section and troubleshoot (Figure 8.11).

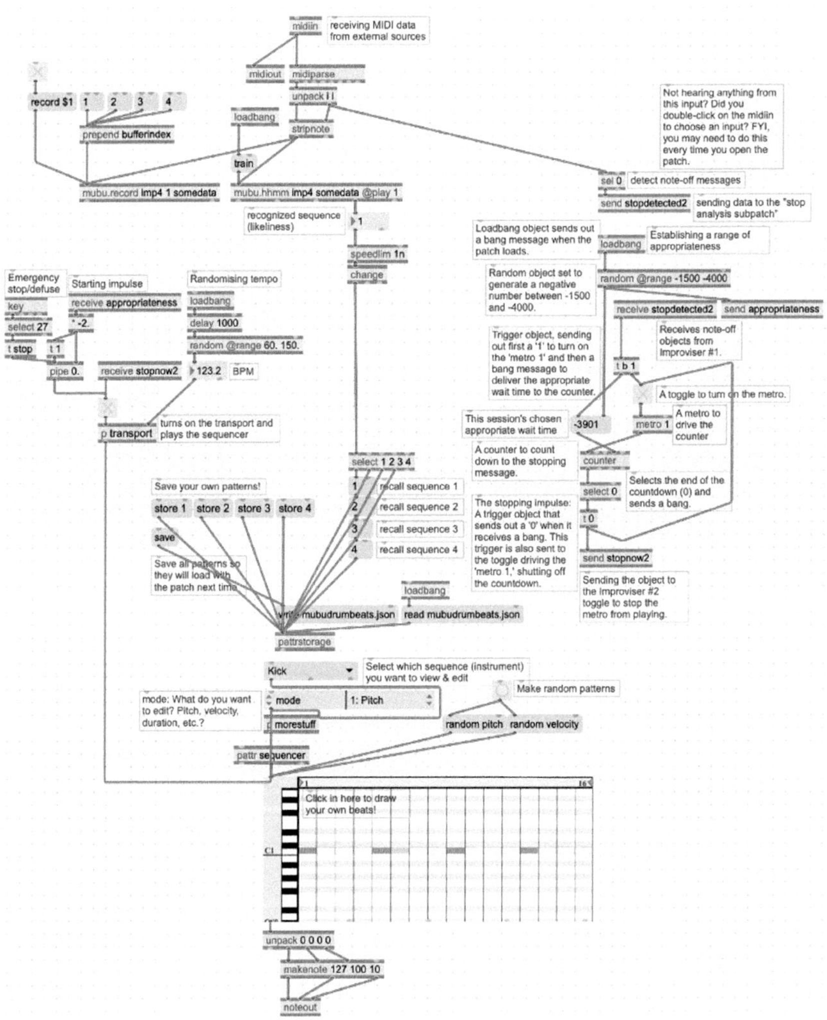

Figure 8.11 The full Imp4 (not counting the mubu setup objects shown in Figures 8.2 and 8.5, which need to be in the same patch).

5th Test—Full Trio Test Drive

- Now that Imp4 is functional, open up Imp3 and jam with both at the same time. Note that Imp3 will only be listening to you, not to Imp4, but you can still have a lot of fun being the only human in a two-thirds AI ensemble.

Going Further

- Change things up...what if Imp3 was listening to both performers? How would you make that happen? Would it create a musical grey goo problem where no one knew when to quit? How would you solve that?
- We created a proactive starting mechanism for Imp4. Could you create a proactive stopping mechanism?
- In the full trio test drive, it is assumed that Imp3 and Imp4 were only listening to one person (Improviser #1, a human). But what if there were four agents with another human (Improviser #2, another human), and either Imp3 or Imp4 were listening to that person?

Conclusion

In building the Imp4 system, we have added a dynamic rhythmic element to the improvisational space we started with Imp3, lending cohesion to your musical ideas. The connection between the training data in the mubu container and the chosen drumbeat creates an unspoken salience that adds prominence to your gestures as you play them. These gestures can also act as a schema the digital drummer can lock into, given the context of the performance. There is also a codified syntax for what must happen when, filtered through a definition of appropriateness that is not fixed, but changeable.

Goodbye (For Now) to the Top-Down Approach

The process of training an HMM to recognise performance data is complicated. However, once a model is sufficiently trained, the reader can see the many ways it could be musically useful. However, three problems remain. Firstly, we have not yet reached the level of human creativity called for in the opening chapter. Humans have an impressive ability to switch and learn new schemas and syntax that an HMM-based system instantiated on a modern computing system cannot compete with.

Secondly the Imp4 system still requires us to train it on the gestures we want it to recognise and there is a limit to how many gestures it can remember. This system recognises and reacts to prepared samples of music, not natural music one might encounter in the wild. Using such a system, how could we scale up the complexity of the music being modelled while also not overtaxing a computer's computational resources? The problems increase greatly as the sophistication of the musical model increases and at each level of musical sophistication, one can expect the complexity problem to compact to the point of making near real-time modelling next to impossible. There is at present no magic solution to this, but in Chapter 9, we will discuss some additional methods for managing the complexity of musical data.

As you can hopefully see, the top-down approach of symbolic AI still allows us great flexibility in designing systems that can learn from natural music in real time, given that the patterns are known and defined ahead of time. There is still much great work to be done in this area, but for now, it is time to leave the top-down approach behind and move in a completely different direction—a direction that models biology from the bottom up.

References

Agawu, K. (2003). *Representing African music: Postcolonial notes, queries, positions.* Routledge.

Barzilay, R., & Lapata, M. (2008). Modeling local coherence: An entity-based approach. *Computational Linguistics, 34*(1), 1–34. https://doi.org/10.1162/coli.2008.34.1.1

Baum, L. E. (1966). An inequality and associated maximization technique in statistical estimation for probabilistic functions of Markov processes. *Inequalities, 1*, 1–8.

Bennett, D. (2019). *What time signature is Radiohead's 'Pyramid Song' in?* [Video]. YouTube. https://www.youtube.com/watch?v=MdZSOoOF5Ms

Boden, M. A. (2006). *Mind as machine: A history of cognitive science.* Oxford University Press.

Brown, P. F., Della Pietra, S. A., Della Pietra, V. J., & Mercer, R. L. (1990). The mathematics of statistical machine translation: Parameter estimation. *Computational Linguistics, 16*(2), 79–85. https://doi.org/10.1162/jcol.1990.16.2.79

Bunt, H. (2010). Musical meaning and interpretation. In *The Cambridge companion to music and philosophy* (pp. 151–167). Cambridge University Press. https://doi.org/10.1017/CCOL9780521814645.009

Chomsky, N. (2006). *Language and mind* (3rd ed.). Cambridge University Press.

Devlin, J., Chang, M. W., Lee, K., & Toutanova, K. (2018). BERT: Pre-training of deep bidirectional transformers for language understanding. *ArXiv.* https://arxiv.org/abs/1810.04805

Elliott, D. J. (1995). *Music matters: A new philosophy of music education.* Oxford University Press.

Forte, A. (1973). *The structure of atonal music.* Yale University Press.

Grosz, B. J., Joshi, A. K., & Weinstein, S. (1995). Centering: A framework for modeling the local coherence of discourse. *Computational Linguistics, 21*(2), 203–225.

Halliday, M. A. K., & Hasan, R. (1976). *Cohesion in English.* Longman.

Huron, D. (2006). *Sweet anticipation: Music and the psychology of expectation.* MIT Press.

ISMM (IRCAM). (n.d.). *MuBu for Max* (Max package) [Software]. {Sound Music Movement} Interaction. https://ircam-ismm.github.io/max-msp/mubu.html

Jurafsky, D., & Martin, J. H. (2020). *Speech and language processing: An introduction to natural language processing, computational linguistics, and speech recognition* (3rd ed.). Pearson Education.

Kostka, S., & Payne, D. (2020). *Tonal harmony: With an introduction to post-tonal music* (9th ed.). McGraw-Hill.
Lerdahl, F., & Jackendoff, R. (1983). *A generative theory of tonal music.* MIT Press.
Meyer, L. B. (1956). *Emotion and meaning in music.* University of Chicago Press.
Nattiez, J.-J. (1990). *Music and discourse: Toward a semiology of music.* Princeton University Press.
Nettl, B. (2005). *The study of ethnomusicology: Thirty-one issues and concepts* (2nd ed.). University of Illinois Press.
Patel, A. D. (2008). *Music, language, and the brain.* Oxford University Press.
Schenker, H. (1979). Free composition (Der freie Satz) (E. Oster, Trans.). Longman. (Original work published 1935)
Schoenberg, A. (1967). *Fundamentals of musical composition.* Faber and Faber.
Sloboda, J. A. (1985). *The musical mind: The cognitive psychology of music.* Oxford University Press.
Snow, C. E. (2010). Academic language and the challenge of reading for learning about science. In M. J. Snowling & HulmeC. (Eds.), *The science of reading: A handbook* (pp. 450–464). Wiley-Blackwell.
Taylor, G. (2018). *Step by step: Adventures in sequencing with Max/MSP.* Cycling '74.
Tenzer, M. (2006). *Analytical studies in world music.* Oxford University Press.
Turing, A. M. (1950). Computing machinery and intelligence. *Mind*, *59*(236), 433–460. https://doi.org/10.1093/mind/LIX.236.433
Weizenbaum, J. (1966). ELIZA – A computer program for the study of natural language communication between man and machine. *Communications of the ACM*, *9*(1), 36–45. https://doi.org/10.1145/365230.365257

Part II

Bottom-Up

The remaining chapters of this book will lay out the approaches to musical AI that model biological systems exhibiting intelligence—the so-called bottom-up approach. Bottom-up approaches begin by breaking down the problem of biological systems into their most minor constituent parts, building larger structures inspired by biological systems, and finally supplying these systems with large amounts of data and training. Bottom-up approaches include the well-publicised neural networks and large language models of our time, as well as lesser-known methods such as genetic algorithms, swarm intelligence, cellular automata, and emergent systems.

DOI: 10.4324/9781003534211-11

9 Connectionism, Part I

MIDI from Audio

In Chapters 6–8, we delved into the top-down symbolic approach that attempts to model human patterns as observed and learned by human music theorists. This method is rooted in the well-known precepts of Western music theory. In the top-down approach, statistical models and rules guide a randomised process down the pathway towards generating a coherent musical output. In the following chapters, we will flip this paradigm and attempt to build a musical mind from the bottom up. A bottom-up approach to AI begins instead by building artificial representations of human biological systems and assumes that intelligence is an *emergent property* that will develop naturally, given that digital simulacra of the necessary biological components are assembled correctly (Rumelhart & McClelland, 1986; Mitchell, 2009).

The theory of intelligence emerging from complex systems, popularised by Douglas Hofstadter's *Gödel, Escher, Bach: An eternal golden braid* (Hofstadter, 1979), originally stemmed from observations made by evolutionary biologists (Edelman, 1987). These scientists observed that complex systems often form patterns that cannot be predicted or even explained by examining individual components. Self-organisation, a type of adaptation observed in biological systems like the human nervous system, allows an organism to adapt to unforeseen changes in the environment and unexpected stimuli (Dehaene, 2021).

Unlike symbolic AI systems (based on logical structures), connectionist approaches are modelled after the human brain's ability to learn over repeated exposure to a set of data. Connectionist systems are increasingly able to learn patterns and thus relationships from virtually any kind of data, and thus, connectionist systems have become the dominant approach to AI systems in the world today. Connectionist systems learn from raw data, developing rules and organising themselves autonomously rather than filtering inputs through preset rules (Camazine et al., 2001). A major strength of this approach is a connectionist system's ability to *generalise* data, an ability humans can do quite well (Tononi & Edelman, 1998). Generalising from a small set of data gives humans the ability to hear only a single word spoken and recognise it as the voice of a loved one. The ability to generalise is a critical component in systems like self-driving cars, which often need to distinguish between things like a full

DOI: 10.4324/9781003534211-12

picture of a human standing on the side of a road, and a partial picture of just a human's legs or arms.

This ability is of paramount importance to a musician, who must discern between instruments and determine what they are playing, even when it is sometimes hard to hear. Musicians on stage often use click tracks to stay in sync with the tempo. These systems are extremely useful but are ultimately dependent on being able to hear the click, which gets hard at times as the stage volume of the band increases. Accordingly, human musicians can use their ability to generalise to follow the click even if they only hear it occasionally.

Musical connectionist systems use these abilities to analyse music from audio sources; a feat symbolic systems struggle to achieve. The ability to generalise allows these systems to make connections between disparate core parameters, leading to a richer understanding of the musical context. Accordingly, this chapter will also begin our exploration of audio, a subject we largely avoided heretofore, including a tutorial showing how to build a rudimentary system which takes in audio signals and turns that audio signal back to MIDI.

It is to be noted at the outset that this enterprise is much trickier than the more well-worn path of creating machines that interact with MIDI signals. We are treading a path that very few have attempted and even fewer have succeeded. While many apps exist that can generate audio using connectionist principles, such things are not done in real time. We have reached the uncharted wilderness of the musical AI frontier. It should also be noted that the tutorials in this section represent, if not true connectionism built upon neural networks, a philosophical connectionism built upon emergent approximations of human biological systems.

Digital Ears

We want to build a system that listens like a human. How do humans hear? Let us use as an example a human clapping their hands once, on one side of the room and a human on the other side of the room listening. The first human strikes their hands quickly together, moving particles of air very rapidly away from their hands. The air pressure in the immediate vicinity of the hands rises dramatically as air pushes out and away from the hands in all directions. The pre-existing air pressure in the room causes air particles at rest to first be pushed away from the hands and then, as it meets resistance, to push back towards the hands.

This wave *propagates,* meaning one wave begets another and another, each with less intensity, again emanating in all directions. The waves pushing away from the hands are called *compression* waves, while the waves pushing back towards the hands are called *rarefaction* waves. Looking at the phenomenon as a cross section, we would see air particles moving up and down like waves of water on the ocean. The water stays in the same general area, but the energy travels upon the waves from one place to another.

As these waves reach the other side of the room, the energy is received by human #2, whose outer ears are shaped perfectly to collect air pressure changes and relay this energy to their ear canal. Once inside, these oscillations strike the tympanic membrane (also known as the eardrum), causing it to move in sync with the in-and-out motion of the sound waves. These vibrations are transferred to three tiny bones that amplify the signal before transmitting it to the cochlea. The cochlea moves another membrane, called the basilar membrane, which in turn moves tiny hair cells called stereocilia. These stereocilia respond to the millions of different frequencies between 20 and 20,000 Hz and subsequently report their vibrations to the brain, where these signals are interpreted as sound.

Truly, the human auditory system is an amazingly complex and sensitive organ. Can we build a digital system as complex and responsive as the human ear? To do so, we must learn how audio operates on the digital level. Since audio is a phenomenon in the real world, it must be represented using continuous data (numbers with decimal points), rather than the tidy discrete data (integers or whole numbers). The reasons for this are subtle and varied, but it suffices to say that sound, being a wave in a *compressible* fluid medium (like air, water, or Jello), can vary in many ways to an infinite degree.

The pitch C4 (MIDI pitch 60) is roughly equivalent to 261.626 Hz and C#4 (MIDI pitch 61) is roughly equivalent to 277.183 Hz. But these divisions do not negate the validity of 274.178 as a pitch a musician might employ, and this is similarly true for every conceivable point on the spectrum between C4 and C#4. The number of pitches between C4 and C#4 is thus continuous, infinite, unending and unknowable. This fact causes significant problems in the detection of pitch. The same can also be said for all audio parameters, which creates an immediate problem for the science of *music information retrieval (MIR)*. For this reason, it must be assumed, when dealing with audio, that all calculations are estimates, not exact figures.

Digital Audio Conversion

Converting real audio into a stream of data involves digital audio conversion via two key processes: sampling and quantisation (Oppenheim & Schafer, 2010). The audio-to-digital conversion process turns the real-world continuous phenomenon of audio into discrete data. It must be noted, therefore, that the process of conversion from audio to data cannot be done without losing *fidelity* to the original. For instance, rather than reacting to audio signals continually (like human ears do in the real world), digital converters sample the audio signal at regular intervals. The number of times the signal is sampled per second is called the *sampling rate*. Since computer processors can at times lose or drop data, and since human hearing can detect frequencies in a range between 20 Hz and 20 kHz, modern digital conversion systems traditionally use a sampling rate above 44.1 kHz (a sampling rate referred to as *CD-quality sound*).

Since this rate is more than double the rate at which humans can hear distinct events (known as the ***human temporal resolution*** of hearing, over which humans experience distinct events as all happening at the same time), errors occurring at these speeds will be unperceivable to human listeners (Moore, 2012). Recordings recorded above 44.1 Hz will tend to be indistinguishable from real world audio, and recordings recorded at a sample rate below 44.1 kHz will sound "digital." There are many good reasons why sample rates above 44.1 kHz exist, but the audible difference between these choices is largely unnoticeable to human ears.

Audio Settings in Standalone Max

- Setting the sample rate in Max can be done by clicking on "Options/Audio status" in the menu bar at the top.
- If this hasn't defaulted to a sampling rate above CD quality sound, click in the pull-down window and set the sample rate to one above 44.1 kHz. (a higher rate is fine, though very-high sample rates will put more strain on your CPU). PC users may see two sample rates, one for input and another for output (if this is the case, set both to a rate over 44.1 kHz.).

Audio in Max-for-Live via Ableton Live

- If the reader is using Ableton Live to access Max, audio is not passed directly from M4L to the computer's audio system, but instead, it is sent out of Max to the channel in which the M4L is sitting in the Ableton Live session. Practically, this means that the Max audio status window shown in Figure 9.1 has little practical use, even though you still can access it. However, Ableton has its own audio status window, which affords the user control over the same parameters. In Ableton, the audio status may be accessed by clicking Live/Settings (on Mac, Options/Preferences on PC) and clicking on the "audio" tab on the left.
- If this hasn't defaulted to a sampling rate above CD quality sound, click in the pull-down window and set the sample rate to one above 44.1 kHz (a higher rate is fine, though very-high sample rates will put more strain on your CPU). PC users may see two sample rates, one for input and another for output (if this is the case, set both to a rate over 44.1 kHz) (Figure 9.2).
- Assuming your Ableton Live audio settings have both an input and an output, you should be able to port audio into a Max-for-Live device and send it back out again.
- To receive audio from your audio input, arm the Live track called "3 audio," (any input from an audio source will work, even the built-in microphone that came installed with your laptop). If you also want to hear the audio through your speakers, set the "monitor" controls to "auto" (Figure 9.3).
- In the browser menu on the left, click on Max-for-Live and look for the blank M4L device called "Max Audio effect" and drag it onto the "3 audio" track.

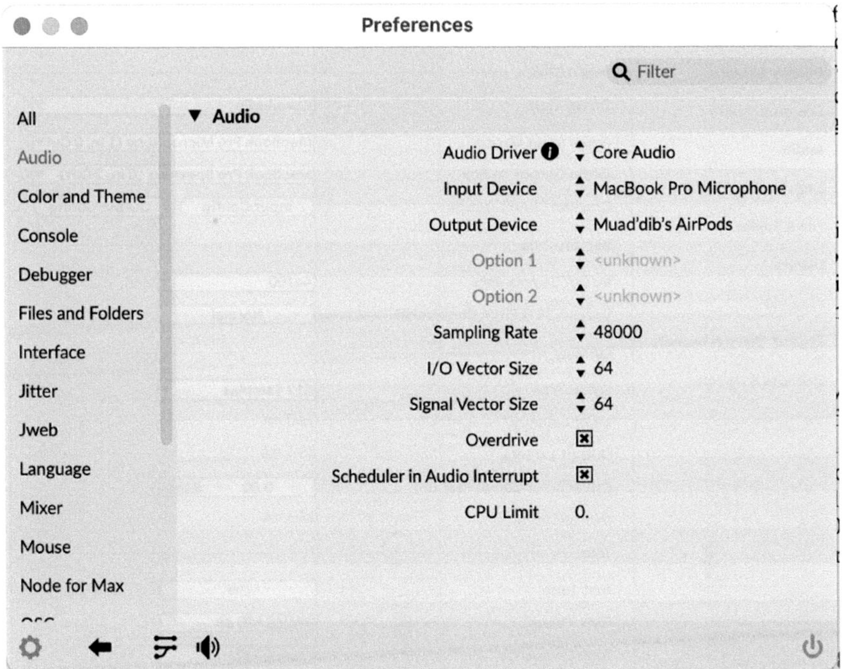

Figure 9.1 Max's Audio status window. N.B., values reflect the Apple standard sampling rate of 48 kHz.

- This device already has a few objects in it, which allow audio to pass through this object from the rest of the track and out to the speakers. The plugin~ object receives audio from the track and the plugout~ object sends audio to the speakers. If an audio effect is placed in the track before this device, it will affect the audio going into the plugin~ object. If an audio effect is placed in the track after this device, it will affect the audio going out to the speakers. There are two cables between these two objects, both carrying audio, one for the left channel and one for the right channel. Deleting the cables between these objects will mute the audio (Figure 9.4).

Editing the Max Audio Effect in Max-for-Live via Ableton Live

- To edit the patch, click the "…" button at the right corner of the Max Audio Effect (Figure 9.5).
- Unlock the patch.
- Select and delete the plugin~ and plugout~ objects and the comments from the Max Audio Effect. This will mute the audio output, a problem we will fix going forward.

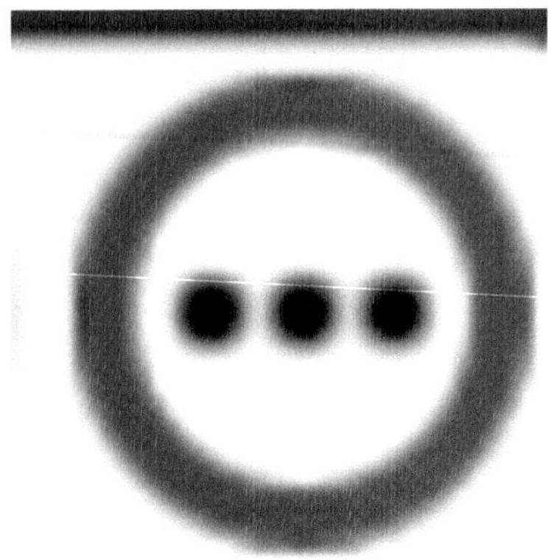

Figure 9.5 The "edit in Max" button.

signal into the live.gain~ object. Note that while this object comes from the Max-for-Live group of objects, one does not actually need Ableton Live to use these objects in Max.

- Create a new "loadmess" object and give it the argument "-70." Make sure to include the decimal point to the argument, as we are dealing with floats, not integers. This object will send out the argument "-70." when the patch loads. Connect the outlet of the "loadmess -70." object to the leftmost inlet of the live.gain~ object. Once this is done, lock the patch and double click on the object to send its argument through (so you don't have to close and open the patch to trigger the message). The fader on the live .gain~ object should drop to -inf dB. Doing this ensures that the live.gain~ object is turned down upon loading, eliminating the possibility of feedback.

In Max-for-Live via Ableton Live

- Create a new object called plugin~. Plug the leftmost outlet of the plugin~ object to the leftmost inlet of the live.gain~ object. Do the same for the rightmost outlet of the plugin~ object, connecting it to the rightmost inlet of the live.gain~. Doing this ensures that audio gain from either stereo channel will be controllable by one fader. All channels in Ableton Live are, by default, stereo, having a left and right output, even if you are only using one mono audio source or microphone.
- Create a new object called plugout~. Plug the leftmost outlet of the live.gai n~ into the leftmost inlet of the plugout~ object. Plug the second-from-leftmost outlet (the "Scaled signal channel 2" outlet) of the live.gain~ into the rightmost inlet of the plugout~ object (Figure 9.6).
- Lock the patch. Slowly bring up the fader to the notch towards the top of the live.gain~. This line represents 0. decibels. Make some noise. You should see the green light of audio coursing through the live.gain~.

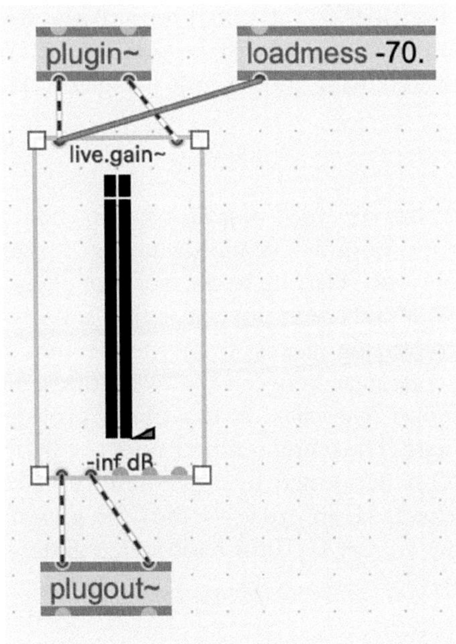

Figure 9.6 Simple audio input and output with a live.gain~ in Max-for-Live.

In Standalone Max

- Create a new object called ezadc~. This object ports audio into Max from external sources like your built-in mic.
- Some computer microphones have two built-in microphones (channels 1 and 2), and some only one. To find out what you have, plug the rightmost outlet of the ezadc~ object to the rightmost inlet of the live.gain~ object. Do you see an audio signal on the live.gain~? If so, then you have a stereo mic pair built into your laptop so all that is left is to connect the leftmost outlet of the ezdac~ to the leftmost inlet of the live.gain~. If not, delete the cord you just connected from the rightmost outlet of the ezdac~ to the rightmost inlet of the live.gain~. Then connect the leftmost outlet of the ezdac~ to the leftmost inlet of the live.gain~ and then connect the leftmost outlet of the ezdac~ to the rightmost inlet of the live.gain~. This will ensure that the output of this object is stereo, whether you have one built-in microphone or two.
- Create a new object called ezdac~. This object ports audio from Max back to the audio output like your built-in speakers.
- Lock the patch and click the ezadc~ object (the one that looks like a microphone). Note that the ezadc~ and the ezdac~ turn on and off together, as these two representations are two halves of the same process.

- Slowly bring up the fader to the notch towards the top of the live.gain~. This line represents 0.0 decibels. Make some noise. You should see the green light of audio coursing through the live.gain~ (Figure 9.7).

What All This Means

It might be obvious that the word *digital* refers to the world existing inside your computer: a world of numbers and data; on/off signals and gates. The word *analog* is less obvious, referring to the world of physical media we live in. It is the world of real sounds from physical sound sources and waves moving through the air. A conversion process from one medium to another is necessary for there to be concourse between the two worlds. The ADC in ezadc~ stands for *analog-digital-conversion*, as this object provides an easy GUI for basic stereo audio input. The plugin~ object does not perform the exact same function, since ADC is performed by Ableton Live before an audio signal reaches the track. The DAC in ezdac~ stands for *digital-analog-conversion*, as this object provides an easy GUI for basic stereo audio input. The plugin~

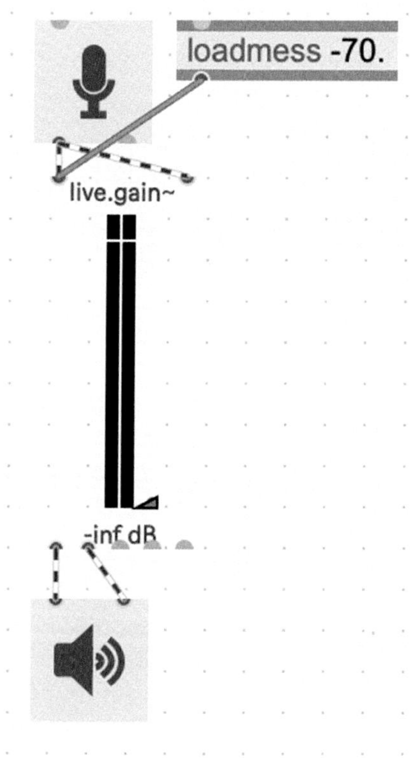

Figure 9.7 Simple audio input and output with a live.gain~ in standalone Max.

object does not perform the exact same function, since ADC is performed by Ableton Live before an audio signal reaches the track.

If for some reason, this did not work, go back to the audio settings and check that the audio input and output are correct. If it has worked, you have successfully achieved audio-to-digital conversion. Or more accurately, you have converted analog audio to digital data (as measured, controlled, and processed by the live.gain~ object) and then converted the resulting data back into audio via your speakers or headphones.

Latency

This process of converting real-world audio to digital data, processing it, and then converting it back again to real-world audio takes some time. The time it takes, called *latency*, is measured in milliseconds. If you've ever worked with a system that has a lot of latency, you know that hearing your own audio in your headphones 500 milliseconds (half a second) later can be a serious impediment to real-time musicality. In the global pandemic that caused much of the world to be "locked down," many musicians struggled with latency while trying to make music online (Zoom and other companies have vastly improved these technologies in the intervening years). It is vital that machine musicians understand this concept and be able to manipulate the settings of a musical system to limit the latency as best as possible. Some digital audio workstations like Ableton Live do an internal calculation to estimate the latency and report on it in the audio settings page. Since the human temporal resolution limit is below 20 milliseconds, latency above 20 milliseconds will be noticeable and may start to adversely affect any collaboration you have with a machine musician. When the latency of an interactive system is low, a sound emitted by the system will seem instantaneous, like the reactions we are used to with humans playing acoustic instruments. Bad latency will make a machine musician seem like it is playing behind the beat.

Buffer Size

Once audio enters the system through the input, it is stored in a buffer, where it is analysed and converted into a batch of samples before being processed by the DAW. The buffer holds only a small number of samples, representing a tiny fraction of the overall sample rate. This *buffer size* has a dramatic effect on the overall latency of an audio system. Since errors are most likely to happen at the changeover between batches (as the process may get interrupted by the myriads of other scheduled tasks your computer is doing at any moment in time), larger buffer sizes will produce better audio. However, since the buffering process causes a natural delay in the system, increasing the buffer size will also increase the latency. Aside from being unfortunate, this trade-off between speed and quality represents a base difference between a machine musician and a human one.

Parsing Data from Audio

Now that we understand the basics of how audio works in a digital space, we can begin to mine the audio signal for relevant data. Our guide for how to parse this signal will be the four core auditory parameters: pitch, duration, timbre, and volume. While duration and timbre are words we still use when speaking of audio, pitch in audio is most often expressed using the term *frequency,* and volume using the term *gain.* The term frequency refers to the number of times a signal oscillates up and down in the air. Gain refers to the relative strength or amplitude of the signal, typically measured in *decibels (dB)*, which is the digital equivalent of how loud the sound will be when perceived in the real world.

Parsing Gain Levels from Digital Audio

There are several different decibel scales, each used for different applications. Somewhat confusingly, each of these scales is often abbreviated simply as dB. Within a computer system or DAW, the scale used is *dBFS*, which stands for *decibels relative to full scale*, so this is the scale used in Max and Ableton Live. The dBFS scale can also be quite confusing to non-audio professionals. In digital audio systems, an audio signal is represented by floats rather than through fluctuations of air pressure. Accordingly, the reference point for amplitude is defined as the maximum representable level within the system (hence *full scale*). 0.0 dBFS denotes the upper limit of the system's dynamic range. All other values are measured as negative decibels relative to the maximum. This explains why in the previous section we created a "loadmess" object and gave it an argument of -70. When the patch loads, the live.gain~ object will be set to -70. dBFS, to avoid feedback hitting us as soon as the patch loads. -70. dBFS is the default lowest gain level the live.gain~ can achieve.

The reader may then ask: if going over 0.0 dBFS, why does the live.gain~ fader (and indeed faders in other DAWs like FL Studio, Logic, and Reason as well) have an upper range of 6.0 dBFS? The answer is complicated and beyond the scope of this text, but shortly, it has to do with what is called 32-bit floating (or sometimes 64-bit) math, which is what DAWs use for their internal signal processing. This gives DAWs a lot more headroom to go over 0.0 without clipping. But how do we know what the signal strength is coming out of the live.gain~?

In Either Version of Max

- Unlock the patch. Below the live.gain~ object, create a new object called "peakamp~" and give it the argument "100." This object will report the peak amplitude of a digital audio signal, with "100" being the interval (in milliseconds) at which it reports the peak. Connect the leftmost outlet of the live.gain~ to the rightmost inlet of the peakamp~.

- Underneath the "peakamp~ 100" object, create a new object called "flonum." This is the object that displays float numbers. Connect the leftmost outlet of the "peakamp~ 100" object to the inlet of the flonum. Chances are you will see nothing unless you make a lot of noise. This is because the flonum object is set to not display any number smaller than 0. To change this setting, select the object and hit CMD + i (on Mac, CTL + i on PCs) to open the Max object inspector window. This window allows the user to change settings and attributes for specific objects in the patch. Find the setting marked "Number of Decimal Places" and change the argument to 5. You should now see float numbers going up and down relative to how much noise you make.
- Be as quiet as you can while you watch the floats report gain levels will show you an approximation of the *ambient noise level* that exists in the room. If there were another human musician in the room with you, listening and waiting for you to begin an improvisation, this level of noise would probably be beneath their notice.
- Sing or play a single note on an instrument at a loud volume. Check the reading to see what your peak is.
- You may be able to catch the highest dBFS reading, but if it goes by too rapidly to read it adequately, change the argument on the "peakamp~ 100" object to a slower rate, like 300 or 500. This doesn't change your peak but rather how often the peak is reported.
- The highest dBFS level you can achieve by doing this is another important reading. If a human musician were playing with you, their brain would be automatically trying to match your volume level so they could match your overall range. Musicians will often notice if there is an imbalance where one person is louder or quieter than another and will work to fix the imbalance.
- Since we've been dealing thus far with MIDI, it would be useful to see these gain levels as MIDI velocities. However, the numbers coming out of the "peakamp~ 100" object are not in the right range for MIDI velocities. Below the "peakamp~ 100" create a new object called "scale." Connect the outlet of the "peakamp~ 100" to the leftmost inlet of the scale object. The scale object scales objects from one range to another. Give the scale object the following arguments:
  - The first number (input low) should be just a bit higher than the quietest gain level you have observed as your ambient noise level. We want to turn this low gain level into a low-velocity note-on message. Anything gain level lower than this should be considered a note-off velocity. (N.B.: this number should be a float number)
  - The second number (input high) should be just a bit higher than the highest (peak) gain level you have observed when you sing or play a loud note. We want to turn this high gain level into a high-velocity note-on message. (N.B.: this number should be a float number)

  - The third number (output low) should be a high enough velocity that the sound will be audible. For reasons that may become apparent as you use this system, we don't want the MIDI output velocity to be too low, so let's start with an output low of 75. (N.B.: this number should be an integer, not a float)
  - The fourth number (output high) should be 127.
- Because the numbers coming out of the peakamp~ are floats, the result will be floating point numbers that don't usually correspond to MIDI velocities like "40.56782." MIDI systems would ignore anything after the decimal place, but there's a handy object to round these outputs to the closest whole number called "round." Create a round object underneath the scale. Connect the left outlet of the scale to the leftmost inlet of the round object.
- Create a new "number" object below the scale object. Connect the outlet of the round object to the inlet of the number object. As you sing or play, you should see numbers that look like MIDI on velocities. If this does not work, go back to the beginning of this section and troubleshoot (Figure 9.8).

Parsing Frequencies from Digital Audio

Parsing pitches from an audio stream is one of the most difficult problems in the subfield of MIR. Recent advancements in this problem have allowed for cutting-edge technologies like Dubler that perform seemingly instant audio to MIDI pitch transfer. But for those of us building our own bespoke systems, this process is still fraught with difficulty. There are many methods tackling this problem that have been devised over the years. Many of these methods are proprietary, require serious computational resources, or special equipment. As such, this section will focus on methods that can be implemented in real time using currently available consumer-grade computers.

Time-Domain Pitch Tracking

Early pitch tracking methods worked directly with the raw waveform, rather than breaking the waveform down into its constituent frequency components. Because these methods focus on the timing of repeating patterns in a waveform, they are referred to as *time-domain* pitch tracking methods. One of the simplest methods for frequency detection involves counting the number of times the energy of the signal crosses over "0," or the number of times the wave transitions from positive to negative pressure (compression to rarefaction). This stat, called the *zero-crossing rate (ZCR)*, can be assessed with little strain on a computer system, but is not reliable in detecting complex timbre sounds that involve harmonics. ZCR is relatively easy to implement in Max using the zerox~ object.

The YIN algorithm is highly reliable for monophonic pitch detection developed by Alain de Cheveigné and Hideki Kawahara (2002). The yin~ object is available via IRCAM's Max Sound Box package, which requires an IRCAM subscription. YIN is also an option to use for FluCoMa's pitch estimation

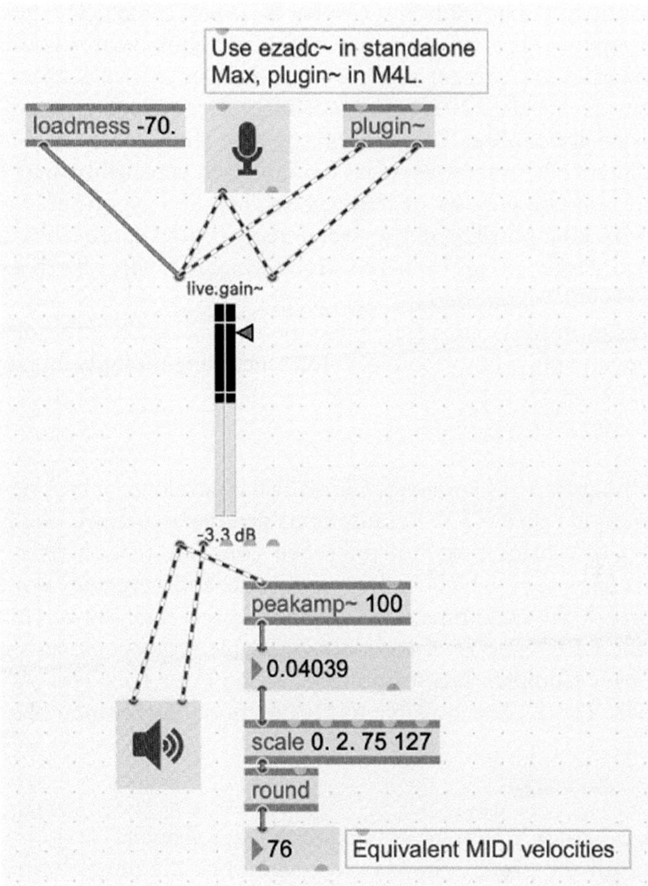

Figure 9.8 A rudimentary system to convert audio signals into MIDI velocities.

object fluid.pitch~ which will be discussed in Chapter 10. Other time-domain approaches include *autocorrelation* (which resists noise and harmonics, making it useful for inclusion in instrument tuners), and *Average Magnitude Difference Function (AMDF)*, which is similarly easily performed with minimal compute power. These methods are useful in many circumstances, but instrumental sounds are typically complex waveforms, consisting of a fundamental frequency (the lowest frequency extant in the waveform) and numerous *harmonics* (multiples of the fundamental, e.g., 880 Hz over a fundamental of 440 Hz).

Frequency-Domain Pitch Tracking

The *Fast Fourier Transform (FFT)* algorithm breaks a complex waveform into individual frequency components (which is sort of like breaking a chord played simultaneously into a list of notes; Cooley & Tukey, 1965). The full scope of how this happens is beyond the scope of this text, but essentially, FFT shows what frequencies are present and how strong they are at a given moment (Oppenheim & Schafer, 2010; Smith, 2007). This process is based on how humans listen for timbre. Two voices may sing the same note, but we can tell the difference between the voices because each voice constructs that note as a unique and complex set of frequencies. The FFT algorithm makes real-time pitch tracking possible and spawned many related approaches, including *Spectral Peak Picking, Cepstrum Analysis, Harmonic Product Spectrum (HPS), and Subharmonic Summation (SHS)*. The fft~ object is the best way to explore these processes in Max. However, these methods struggle with noisy signals, rich timbres, and polyphony (sound sources including multiple fundamentals).

ZTX

The Zynaptiq group of Hannover, Germany has developed a proprietary pitch tracking method called *ZTX*. Because of its proprietary nature, the ZTX process is a bit of a black box, but published company reports refer to *adaptive wavelet technology*, which analyses both time and frequency domains of a sound source at the same time. ZTX operates in real time but can put a lot of strain on the CPU. The ZTX code is a licensable technology, also powering Ableton Live's Complex Pro warp mode, Logic Pro's Flex Time/Pitch, and other DAWs. The ZTX is available to Max users via the retune~ object.

In Either Version of Max

- Unlock the patch you've been building for this chapter.
- Underneath the ezadc~ (in Max standalone) or the plugin~ (in Max-for-Live), create a new object called "retune~." This object performs automatic pitch correction (hence the name), in the manner of Antares' Autotune, but a side benefit of this processing is that retune~ can also perform ZTX-based pitch detection. After the name retune~, add the attribute "@pitchdetection 1." This will turn on the retune~ object's pitch detection abilities, which are mutually exclusive with its pitch correction abilities. Connect the leftmost outlet of the ezdac~ or the plugin~ to the leftmost inlet of the "retune~ @pitchdetection 1" object. Assume the mic or input you are using is essentially the same as channel 2; there is no need to worry about a second channel.
- Delete the patch cord going from the live.gain~ to the "peakamp~ 100." Connect the leftmost outlet of the retune~ object to the leftmost inlet of the "peakamp~ 100." In pitch detection mode, the leftmost outlet of the retune~ object simply passes the signal back out of the object. This connection will ensure that the system will be parsing pitch and amplitude from the same sources but may necessitate changing the arguments on the scale object you set in the previous section.

- Under the retune~ object, create a new object called "route" and give it the argument "onset." When data signals are complicated, the route object can be used to parse complicated data signals by ignoring some signals and routing any data that starts with a given argument to its output. When the retune~ object hears a new note, it outputs a data list that looks like: "onset 5 -14.089933." In this list, we can see the word onset, which refers to the beginning of a newly detected note. The integer 5 refers to the fundamental frequency of the pitch detected (0=C, 1=C#, etc., 5=F). The float refers to the deviation in *cents* from the centre of the fundamental frequency. In the Western equal-tempered tuning system, each semitone (half-step) is divided into 100 cents, meaning there are 1200 cents in an octave. A deviation of +50 cents places a pitch halfway between two semitones, and a tuning of -100 cents would be the same as the note a half-step (one semitone) below the original pitch. This number is useful in some contexts, but not here except to note that if your pitch is off by a significant margin, the system may assume you mean a different note. The "route onset" object will route any message starting with the word "onset," and will also eliminate that word from the data stream, leaving just the two subsequent numbers. Connect the rightmost outlet of the retune~ object to the leftmost inlet of the "route onset" object.
- Underneath the "route onset" object, create a new unpack object with the argument "i f," indicating that we are unpacking a list including an integer and a float. Connect the leftmost outlet of the "route onset" to the inlet of the "unpack i f." Create a new message object under the "unpack i f." Connect the leftmost outlet of the "unpack i f" to the rightmost inlet of the message box so you can see the data coming out of the unpack object. You may notice that when you are quiet the message box shows -1 and when you sing or play it returns numbers from 0-11.
- The system is often returning -1, which is the retune~ object's way of distinguishing between discernible frequencies and indistinct noise. Let us use a conditional argument to filter this message out. Create a new "if" object and give it the arguments "$i1 > 0 then $i1." Connect the leftmost outlet of the "unpack i f" to the inlet of the "if $i1 > 0 then $i1" object. Create a new message object. Connect the outlet of the "if" object to the rightmost inlet of this second message object to see that the "-1" messages are being filtered. Sing or play some notes to see the retune~ object tracking your pitches.

Adding MIDI Output

- You may have noticed that the output of the retune~ object changes at a blinding speed, and probably it's too fast to make intelligible music out of this stream. This illustrates one of the stickier problems inherent in the exercise of turning audio into MIDI: how to get the system to understand when a pitch has started vs. when it is simply sustaining. A total fix for this problem requires a much longer conversation, but there is a quick fix that will get us making music in a hurry. Create a new object called "speedlim" and give it an argument of "100." As stated previously, the speedlim object gates inputs faster than its argument (either in milliseconds or time values like 4n, 8n, etc.), so we can use it to limit these fast signals. Connect the outlet of the "if" object to the leftmost inlet of the "speedlim 100" object.

- The pitches identified by the retune~ (0-11) are too low to be usable by a MIDI system. Create a new "+" object and give it the argument "60." Connect the outlet of the speedlim to the leftmost inlet of the "+ 60" object. In this way, we can boost the pitches from the retune~ object up a few octaves into a more audible range.
- Create a new makenote object with the arguments "127 100 1." Connect the outlet of the "+ 60" object to the leftmost (pitch) inlet of the makenote.
- Create a new noteout object and connect the three outlets of the "makenote 127 100 1" object to the corresponding three inlets of the noteout.

Using Audio-to-MIDI Velocities

- The MIDI velocities are changing rapidly in response to the continuous nature changes in air pressure pressing on the microphone. Let's filter this a bit further. Above the makenote object, create a new message object. Connect the outlet of the message object to the second-from-the-left inlet of the makenote (the velocity inlet). Connect the outlet of the number object showing the equivalent MIDI velocities to the rightmost inlet of this message object. The message in the message object should start changing immediately, but it is not being sent to the makenote yet.
- We only want to change the velocity when the system detects the onset of a new note. Under the "+ 60" object, create a new "t" (trigger) object and give it the argument "b" so it will send out a bang every time it is triggered. Connect the outlet of the "+ 60" to the inlet of the "t b" object. Connect the outlet of the "t b" object to the leftmost inlet of the message box above the makenote. This will cause the velocity to be passed to the makenote only when a new onset is detected by the retune~ object (Figure 9.9).

Standalone Max

- Lock the patch and test it by singing or playing some notes. You will discover that it works best with sharp sounds, e.g., singing notes on the syllable "tah" rather than "la." Sounds with sharp formants are easier for the system to pick up. You will also discover that polyphonic sounds are practically meaningless to the system, producing merely a jumble of notes.

Max-for-Live via Ableton Live

- Since the system you've been building is residing in an audio track in Ableton Live, there is no MIDI output. There is unfortunately no way to

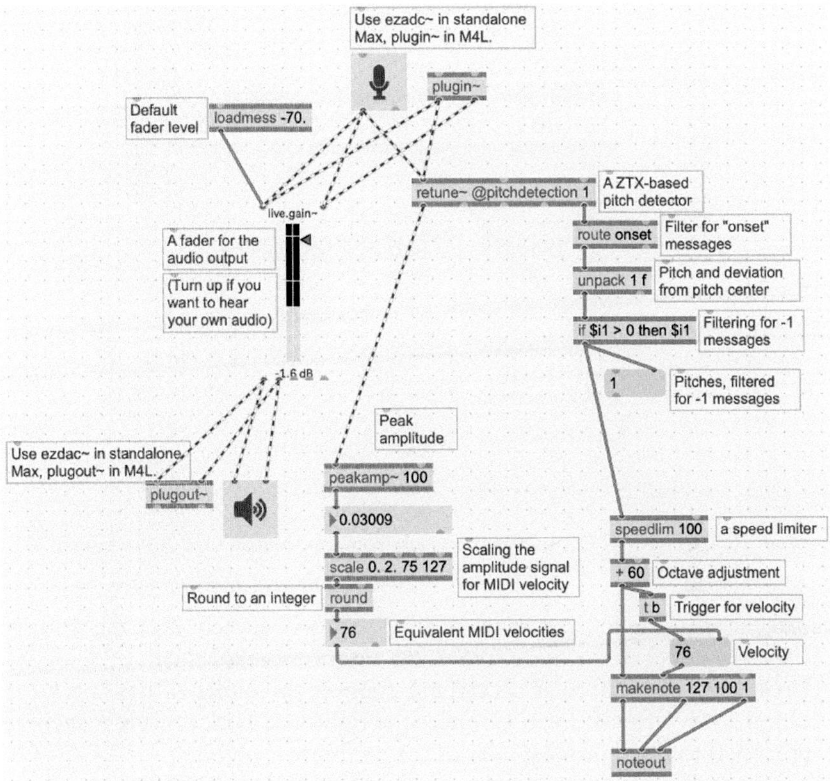

Figure 9.9 A rudimentary system to perform audio-to-MIDI conversion.

send raw MIDI data out of an audio channel directly to Ableton's MIDI system. In fact, if you lock the patch and double-click on the noteout object at the bottom of the patch nothing will happen. The object is dead. Luckily there is a workaround that will allow you to connect this patch to MIDI.

- In Ableton Live's browser, click on Max-for-Live and look for the blank Max MIDI Effect. Drag it onto the track called "1 MIDI." Next find an instrument in the browser called "Grand Piano" and drag it onto the same track, to the right of the Max MIDI Effect. Right-click on the Max MIDI Effect and click "Edit in Max." The patch will open with a midiin object, connected to a midiout object. These objects allow MIDI to pass through the effect. Leave these where they are.
- Unlock the patch. Create a new receive object and give it the argument "MIDIfromAUDIO." Connect the "receive MIDIfromAUDIO" object directly to the midiout object (Figure 9.10).
- In the other patch, create a new pack object and give it the argument "i i" so it will pack two integers. Connect the pitch (leftmost) outlet of the

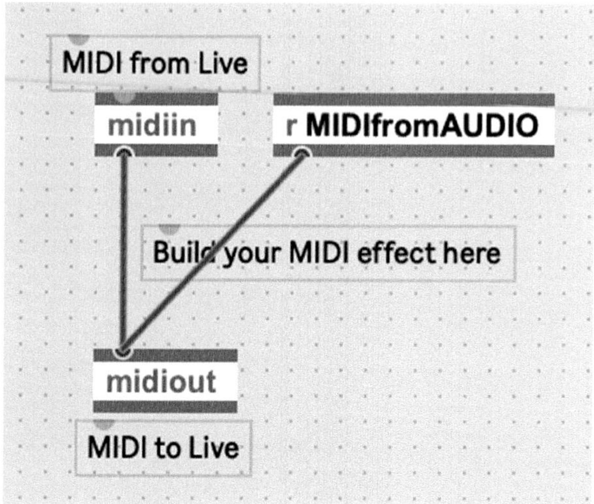

Figure 9.10 Passing MIDI into a MIDI track from an Ableton Live audio effect.

makenote to the leftmost inlet of the "pack i i" and connect the velocity (middle) outlet of the makenote to the rightmost inlet.

- Create a new midiformat object and connect the outlet of the "pack i i" object to its leftmost inlet. Connect the rightmost outlet of the makenote (channel) to the rightmost inlet of the midiformat object.
- Create a new send object and give it the argument MIDIfromAUDIO. Connect the outlet of the midiformat object and connect it to the "send MIDIfromAUDIO" object.
- Sing or play your instrument. You should hear the piano playing and responding immediately.
- Save this device for anytime you want to send MIDI from an audio track (Figure 9.11).

Either Version of Max

- Is the system not responsive enough? Try changing the timing arguments for the speedlim and the peakamp~ to a higher or lower setting.
- Save the patch and add comments as shown above. We will continue adding to this system in Chapter 10.
- Play with this system for a while; test its strengths and weaknesses.

Controlling Imp3 or Imp4 with Your Voice

- As interesting as it may be to turn your audio into MIDI, this system could do a lot more if it were used in place of the MIDI controller you've been

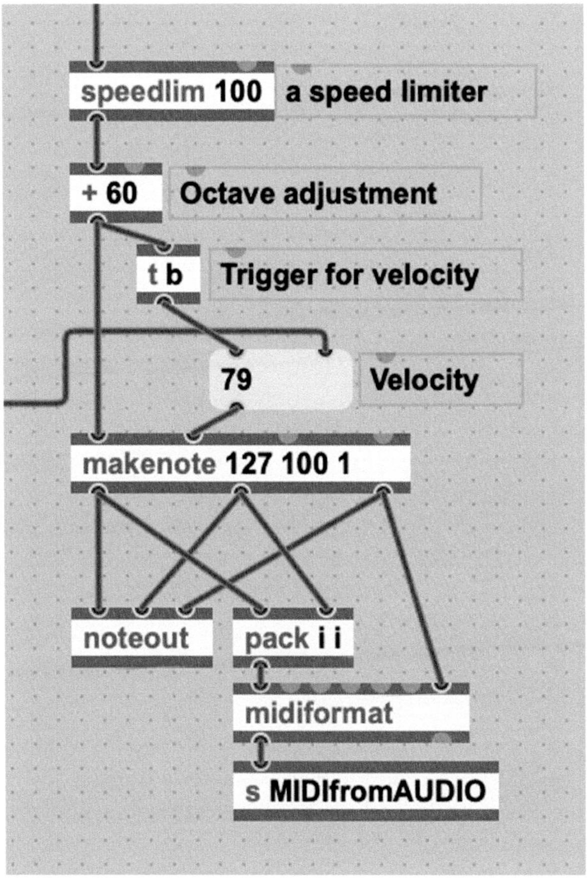

Figure 9.11 Passing MIDI out of an Ableton Live audio effect.

using to interface with Imp3 and Imp4. To connect this system to Imp3, we simply must create a bridge between the two programs via the "send MIDIears" data channel. Under the makenote object at the bottom of the audio-to-MIDI system, create a new "pack i i" object to pack the pitch and velocity together into a list. Connect the makenote's pitch and velocity outlets to the inlets of the pack object.

Connecting to Imp3

- Under the "pack i i" create a midiformat object and then connect the outlet of the pack to the leftmost inlet of the midiformat. Connect the rightmost (channel) outlet of the makenote to the rightmost (channel) inlet of the midiformat object. While we're there, let's change the default channel of

the makenote so it doesn't clash with anything else we've used thus far (channel 5 is free).
- Next, create a "send MIDIears" object under the midiformat object. Connect the leftmost outlet of the midiformat to the inlet of the "send MIDIears."
- Finally, open Imp3 and improvise.

Connecting to Imp4

- Since we did not use a MIDIears send channel for Imp4, we will need to create a way for this system to listen to the output of the system we've been building in this chapter. However, we don't want signals from the MIDIears channel (which pertain only to Imp3) to also be received by Imp4. Duplicate the "send MIDIears" object in the present patch and rename the new send object using the channel "MIDIears2." Connect the outlet of the midiformat to the new "send MIDIears2" object.
- Open the Imp4 patch. Up towards the top, near the midiin object, create a new "receive MIDIears2" object. Connect the outlet of this object to the midiparse object. There is no reason to connect it to the midiout, since we can already hear our performance via the patch we've been working on.

Wrapping up with a Test Drive of the New Trio

- Save the patch and add comments to the novel objects so you can remember what you did later. The following chapter's tutorial will not take this system as a starting point, but instead we shall build a similar system while introducing some new objects.
- Take some time to try out this new AI trio. This will involve singing or playing an instrument into your microphone, which is quite different from what we've done with previous improvisations. Along the way, ponder these questions: What does this system do that previous systems could not? What is still missing from this ensemble? Is the ensemble playing too much? Or do you feel like you need to keep playing so constantly so it doesn't stop all the time?

Conclusion

Although this prototype is simple, it points towards the possibility of systems that can listen and respond to human-made sound in real time. At this stage we have not addressed higher-level parameters such as duration or timbre, nor incorporated machine learning in a substantial way. The system is reactive rather than improvisational—closer to an approximation of a human ear waiting for the addition of a mind. Yet this is precisely how pioneering projects like George Lewis's Voyager began: as frameworks that could listen and react in real time. In that sense, even a rudimentary design positions us squarely on the shoulders of giants. Crucially, every step in this direction helps redefine what it means to collaborate with a machine as a genuine musical partner.

References

Camazine, S., Deneubourg, J.-L., Franks, N. R., Sneyd, J., Theraulaz, G., & Bonabeau, E. (2001). *Self-organization in biological systems*. Princeton University Press.

Cooley, J. W., & Tukey, J. W. (1965). An algorithm for the machine calculation of complex Fourier series. *Mathematics of Computation*, *19*(90), 297–301. https://doi.org/10.2307/2003354

de Cheveigné, A., & Kawahara, H. (2002). YIN, a fundamental frequency estimator for speech and music. *The Journal of the Acoustical Society of America*, *111*(4), 1917–1930. https://doi.org/10.1121/1.1458024

Dehaene, S. (2021). *How we learn: Why brains learn better than any machine... for now*. Viking.

Edelman, G. M. (1987). *Neural Darwinism: The theory of neuronal group selection*. Basic Books.

Hofstadter, D. R. (1979). *Gödel, Escher, Bach: An eternal golden braid*. Basic Books.

Mitchell, M. (2009). *Complexity: A guided tour*. Oxford University Press.

Moore, B. C. J. (2012). *An introduction to the psychology of hearing* (6th ed.). Brill.

Oppenheim, A. V., & Schafer, R. W. (2010). *Discrete-time signal processing* (3rd ed.). Prentice Hall.

Rumelhart, D. E., & McClelland, J. L. (1986). *Parallel distributed processing: Explorations in the microstructure of cognition*. MIT Press.

Smith, J. O. (2007). *Introduction to digital filters: With audio applications*. W3K Publishing.

Tononi, G., & Edelman, G. M. (1998). Consciousness and complexity. *Science*, *282*(5395), 1846–1851. https://doi.org/10.1126/science.282.5395.1846

10 Connectionism, Part II

Turning Estimations into Actions

It is of paramount importance that a machine musician be able to sense the context of the musical world it is reacting to and respond in a musically appropriate way. In Chapter 9, we built a rudimentary system that, like Commander Data, interacts with audio, rather than MIDI, even though MIDI remains very useful for controlling sound output. Through this experience, you have begun to understand that audio is a tangled, complicated, multidimensional mess of interconnected phenomena that often lacks a single standardised representation.

Briefly mentioned in the last chapter, MIR (Music Information Retrieval) is the study of how to get machines to understand, parse, *classify* (label and explain), and transcribe raw audio as data (Downie, 2003). MIR researchers use various methods to process audio signals, searching the stream of data for musical features like pitch, rhythm, duration, timbre, and dynamics (Casey et al., 2008). However, the study of perceptual features like range, contour, contrast, repetition, and frame discussed in this text was widely addressed by the MIR field until somewhat recently (Lerch, 2012). In this chapter, we will dive deeper into audio problems and how to deal with them in interactive systems using some MIR techniques. However, this chapter is not meant as a full explanation of MIR methods, but rather a brief introduction to MIR as a pathway to understanding more advanced connectionist approaches to real-time music improvisation.

Arguably, the study of MIR began in the 1950s with the work of famed computer scientist Max Matthews. Coinciding roughly with the rise of symbolic AI, Matthews' work focused on vocal synthesis and resulted in the development of the LISP (standing for LISt Processing) system, a computer programming language with applications in natural language processing and AI (McCarthy, 1956). Matthews' vocal synthesisation work inspired the voice of the HAL computer in the movie *2001: A space odyssey*, earning this work a greater degree of cultural visibility (Matthews, 1960). With the advancements of digital audio technology in the 1980s and '90s, audio technologists made advancements in the limited extraction of some audio features like pitch, rhythm, and timbre (Backer, 1996). Importantly, the implementation of FFT-based algorithms gave researchers the ability to analyse audio spectrally, greatly

DOI: 10.4324/9781003534211-13

enhancing their ability to retrieve information from musical data (Cooley & Tukey, 1965; Oppenheim, 1989).

The deep learning boom of the 2010s brought many advancements to the MIR field. New connectionist models, such as convolutional neural networks (CNNs), enabled much greater accuracy in audio classification (in the context of MIR, "classification" refers to explaining or labelling features of audio; Choi et al., 2016). As of this writing, the field of MIR is advancing steadily, with funding from many successful private sector firms like Spotify, Google, Apple Music, Yamaha, and Sony spending more money than ever on music technology. The *International Society for Music Information Retrieval (ISMIR)* was founded in 2000 to promote research that intersects with computer science, music theory and audio signal processing (Downie, 2008). Since its founding, ISMIR has continued to provide a public forum for the advancement of MIR research.

Feature Extraction

The audio parsing processes we undertook in Chapter 9 are often referred to as *feature extraction*, a major focus of the MIR field. Audio features are essentially anything about a stream of digital audio we might want the system to notice. MIR researchers typically classify these features into three general categories: low-end (signal-based) features, mid-level (musical and perceptual) features, and high-end (semantic or contextual) features (Peeters, 2004). The following is a necessarily limited list of features that may be extracted, accompanied by a truncated list of some methods commonly used for their extraction:

As one can see from this non-exhaustive list, MIR methods are deep and complex. MIR researchers may base their entire careers on investigating a limited set of features for recommender systems like Spotify or Apple Music. While there are many uses for these extraction techniques, our goal demands investigation into methods that will give our machine musician a context for what is appropriate when playing music in real time. In this chapter we will complete our final real-time improvisation system, one which will listen to audio and (like its ancestors Imp3 and Imp4) produce music via a MIDI output.

Approaching Loudness

There is an unavoidable level of noise (unwanted or unintentional sound) in all electronic audio systems. As the gain of the output increases, the level of noise increases as well. Yet most audio situations (beyond the music of John Cage) call for a high level of signal and a low level of noise. To combat this, audio engineers often increase the gain of the input (the microphone or other source) and lower the output volume, thus increasing what is called the *signal-to-noise ratio*. Similarly, one thing that will impair our autonomous music system is not being able to hear the signal through the noise. You may have

Table 10.1 A brief list of audio features and example extraction methods

Low-end features	*Example extraction methods*	
Pitch	autocorrelation	YIN algorithm
Loudness	root-mean-square (RMS) energy	perceptual loudness models (LUFs, etc.)
Timbre	Mel-frequency cepstral coefficients (MFCCs)	spectral centroid/flux/ rolloff
Mid-level features	**Example extraction methods**	
Melody	derived from pitch-tracking	contour analysis
Harmony	chroma features	constant-Q transform (CQT)
Key	Krumhansl-Schmuckler key profiles	tonal centroid
Tempo	derived from onset detection	beat histograms
Rhythm	derived from inter-onset intervals (IOI)	periodicity analysis
High-level features	**Example extraction methods**	
Genre	inferred from supervised machine-learning performed on timbral features	convolutional neural networks (CNNs)
Mood	modelled using audio descriptors mapped to emotion spaces (valence/arousal)	regression models
Instrument recognition	timbre-based features (MFCCs)	spectral-temporal patterns
Formal structure	segment boundary detection	hidden Markov models (HMMs)

already discovered with the system we built in Chapter 9 that turning audio into MIDI pitches involves putting up with a lot of false triggers. Moving the system to a very quiet environment will improve this performance somewhat.

In strictly MIR-focused studies, we could just set up the machine in an anechoic chamber (a room built to negate nearly all reverberation, like the one at the University of Iowa's Wendell Johnson Speech and Hearing Lab), but we are building a machine musician that has the ability to react like a human musician to natural music situations. Real-world situations are often less than ideal. Some performance venues are noisy, and some are quiet. In some venues, there is an incessant 60-cycle hum coming from every electrical outlet that infects all audio systems. Even in the best situations, where music aficionados are culturally trained to maintain complete silence in a performance, there will always be unexpected noises like audience coughing, sneezing, and unexpectedly loud page turns. A true machine musician requires a noise filter that can discriminate between noise and a listened-for sound in real time. Unfortunately, this one-stop perceptual noise gate does not yet exist (at least not as a Max object).

Up until now, the systems we have developed have required minimal human intervention to operate once they are set up. That will be decreasingly possible going forward. As a stopgap measure, we will utilise some objects from the *FluCoMa* package developed by the *Fluid Corpus Manipulation* team. Researchers and artists at the University of York developed this project focusing on building new tools for sound analysis, synthesis, and performance using machine learning and AI. Most of their work is open source, enabling other researchers to build upon their efforts. They have developed many audio manipulating objects for this Max package, a full list of which would be well beyond the scope of this text. However, those interested in carrying the learning in this text further should give the FluCoMa package a high priority.

Downloading and Installing the FluCoMa Package

1. Open Max (or alternatively, Max-for-Live, within Ableton Live)
2. Click on File and then click "Show Package Manager"
3. Search for *machine learning*.
4. Locate the FluidCorpusManipulation (FluCoMa) package, click on it, and then click the install button (Figure 10.1).

In Max-for-Live via Ableton Live

- Create a new Ableton Live session.
- Drag a blank audio effect device into an audio track and arm the track to record.
- Open the new blank audio effect device in Max by right-clicking on the device and clicking "edit in Max."
- Delete the plugin~ and plugout~ objects (we will create our own later).

In Standalone Max

- Create a new blank patch.

In Either Version of Max

- Create an audio input (either plugin~ for Max-for-Live or ezadc~ for standalone Max).
- Under your audio input create a new live.gain object. Connect the outlet or outlets of your audio input to the live.gain (whichever configuration makes the most sense for your setup, e.g., two channels, one channels, etc.).

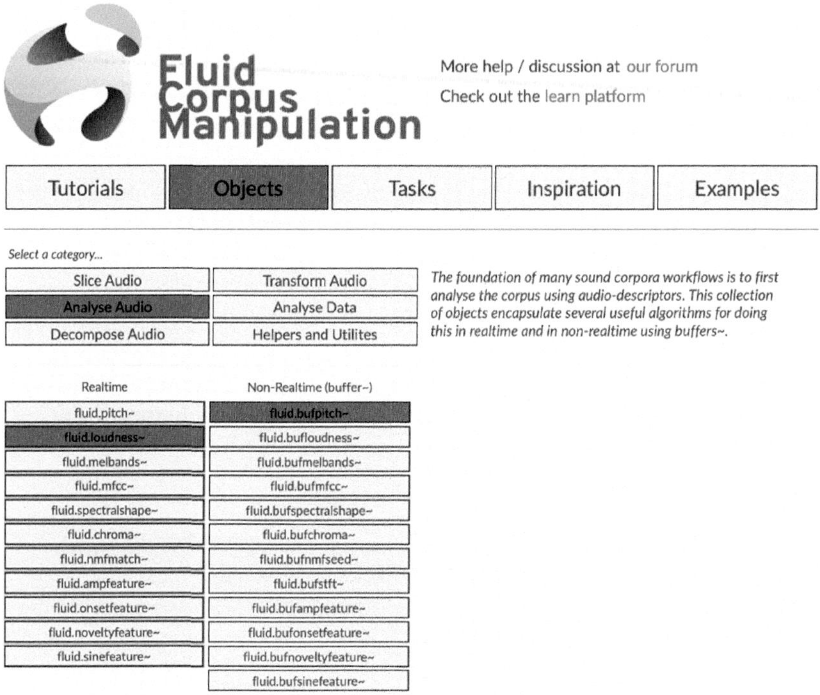

Figure 10.1 The FluCoMa overview patch.

Audio Output

- The live.gain we have created will need to send audio both to the audio output and the rest of the system. However, it would be useful to have a separate fader to control the audio output we hear. Create a second live .gain~ object beneath and to the left of the first. Connect the two leftmost outlets of the first live.gain~ to the inlets of the second.
- Under this second live.gain~ create an audio output (plugout~ in M4L or ezdac~ in standalone Max). Connect the two leftmost outlets of the second live.gain~ to the inlets of the audio output object.
- It is often useful to start an audio system with the sound turned down. Above the second live.gain~, create a new "loadmess -70." object so it sends out the -70 float when the patch loads. Connect the outlet of this loadmess object to the inlet of the second live.gain~ (Figure 10.2).
- Since the loadmess object wasn't in the patch when it loaded, lock the patch and then double-click the "loadmess -70." to turn the live.gain~ down.

In Standalone Max

- Lock the patch and click the ezadc~ object to turn on audio.

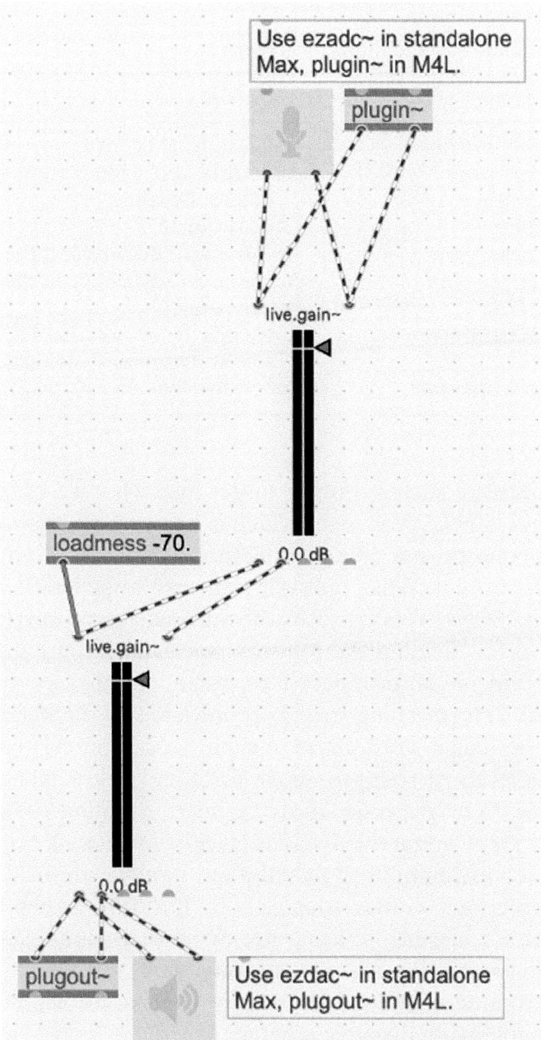

Figure 10.2 Audio input and output (stereo configuration shown, your results may vary).

Loudness

Now that we have some degree of control over the audio passing through our system, it is time to begin extracting features we will be able to use to generate context-appropriate music. In the last chapter, we converted raw audio peaks into velocities by changing the scale of the data, but you may have noticed that the velocity output still ended up being quite glitchy. This is due primarily to the continuous nature of audio. Amplitude levels are in constant flux, and it

Table 10.2 A common scheme for musical dynamics.

Dynamic	*Name*	*Meaning*
fff	*fortississimo*	Loudest dynamic on a particular instrument.
ff	*fortissimo*	A dynamic above loud, but less than the loudest dynamic.
f	*forte*	Loud dynamic.
mf	*mezzo-forte*	An "average" dynamic, on the side of loud.
mp	*mezzo-piano*	An "average" dynamic, on the side of soft.
p	*piano*	Soft dynamic
pp	*pianissimo*	A dynamic below soft, but louder than the softest dynamic.
ppp	*pianississimo*	Softest dynamic on a particular instrument.

is difficult to translate such a moving target into what we normally think of as a *loudness level.* Unlike peak gain (which is a feature of amplitude), *loudness* is a perceptual concept, not an actual feature of the audio but more a sense our brains derive from it. While musicians of every stripe have terminology for various loudness levels, Western classical musicians have developed a useful cognitive system for dividing the loudness spectrum from loudest to softest volume an instrument can produce. This system classifies loud volumes with the Italian word *forte* (meaning strong, abbreviated by the letter *f*), and quiet volumes with the Italian word *piano* (meaning soft, abbreviated by the letter *p*). The various levels of strength above forte and below piano are denoted by adding either *f's* or *p's*, respectively (as in *ff,* meaning the dynamic level above *forte* and *pp*, meaning the dynamic level below *piano*). Some composers have added an intense amount of *f's* and *p's* to signify extreme dynamic levels. The Austrian composer Gustav Mahler is traditionally tagged as one of the worst offenders, for instance utilising the extreme dynamic *ppppp* in his 2nd Symphony, signifying a dynamic of very, very, very, very, soft). Thus, despite the periodic extremes mentioned above, many musicians will recognise some variation of the following dynamic scheme:

Dynamics as MIDI

When musicians are improvising, they are most likely not taking note of their dynamics by keeping this list in mind. The dynamic scheme above is mostly useful as a way of communicating an intended dynamic level to a musician reading from a score composed by a composer who is often not present. Each level slices a musician's total potential loudness into eight bands or sub-spectra. Dynamics and loudness values are often calculated on a *logarithmic* curve, a mathematical function that increases rapidly at first and then gradually levels off. This scheme of logarithmic loudness values more adequately maps to

Table 10.3 Common dynamics translated to LUFS and equivalent MIDI velocities.

Dynamic	*Name*	*LUFS*	*MIDI velocities (logarithmic)*
fff	*fortississimo*	-2. to 0.	121–127
ff	*fortissimo*	-5. to -2.1	106–120
f	*forte*	-10. to -5.1	86–105
mf	*mezzo-forte*	-20. to -10.1	66–85
mp	*mezzo-piano*	-30 to -20.1	46–65
p	*piano*	-40. to -30.1	26–45
pp	*pianissimo*	-50. to -40.1	11–25
ppp	*pianississimo*	-60. to -50.1	1–10

the human perception of sensory information like sound (Hartmann, 1998; Roederer, 2008).

Loudness Representation

Dynamics in audio are commonly measured using many different scales. When audio engineers talk about sound levels, they are usually referring to the *Decibel Scale* (dB), which measures the physical air pressure exerted by a sound wave. Inside a software application or even inside a piece of hardware, where audio is no longer a physical phenomenon, loudness is measured in the *Decibel Relative to Full Scale* (dBFS). dBFS measures digital audio amplitude relative to the loudest possible signal. As useful as these scales are, they do not replicate human perception, which will be important in building a machine musician with a human-like appreciation of loudness. Accordingly, in 2006, the *Loudness Units Full Scale* (LUFS) was introduced by the International Telecommunication Union (International Telecommunication Union, 2006). The LUFS scale was designed to account for how humans perceive loudness differently depending on the frequencies extant in the signal. While a full translation of musical dynamics to LUFS would require a complex interweaving of both loudness and frequency ranges, a rough translation of the one to the other might look something like this:

Unfortunately, since the scale is a recent invention, there is not a standard object in Max that allows for it (the default scale for MSP audio objects in Max is dBFS), but luckily the FluCoMa has solved this problem.

In All Versions of Max

- Unlock the patch.
- Beneath the first live.gain~ object, create a new object called "fluid.loudness~." This object takes in an audio signal and translates that signal into LUFS. The fluid.loudness~ object assumes a mono signal, so we only need

one channel as an input. Choose whichever one of the two leftmost outlets of the live.gain~ is appropriate and connect it to the inlet of the fluid.loudness~.

- Under the fluid.loudness~ object, create a new "unpack f f," which we will use to break apart the list coming out of the fluid.loudness~ object into two floats (loudness and peak amplitude, the latter of which we will not need). Connect the leftmost outlet of the fluid.loudness~ to the inlet of the "unpack f f."
- Under the unpack object, create a new message object. Connect the leftmost outlet of the unpack (loudness) to the rightmost inlet of the message object. You should immediately see float numbers changing rapidly. These numbers are the LUFS equivalent of your live audio.
- Click on the fluid.loudness~ object and go to the Max Inspector window (Command + I on a Mac, Control + I on a PC). Look down at the attribute called "Latency." Using the default settings of this object will involve a latency of 1024 samples, meaning any system we build upon this object will always be slightly behind any beat we give it. We can make this number smaller by decreasing the *window size* (the *window* is the chunk of audio samples currently being evaluated). If we were using fluid.loudness for analysing, recording, or generating audio, this could have a deleterious effect on our audio quality, but in this instance, we are only using this reading so we can calculate LUFS into MIDI velocities, so change the window size to 512 samples. The latency should go down as well. Close the Inspector window.

Play Detection

- When we were building Imp3 and Imp4, it was quite easy to tell whether the human creating the signal was playing or not. It will not be as easy to build an audio system that does the same, but this signal is vital to the overall performance of the system. Below the "unpack f f," create a new object called live.text. The live.text object is much like the toggle object, but it also holds a message. Click on the live.text. In the Inspector window, change the Text Off Label to "Silent." Then change the Text On Label to "Playing." We will use this object as a visual indicator of when the human collaborator is silent or playing.
- Above the live.text, create a new object called ">" (greater than). This object compares two numbers or floats (sending out a 1 if the number in the left inlet is greater than the number in the right inlet and sending out a 0 if not). Connect the outlet of the > object to the inlet of the live.text. Connect the leftmost outlet of the "unpack f f" to the leftmost inlet of the > object. Since the audio is turned on, the live.text indicator should immediately turn to "Playing."
- To set the threshold of the > object, create an object called live.slider. This object is much like live.gain but sends data instead of audio. Click on this object and open the Inspector window and find the attribute called

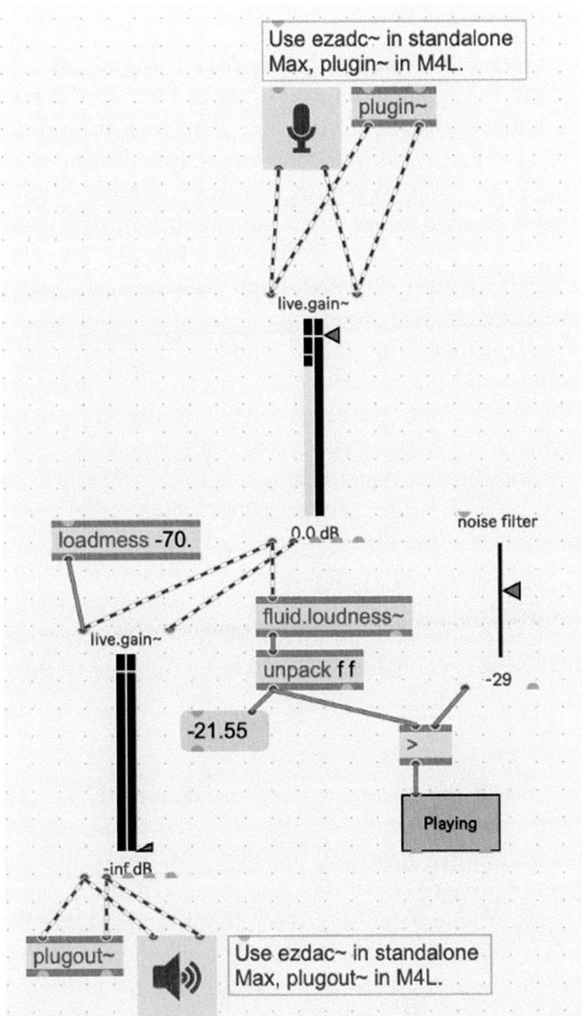

Figure 10.3 Using fluid.loudness~ to create a play detection indicator.

Range/Enum and change it to "-70. 1." (don't forget the decimal points to indicate that the output should be a float). Find the attribute called Short Name and change it to "noise filter." Close the Inspector window. Connect the leftmost outlet of the live.slider to the rightmost inlet of the > object. Lock the patch and drag the noise filter slider up and down while making some noise into your microphone or playing an instrument. There should be a "sweet spot" where the live.text indicator switches to "playing" when you are playing and "silent" when you are not playing. Set the noise filter to that sweet spot. You will need to do this whenever you use this patch, or the system will be either too active or not active enough (Figure 10.3).

LUFS to MIDI

- Doing the calculation from LUFS to MIDI would take an inordinate amount of time to explain, so in the Chapter 10 Snippets folder there is a file called "loudness2dynamics.maxsnip." Find that file and drag it directly into the patch. This snippet contains a subpatch that takes in LUFS and outputs equivalent MIDI velocities and dynamics according to the logarithmic scheme detailed above (with one exception, that will be explained later).
- This patch is getting quite crowded. Under the unpack object, create a new send object on the channel "loudness." Connect the leftmost outlet of the "unpack f f" to the inlet of the "send loudness." Next create a new "receive loudness" object and place it above the object called "p loudness2dynamics." Connect the outlet of the receive object to the leftmost inlet of the "p loudness2dynamics." Now as you make noise you should see the objects below the "p loudness2dynamics" object change. The "p" object is a way to encapsulate a patch within another patch (often called a subpatch), so if you are curious how this is being done, lock the path and double-click on the object. One thing you should know about how the "p loudness2dynamics" is that it is calculating an average of dynamics over time, so as you play it is going to eventually smooth out all your dynamics to a single value. To reset this average, you need to send a bang message to the middle inlet.

Slicing

- It would be nice if the necessary bang message could be extracted from the impulse to play. We could do this with the retune object, extracting the onset as we did in Chapter 9, but FluCoMa provides another option. FluCoMa's fluid.noveltyslice~ finds *slicing points* in an audio signal, which are dividing points where one sonic event ends, and another begins. Above the "p loudness2dynamics" object, create a new object called fluid.noveltyslice~. The fluid.noveltyslice~ object sends out an audio signal that vacillates between -0. (when the incoming signal is not a new audio event) and 1. (when the incoming signal is new).
- To convert this signal into a bang message, we will use an object called edge~, which detects transitions in audio signals going from 0. to 1. Create this object and connect the leftmost outlet of the fluid.noveltyslice~ to the inlet of the edge~ object.
- Under the first live.gain~, create a new send~ object (note the tilde, indicating we are sending audio) and attach it to a new channel named "audioL." Connect the leftmost outlet to the new "send~ audioL" object. Next, create a "receive~ audioL" object and connect its output to the inlet of the fluid.noveltyslice~ object.
- Now when you make a noise into your microphone or with your instrument, the average within the dynamic system will be reset.

- Lastly, we will use the velocity states elsewhere in the patch, so under the number object displaying velocity, create a new send object and give it a new channel called "VLCTYstates."
- The fluid.noveltyslice~ object uses the FFT algorithm in its slice extraction, which (as with the window size of the fluid.loudness object) adds some latency. Since the audio quality is not mission-critical currently, let's lower the latency (which defaults to 2048 samples) by clicking on the object, opening the Inspector window and changing the FFT Settings attribute from "1024 -1 -1" to "256 -1 -1." This should bring the object's latency down to 512, putting it on par with the fluid.loudness~ object (Figure 10.4).

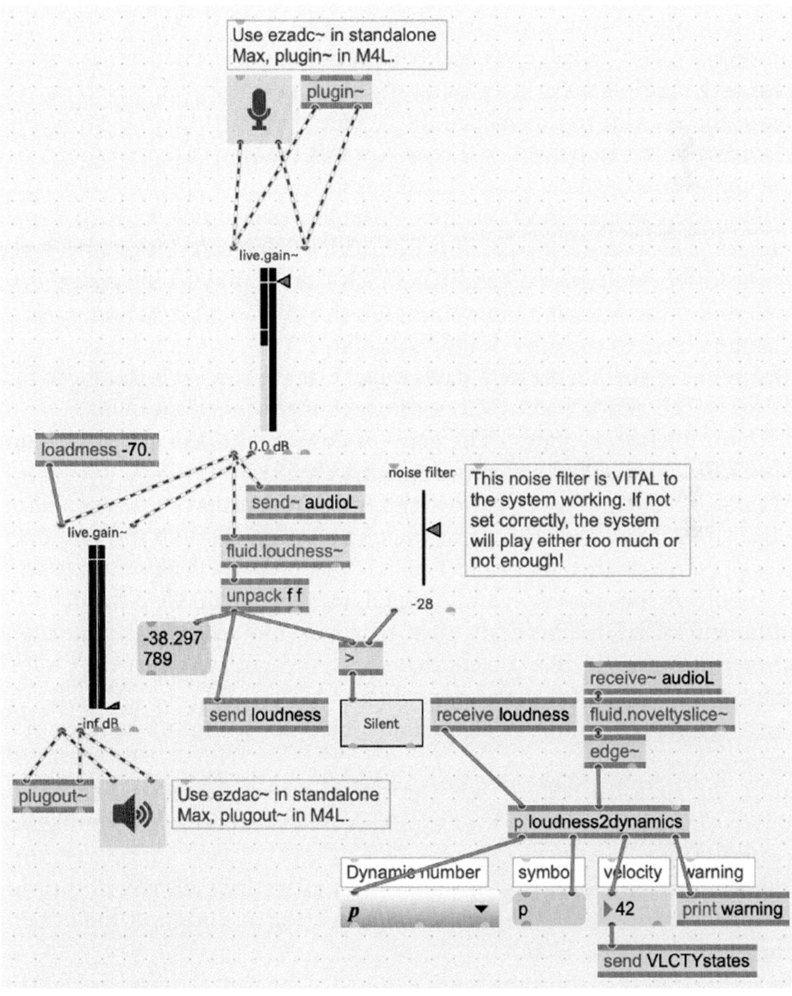

Figure 10.4 Converting LUFS into MIDI velocities and stable dynamics.

Extracting for Duration

- To generate music using this system, we will also need to extract duration via the onsets of notes received by the audio input. Since FluCoMa has its own onset extraction object, create a new object called fluid.onsetslice~. This object is rather simple and works quite well.
- Under the fluid.onsetslice~, create a new edge~ object. Connect the left-most outlet of the fluid.onsetslice~ to the edge~ object.
- Under the edge~ object, create a button and connect the leftmost outlet of the edge~ to the inlet of the button.
- This system will tend to react to every onset in the room, both intentional and unintentional, so it would be good to filter the audio a bit before sending it to the fluid.onsetslice~ object. Luckily, we have already created a play detector which we can use to control a gate. Under the live.text, create an object called "change" (which will pass a number whenever it changes, stopping multiple 1's or 0's passing through continually). Connect the outlet of the live.text to the inlet of the change object.
- Amazingly, this signal will still tend towards sending data faster than once per millisecond, which will eventually result in a very glitchy performance. Under the change object, create a speedlim object and set it to 1 millisecond. This part of the patch is eventually going to control MIDI playback, so we don't want to add too much latency, but 1 millisecond is still well under the human temporal resolution rate. Connect the outlet of the change object to the inlet of the "speedlim 1."
- Below the speedlim, create a gate~ object (make sure to include the tilde, as we will be gating audio). Connect the outlet of the "speedlim 1" to the leftmost inlet of the gate~. The gate~ is now opened and closed whenever you begin playing and will close immediately after.
- We now need to put some audio in the gate. Create a new "receive~ audioL" object. We don't want the audio to attempt to go through the gate before it is open, so create a new object called "delay~," which acts much like the delay object, but passes an audio signal instead of data. Give the delay~ an argument of 1.5 milliseconds, such that its audio will be 0.5 milliseconds slower than the speedlim object that opens the gate. Connect the outlet of the "receive~ audioL" to the inlet of the "delay~ 1.5."
- Next connect the outlet of the delay~ object to the rightmost inlet of the gate~.
- With the audio turned on, test the system to see if it is reacting to your onsets. If not, go back to the beginning of this section and troubleshoot (Figure 10.5).
- We will extract the timing of note onsets as we have done with previous systems. Create a timer object below the button and connect the outlet of the button to both inlets.
- Since the timing of the signals we've been dealing with thus far has been very fast, it would be good to filter the signal with some conditional arguments.

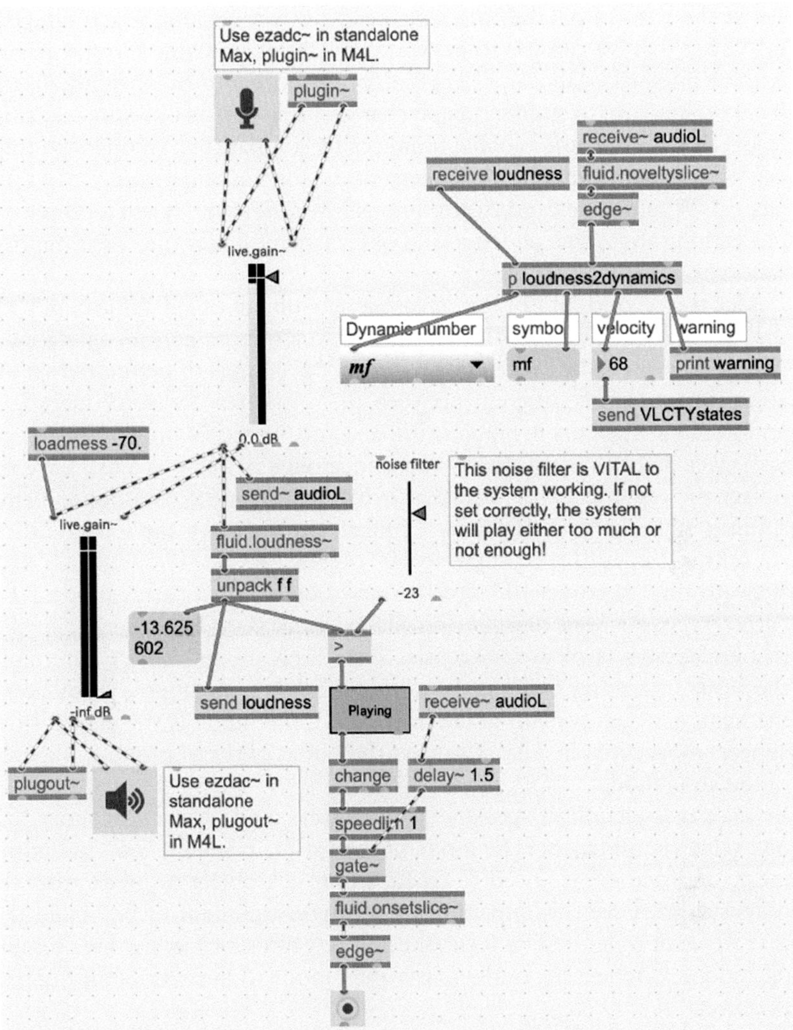

Figure 10.5 Using fluid.onsetslice~ to extract onsets of notes.

Under the timer, create an "if $fl > 10. then $fl" object, meaning, "if the incoming float is greater than 10., allow it to pass." This will filter out timing messages shorter than 10 milliseconds. Connect the leftmost outlet of the timer to the inlet of the "if" object.

- Create a second conditional object to filter out long pauses between onsets: "if $fl > 4001. then $fl." This object will filter out timing messages longer than 4 seconds. Connect the outlet of the first "if" object to the inlet of the second.

- As we did with Imp3 and Imp4, we need a way to group these timing data into a list that we can use to generate new duration states. To stay in time with its human collaborator, Imp3 plays only a beat or two behind, making it very responsive to sudden tempo changes. Imp4 is the opposite—a tempo leader that ignores the variable timing of its compatriots. In this way, Imp4 can act as a sort of unchanging metronome for the other musicians to play against. What if our third Autonomous Music System lagged all three and played long tones that added a kind of firmament under the entire improvisation like a bass player might?
- Under the second "if" object, create a new object called "zl.group." The "zl" class of Max objects allows the user to structure and manipulate lists of data in a myriad of ways. For instance, "zl.compare" evaluates two lists and returns what is different between them, whereas "zl.sort" takes a list and sorts its elements in alphabetical and/or numerical order. The "zl.gro up" takes in a stream of data points and groups N items as a list. Give this object the argument 10, such that it will listen for 10 data points before spitting out a list with 10 items. Connect the outlet of the second "if" to the leftmost inlet of the "zl.group 10" object.
- Beneath the "zl.group 10," create a new object called "array.mode." The "array" class of Max objects (introduced in Max 8) is similarly aimed at manipulating sets of data like lists. The "array.mode" object determines the *mode* of a numerical list. In case you don't remember it from Year 6 mathematics class (or 6th grade in the US), the mode is the element that appears most often in a list. Connect the outlet of the zl.group to the inlet of the array.mode.
- Because it is technically possible for the array.mode to output more than one value (consider that the mode of the list "1 2 3 3 4 4 5 6" has both a mode of 3 and 4), we need to create an unpack object to break apart this potential list. Give this unpack object a single argument of "f," indicating that we want only the first float (the shortest duration) in any list of multiple modes. Connect the outlet of the array.mode to the inlet of the "unpack f" object.
- We want this system to play long tones derived from the mode of the human's onsets, but we also want some rhythmic diversity so it's not just playing one rhythmic value. Under the "unpack f" object, create four "*" (multiply) objects. Give these objects four different arguments: 2., 4., 8., and 16. (make sure to include the decimal points as we don't want to round all our rhythmic values up to the nearest integer). Connect the outlet of the "unpack f" to the leftmost inlet of each "*" object so the mode will be multiplied by these values.
- We need a way to trigger these values randomly. Beneath the "*" objects, create five message objects. Connect the outlet of each "*" object to the rightmost inlet of one of the five message objects. You will have one left over. Connect the outlet of the "unpack f" directly to the rightmost inlet of

the fifth message object (this is the same as multiplying the mode by 1, but easier). Now as you sing into the mic or play your instrument, the mode of your durational data will be lengthened into long tones.

- Depending on the duration of the onsets you sing or play, the durations calculated by this system might be longer than is appropriate. It would be good to shorten these long tones with yet another conditional argument as a final filter. Below the message objects, create a new "if $f1 > 8001. then $f1" object. This object will filter out any duration messages longer than 8 seconds. Connect the outlets of all five message objects to the inlet of the if object.
- The outlet of this third if object is a duration state the system will use to generate new material. Create a new "send DURstates" object and connect the outlet of the third if object to its inlet. We will create an accompanying receive object later.
- Above the message objects, create a new "select 0 1 2 3 4" object so it will send out a bang corresponding to numbers between 0 and 5. Connect the five leftmost outlets of the select object to the leftmost inlets of each of the five message objects so that when the select object sends out a bang message, the data in these messages will be triggered.
- Above the select object, create a new "drunk 4" object so it will generate a drunken walk of integers between 0 and 4. Connect the outlet of the "drunk 4" to the leftmost inlet of the select object.
- Above the drunk object is where we need to provide a signal to trigger new duration states to be sent to the output system we haven't built yet. Create a new object called "receive generate!" Later, we will create a send object to accompany this object, and duration data will be turned into MIDI output (Figure 10.6).

Test of the Duration System

- This system doesn't make any sound yet, but you should be able to see it working. Lock the patch, turn on the audio (if it is off) and make some sounds in your microphone or on an instrument. Are timing data points being calculated in the message boxes at the bottom? If not, go back to the beginning of this section and troubleshoot.

Estimating Pitch

Now that we have generated duration data from audio input, let us turn our attention to the estimation of pitch. Though we have done this to a certain extent in a previous chapter, we will start over from scratch here, going in a slightly different direction. At the end of this tutorial, we will also create the final system that triggers music generation.

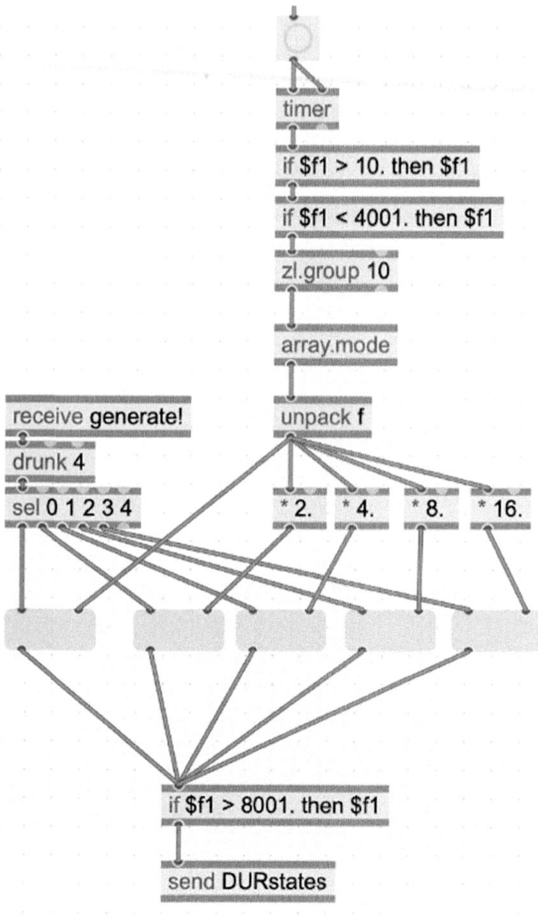

Figure 10.6 Turning timed onsets into new long-duration states.

Autotuning the Pitch Pre-Emptively

- When estimating a pitch digitally, it really helps to be robotically accurate with your performance. The tendency of acoustic instruments to almost never be directly on-pitch makes pitch estimation all the harder. Luckily, we already know an object that can fix this to a certain extent. Below the gate~ object, create a new retune~ object. We will use this retune~ object not to detect onsets, but to pitch correct the signal before we try to estimate pitch. Connect the outlet of the gate~ to the leftmost inlet of the retune~ object.
- Under the retune~, create a new object called fluid.pitch~. This is FluCoMa's pitch estimation object, which is in some ways superior to retune~. Connect the leftmost outlet of retune~ to the inlet of fluid.pitch~. Click on this new object and open the Inspector window. Note that the default latency

is 1024 samples. Like the other FluCoMa objects we've been using, this object's audio output performance is not mission critical since we won't be listening to it directly. Find the attribute called FFT Settings and change the setting to "512 -1 -1." The latency should drop to 512 samples. If you later find the latency of this system to be too much, drop the FFT setting to 256 or lower to improve it.

- While we are in the fluid.pitch~ object's Inspector window, note that the algorithm driving the pitch estimation is based on the YIN algorithm (mentioned in a previous chapter).
- The output of the fluid.pitch~ object will be a list consisting of the estimated pitch and a confidence level (from 0. to 1.). We will use both data points. To break this list apart, create an "unpack f f" below the fluid.pitch~. Connect the outlet of the fluid.pitch~ to the inlet of the "unpack f f."
- Since audio signals are continuous, even when there is not an estimated pitch being outputted from the unpack object, the most common signal will be 0. We can filter out this signal with the conditional argument "if $f1 > 0. then $f1." Create this if object, set its arguments and connect the leftmost outlet (pitch) of the "unpack f f" object to its inlet.
- The other number from the fluid.pitch~ represents the system's confidence level in its estimation. This number will also most commonly be 0., which we should filter out. We can do this with another conditional argument: "if $f1 > 0. then $f1." Create this if object, set its arguments and connect the rightmost outlet (confidence) of the "unpack f f" object to its inlet.
- Having filtered out the nonstop 0. messages, we should also filter out any pitch estimations that are low confidence. We can do this with yet another conditional argument, but we will need to add a second inlet. Create a new "if" object and give it the condition: "if $f2 > 0.5 then $f1." This means, if the pitch confidence (inlet 2) is greater than 0.5, pass the pitch from inlet 1 out of the outlet. You may find a different setting works better, but start with 0.5 and adjust it after you've tested it fully. Connect the outlet of the first (pitch) if object to the leftmost inlet of the third if object and then connect the outlet of the second (confidence) if object to the rightmost inlet of the third if object.
- Under the third if object, create a new message object. Connect the outlet of the third if object to the rightmost inlet of the message object to set the message with the estimated pitch.
- We will need a way to trigger this message's output. We will do this with the button below the edge~ object we previously created. Remember that this button is reacting to the onset of new notes from the audio input. Connect the output of the button to the leftmost inlet of the message object.
- Since we want to eventually generate MIDI data, we will need to translate the frequency floats from the fluid.pitch~ object into MIDI data. The "ftom" (frequency to MIDI) object does this easily. Create a new ftom object and connect the outlet of the message object to its inlet.

- This method will still tend to pass the same note many different times, so it is recommended that you create a "change" object under the ftom object to filter out repeated pitch repetitions. This will make performing repeated pitches more difficult, so if this adversely affects your performance, feel free to delete it. Connect the outlet of the ftom to the inlet of the change object.
- Below the change object, create a new "send PTCHstates" object to send the pitch states to the generator we will build later (Figure 10.7).

Test of the Pitch System

- This system doesn't make any sound yet, but you should be able to see it working. Lock the patch, turn on the audio (if it is off) and make some sounds in your microphone or on an instrument. Are frequency data points being calculated in the message box at the bottom? If not, go back to the beginning of this section and troubleshoot.

Putting it Together—Imp5

We have derived from the audio input states estimating pitch, velocity duration, and both starting and stopping impulses (in the form of 1's and 0's from the live.text play detector). This system is nearing completion. Let's christen the system *Imp5* and let the bot join the band.

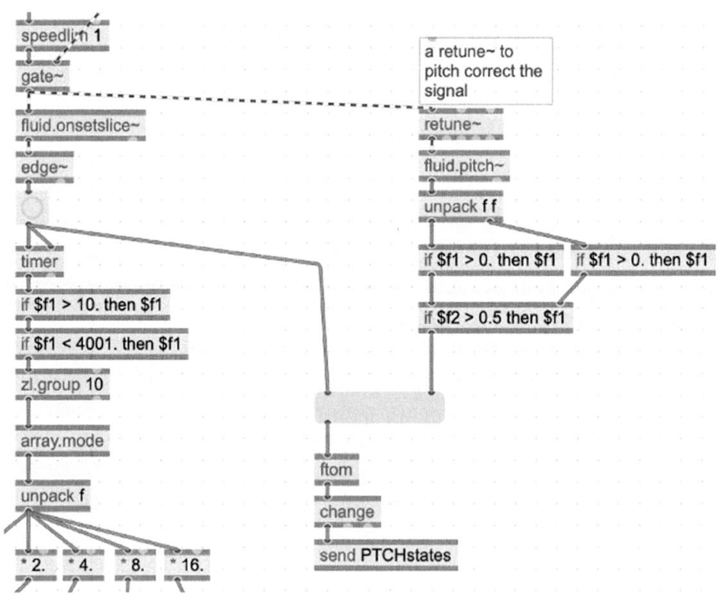

Figure 10.7 Estimating pitch using fluid.pitch~.

Range of Appropriateness

- We once again need to define appropriateness for how long Imp5 will play when the human is silent.
- That said, we will need to add a new "send playingorsilent" object below the live.text so the patch doesn't get too cluttered. Connect the outlet of the live.text to the inlet of the send object. The range of appropriateness subpatch includes a corresponding "receive playingorsilent" object (Figure 10.8).
- You have built two versions of the range of appropriateness subpatch thus far, and it is probable that you can follow the diagram below to build a third without too much added verbiage.
- This subsystem uses a new object called "onebang." At this point, you should be able to look up the Help file (right-click on the object and click on "Open onebang help") and determine how and why it is being used.
- Build the following system from scratch (Figure 10.9):
- Note the subtle differences between this system and those we used for Imp3 and Imp4. This system results in the "send generate!" we referenced earlier with a "receive generate!" object.

Generating Musical Output

- Similarly, the output generation system is built mostly from objects you've encountered before.
- The one novel thing this patch does is change to reduce the pitch states to a single octave using the "% 12" object. Going with the idea previously stated that Imp5 will be akin to a bass player (playing low tones and generally changing at a slower rate than the other musicians to add a firm foundation

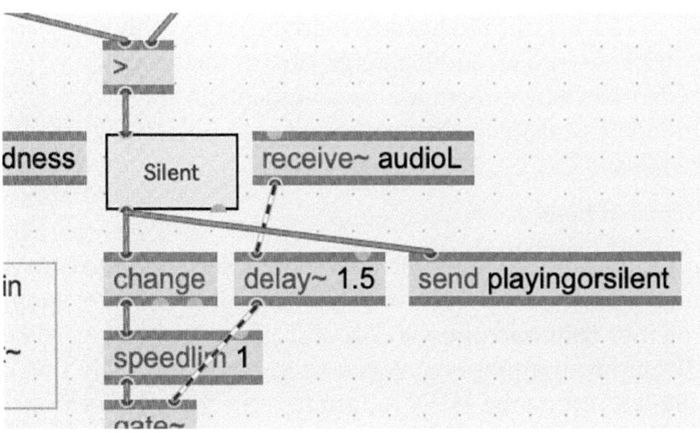

Figure 10.8 Sending a message from the live.text object.

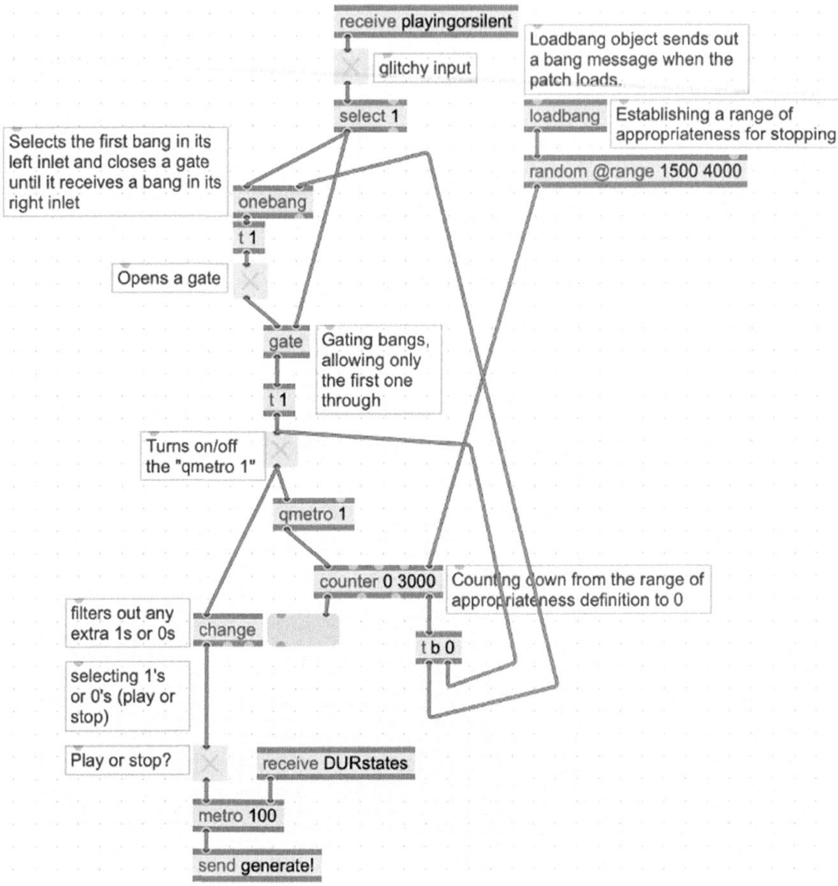

Figure 10.9 A third system for defining a range of appropriateness.

upon which to jam), the pitches are first reduced to a single octave and then brought back up into an audible range later in the system.

- As an added challenge, there are no comments in the diagram. Add your own comments explaining the function of each object (Figure 10.10).

Initial Test Drive of Imp5

- After you've finished building the final system, turn on the audio (if it's not on already) and give it a test drive by playing some notes on an instrument or singing into your microphone. You will also need to set up some manner of MIDI output, but presumably you've learned how to do that already. I would suggest setting the MIDI output to something with a long decay like a bass synth or organ sound. If using Ableton Live as an output, search for the tags "ambient" and "evolving" in the browser window.

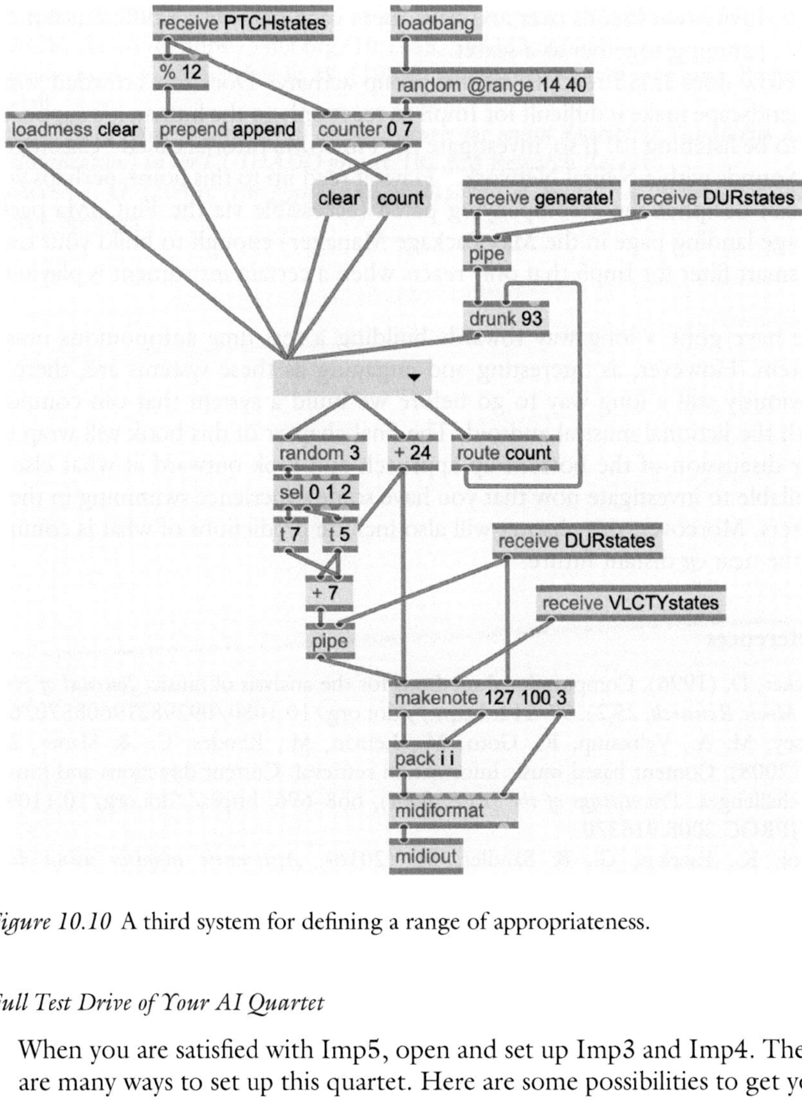

Figure 10.10 A third system for defining a range of appropriateness.

Full Test Drive of Your AI Quartet

- When you are satisfied with Imp5, open and set up Imp3 and Imp4. There are many ways to set up this quartet. Here are some possibilities to get you started:
  - Modify Imp5 so it sends out MIDI data on the MIDIears channel (so Imp3 can hear it).
  - Modify Imp4 so it can send out MIDI data on the MIDIears channel (so Imp3 can hear it).
  - Go back to playing a MIDI controller into Imp3 and Imp4 but find a way to pass the audio output from Imp3 or Imp4 into Imp5 (this is somewhat easy to do on Ableton Live using the I/O setup controls, most difficult on PCs with standalone Max).

11 Continuation...

While connectionist systems have recently made a strong impression on the public, they have also been highly controversial. The high-profile lawsuit alleging intellectual property theft brought by Universal Music Group against Suno and Udio has been settled, and another lawsuit has been filed by independent artists against Suno and Udio alleging stream-ripping and market harm (Dalugdug, 2025). These legal difficulties illuminate a significant drawback in using AI to generate music, which is intensified by the speed with which connectionist systems can produce convincing musical outputs. These systems do not generate novel music in the way the previously discussed symbolic systems do; instead, they learn patterns in a dataset and remix these variables to generate seemingly novel material. But the appearance of novelty in these outputs can be deceiving.

To illustrate this, consider the *Lost Tapes of the 27 Club's* 2021 song, "Drowned in the Sun" (produced by Over the Bridge, 2021). The song was generated by training a neural network on the music of Nirvana and then generated several new songs in the style of the band that broke up after lead singer Kurt Cobain's death in 1994. At first listen, this seemingly new song may impress an ardent fan of the band whose output ended so tragically. But further hearings of the track reveal a sad truth: the song bears a striking resemblance to other songs released by Nirvana before Kurt Cobain's tragic death. This song is not new material as Nirvana would write it today. A close listen to the song reveals it is strongly influenced by other Nirvana songs, including "Pennyroyal Tea" (chord progression and rhyme scheme), *In Bloom* (the vocal timbres and overall range), "Lithium" (specifically the guitar tone), All Apologies (the lyrics, particularly the oft-repeated line *"In the sun, in the sun, I feel as one,"* which is mimicked in the AI song by lines in the chorus *"I don't care, I feel as one, Drowned in the sun, drowned in the sun.")*.

This is not to denigrate the song (which is quite listenable) or the efforts of the *Lost Tapes of the 27 Club's* efforts, which were ahead of their time for 2021. But if the music world discovered to its surprise that Kurt Cobain had faked his death and he subsequently released a new album of newly recorded and composed songs with Krist Novoselic and Dave Grohl, the results would most

DOI: 10.4324/9781003534211-14

likely sound nothing like "Drowned in the Sun." The truth of this claim can be tested in the similar situation of fellow Seattle grunge band Soundgarden.

Soundgarden, a band with a similarly successful career compared to Nirvana, broke up amicably after the release of their 1996 album *Down on the Upside*, and then reunited in 2012 to record a new album entitled *King Animal.* After a very long hiatus, Soundgarden guitarist Kim Thayil thought it would be interesting to "hear how Soundgarden-ish" the results would be after 16 years had passed (Bray, 2012). Some strong musical tropes extant in Soundgarden's previous output carried over into *King Animal.* As Washington Post reviewer Allison Stewart wrote shortly after the album's release, "King Animal is the best and rarest kind of reunion disc, one in which members of a band's classic line-up make an album that sounds like a reasonable version of the albums they made before, without wallowing in nostalgia or bringing in contemporizing touches like electro beats or duets with Ne-Yo." (Stewart, 2012).

A Rolling Stone review went on to note how themes in the songs have been updated to reflect the band member's current life context. "Being from Seattle in the Nineties, helplessness suggested drug abuse. But *King Animal* was recorded by sober dudes in their forties...'Bones of Birds' is about the challenges of parenting" (Dolan, 2012). Musically, while many Soundgarden songs before their hiatus featured odd or changing time signatures (1994's "Black Hole Sun" featured a section in 9/4), the song "By Crooked Steps" (the third track on King Animal) features a drum beat in 15/8, something they had never tried before. Moreover, the verse's main guitar riff, while often repeated verbatim throughout, features a confusing division between beat (which sounds like it should be divided in crotchets) and rhythm (which is more easily divisible in quavers), as if a somewhat mundane 4/4 drumbeat had been interrupted by a measure of 2/8 after the first beat (Figure 11.1).

These differences and the overall willingness to try new musical schticks show the growth in the individual members of the band since their breakup. By comparison, "Drowned in the Sun" sounds like a long-lost track recorded by Nirvana at a time shortly before Cobain's death. Everything heard in this track had been done before by Nirvana on previous recordings. Thus, this track does not represent in any meaningful way "new" music by Nirvana. This tendency to overfit is the premise of the lawsuits against Udio and Suno, but it is a tendency AI systems share at every level.

Figure 11.1 Transcription of the main riff from Soundgarden's "By Crooked Steps" (Soundgarden, 2012; author's transcription).

Black Boxes

Another major drawback of the connectionist approach is the lack of interpretability. Neural networks are often described as "black boxes," meaning that the processes that lead them to a given output are difficult or impossible to understand after the fact. Reasons for this are varied, but it should suffice to say that as music is an artistic pursuit characterised by a near obsession with process (Neely, 2024), a musical output machine that cannot be explained or justified in any way is not going to have much of a future of musicking with humans (Small, 1998).

These issues, the energy and computational resources necessary to pull off connectionist-based music in real time, plus the steep learning curve involved in understanding the root problems of the endeavour, have kept musicians largely out of this discussion until very recently. Hopefully, this text has assisted the reader's entry into the AI discussion and shed some light on where things are and where they need to go in the future. The following sections detail some options for going further with this topic that did not fit elsewhere in the book.

Other Resources

ml.lib

Max has many packages available that may be helpful to those wanting to go further with building and learning about machine learning systems. Nick Gillian's *ml.lib* package shares some similarities with Ben Smith's ml.star but allows for the inclusion of continuous data in most objects (Gillian, 2014). The learning curve of the package is steep, and the documentation is minimal, but the objects are solid and functional. The objects in this package could be used for feature extraction or for creating Markov models and HMMs of continuous data.

More MuBu

There are many objects we did not cover in the MuBu package which could be quite useful. Many of these objects are aimed at gesture recognition. In this text we focused mainly on machine learning "in the box," i.e., what we can accomplish inside the computer. Gesture recognition could give your autonomous music system the ability to watch other players for visual cues, responding to gestures with musical gestures it has been trained to associate with visual motion. If you are curious to investigate, begin with the mubu.gvf object. The MuBu setup should be familiar to you now, having read this text. Other objects like mubu.xmm instantiate higher-level machine learning algorithms like *Hierarchical Multimodal Hidden Markov Models* (mubu.xmm), *K-nearest neighbour* (mubu.knn), or *Gaussian Mixture Regression* (mubu.gmm). Unfortunately for the uninitiated, the intense learning curve inherent in these endeavours is exemplified by sentences like this one from a MuBu help file: "The external creates an internal data structure—a multidimensional binary search tree—from the data of a MuBu track to allow for an optimised k-nearest neighbour search in a track." (Schnell et al., 2023).

CataRT-MuBu

Partially created to assist with learning this package, a second package called CataRT-MuBu (Schwarz, 2007, 2013) was released by Diemo Schwarz. This package is based on the work of other packages including primarily MuBu, but also Cage, Bach, sensel, blocks, and spat5. Cata-RT includes many helpful abstractions (another word for a subpatch, or encapsulated code), extending the functionality of each. One abstraction, camu.taboo, avoids repetition when running through data points in an output. Throughout the tutorials in this book, the change object was used to avoid unnecessary repetitions. The camu.taboo patch could do essentially the same thing, but without the data point being exactly the same (a definite probability when estimating pitch), using the mubu.knn (K-nearest neighbour) object.

Data Knot

Similarly, Rodrigo Constanzo's *Data Knot* package extends the functionality of FluCoMa, providing helpful abstractions for tasks such as onset detection, audio descriptor analysis, and regression (Constanzo, 2025). The *Data Knot* landing page also links to several valuable YouTube tutorials by Constanzo, Ted Moore, and others. In addition, the project is supported by a thriving Discord community, accessible at https://discord.gg/Vy2zuKQkqN. These tutorials generally assume a basic familiarity with Max and audio concepts, but they represent an excellent next step for those seeking to go deeper after reading this text.

MC Movement Studies

Dillon Bastan (maker of the Tree Tone synth, discussed in Chapter 3; Bastan, 2022) has also released a Max package that provides open-source JavaScript that models extremely complex and chaotic natural phenomena in Max via the JSUI object (Bastan, 2021). Modelling complex behaviour of natural phenomena is not necessarily machine learning, but along the way, Bastan created helpful abstractions including one called db.geneural, which instantiates a simple neural network using the Gen class of Max objects. Additionally, since the interfaces used in this package are built on the JSUI object, which allows users to open the code and modify it, users of this package can use these abstractions as a jumping-off point to create their own complex interfaces using a Large Language Model in a process called Vibe Coding.

Vibe Coding

Using Bastan's db.mc.particlegrains abstraction as an example of this, with the patch locked, follow the numbers and instructions to make some sound using the three JSUI interfaces in the middle of the patch. The following brief tutorial involves using a large language model (like ChatGPT, Claude, or Grok) to edit JavaScript.

- Unlock the patch and right-click on the middle interface (as shown in Figure 11.2):
- Click on "Object," and then "Edit flowfield.js." A second window opens, revealing the underlying JavaScript. Click on this window and copy this code entirely (CMD + C on a Mac, CTL + C on a PC).
- Open the large language model of your choice in a browser window and ask it to edit the code using a prompt like, "I'd like to do some vibe coding. Please edit this code to change the colour variables to make the dots and lines blue instead of gold. Output the entire code so I can copy it directly into a Max JSUI object." Then paste the code (CMD + V on a Mac, CTL + V on a PC) directly into the chat window and hit enter.

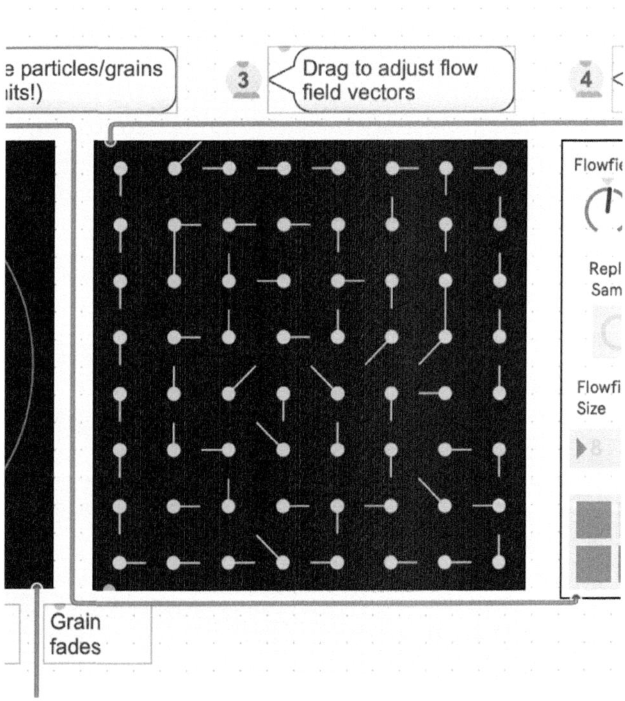

Figure 11.2 Dillon Bastan's "flowfield" interface (available via the MC Movement Studies Max package, Bastan, 2021), image reprinted by permission.

- When the LLM returns the code, copy it and paste it into the JavaScript window, then save that window with a name other than “flowfield.js” (this way you can always reload the original file back in again if this experiment doesn’t work).
- Returning to the db.mc.particlegrains abstraction. Did the dots and lines turn blue? If not, report this to the LLM and ask it to try again, repeating the process until the results are satisfactory (Figure 11.3).
- Eventually, the LLM should change the lines of code that say “var col_arrows = [1., 0.71, 0.196];” and “var col_circles = [0.5, 0.5, 0.5, 1];” to something like this (Figure 11.4):
- The possibilities of this kind of adaptation are astounding, putting nearly limitless coding power in the hands of completely uninitiated non-coders. While this certainly democratises computer science to a great degree, it also may strike some as unethical or at least appropriative of the work of others.

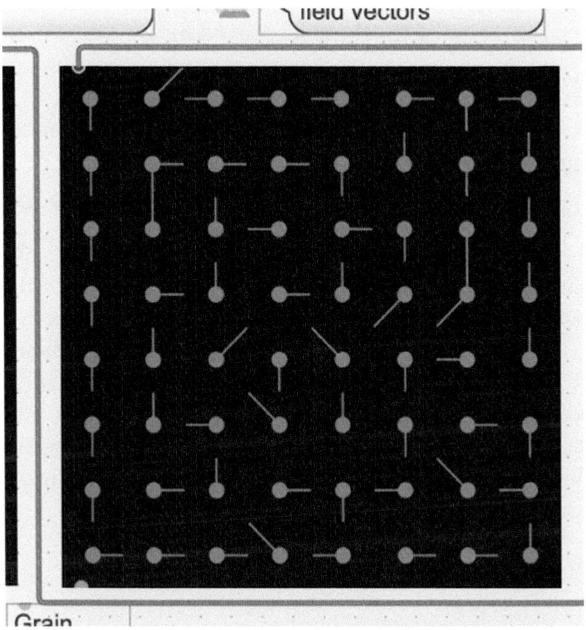

Figure 11.3 An edited version of Dillon Bastan’s JavaScript “flowfield” interface edited by ChatGPT, prompted by the author, image reprinted by permission.

```
var col_positive = [0.427, 0.843, 1.];
var col_arrows = [0.2, 0.6, 1.0, 1.]; // bright sky blue
var col_background = [0.157, 0.157, 0.157, 1.];
var col_circles = [0.2, 0.6, 1.0, 1.]; // matching blue
```

Figure 11.4 An edited version of Dillon Bastan’s JavaScript for “flowfield.js,” edited by ChatGPT, prompted by the author, image reprinted by permission.

Still others may balk at the use of LLMs in general, which are said to be unethical and appropriative from first principles, so some caution should be used in this line of work.

Beyond Max

While Max is extremely versatile and musician-friendly, not every machine learning algorithm can be instantiated in a Max patch—at least not yet. Some AI endeavours will require branching into other programming languages and ecosystems. Python remains the most common entry point, with libraries such as *TensorFlow*, *PyTorch*, and *scikit-learn* forming the backbone of most hard-science music-related ML research. For music-specific applications, tools like Magenta's *Python API*, *MusPy*, and *Essentia* offer frameworks for working with symbolic, audio, and feature-based data. Languages like JavaScript (via TensorFlow.js or ml5.js) allow for interactive, browser-based sound projects, while C++ remains essential for those interested in low-latency, embedded, or plugin development. Together, these environments provide musicians with multiple pathways to explore machine learning beyond Max, extending creative and technical possibilities well into the domain of autonomous performance systems.

Magenta

The Magenta project, mentioned in Chapter 7, is a side venture of Google Brain that applies machine learning to creative musical research (Hawthorne et al., 2018). Initially, Magenta focused on offline, plugin-based tools such as Magenta Studio, which generated melodies, harmonies, and rhythms for later editing in a DAW. Recently, the project has shifted towards real-time interaction with the release of *The Infinite Crate*—a plugin powered by Lyria RealTime through Google's Gemini API. This marks an evolution from static, batch-generation workflows to live, responsive systems.

Wekinator

Wekinator is an open-source software environment that enables artists and musicians to create interactive systems using machine learning without extensive coding. Developed by Rebecca Fiebrink, it provides an intuitive interface for mapping inputs—such as gestures, audio features, or sensor data—to real-time musical or visual outputs (Fiebrink, 2011). Fiebrink's online tutorials (accessible via http://www.wekinator.org) offer a clear, hands-on introduction to these concepts, guiding users through building systems based on classification, regression, and data representation. A key idea introduced is the *tensor*, a multidimensional array that underlies many modern ML models. Tensors are particularly valuable for musical applications because they can efficiently encode complex, time-varying data—like the Core Audible and

Perceptual Parameters—into a structure that algorithms can process and learn from.

Robots, Hybrids, and Holograms

While firmly outside the scope of this book, some mention of these other avenues for musical exploration practically demands inclusion. The discussion in Chapter 2 outlined several philosophical frameworks for understanding mind—dualism, materialism, functionalism, and phenomenology—each carrying different implications for machine musicianship.

This text has, for the most part, sidelined dualism and phenomenology, both of which depend upon a notion of *embodiment*: the idea that consciousness and perception arise not solely from disembodied cognition but from the body's lived, situated engagement with the world. To speak of an embodied mind is to reject the notion that thought can exist in isolation from sensory experience and physical context. If we take this idea seriously, then we must also consider musical systems that emulate bodily presence, mechanical gestures, generating sound, hybrid organisms that conjoin human and nonhuman intelligences, or holographic projections that simulate corporeality while remaining disembodied and immaterial. These forms complicate the disembodied logic of algorithmic composition and gesture toward a more phenomenological understanding of machine musicianship, one that treats musical meaning as inseparable from the bodies through which it is enacted.

Robots

For those wanting to explore this direction more concretely, the Max-for-Live *Connection Kit* provides an ideal bridge between the conceptual work of this text and the physical realities of embodied musical systems. Developed as a suite of Max-for-Live devices that connect Ableton Live to hardware and web-based platforms such as Arduino, LEGO MINDSTORMS EV3, OSC, and webcams, the Connection Kit allows users to construct primitive robotic systems capable of sensing, responding to, and manipulating their environment (Ableton, 2016). Through these devices, artists can easily extend their AI experiments with machine musicianship beyond algorithmic cognition into physical gesture and interaction, creating systems that pluck strings, strike drums, or vibrate air via acoustic instruments.

Few projects exemplify this embodied frontier more vividly than Gil Weinberg's work with *Shimon*, the robotic marimba player developed at the Georgia Tech Center for Music Technology. Shimon listens, improvises, and composes in real time, embodying an ideal of mechanical empathy and creative responsiveness that has redefined human-robot collaboration in music (Weinberg, 2021). Shimon's performance with the band COIN on *Jimmy Kimmel Live!* playing the song "Chapstick" signalled a cultural moment in which robotic musicianship moved from the laboratory to the mainstream stage.

For a more comprehensive exploration of the field's theoretical and technical dimensions, Richard Savery's *Robotic Musicianship: Embodied Artificial Creativity and Mechatronic Collaboration* (2020) provide an indispensable foundation. These developments represent a fundamental reconsideration of musical intelligence as a situated, embodied, and collaborative phenomenon enacted through motion and sound.

Bayesian Logic Systems

To counter the drawbacks and limitations of the symbolic and connectionist approaches, many researchers have ultimately favoured a hybrid approach that is tempered with so-called Bayesian reasoning (Temperley, 2004). The Bayesian approach, named after the mathematician Thomas Bayes (1702–1761), allows for the calculation of conditional probability, which is used to determine the likelihood of a specific outcome by evaluating the outcome of the system tackling a similar problem. Bayesian reasoning is not as easy to understand as a purely symbolic or connectionist approach, as it involves similar processes depending on the use case. For an example, imagine you are a band leader wondering, "Will my drummer show up for today's rehearsal?" In the past, they have usually proven reliable, such that you think there is an 80% chance they will show up. But then they text you saying, "Running late!" This statement causes you to lower your internally calculated likelihood to a 50% chance that they will prove reliable today.

Bayesian/Symbolic Hybrids

As Bayesian approaches are based on formal rules, it is often easy to integrate with symbolic systems. Both approaches also use variables and explicitly defined relationships. For instance, a Bayesian approach could be used to modify the volume of a backup piano part given the probability that another player is performing a solo. Whereas purely symbolic approaches often struggle to adapt to unfamiliar situations, Bayesian networks can provide clear reasoning amid uncertainty.

While David Cope's Experiments in Musical Intelligence (EMI) system was primarily a symbolic system, Cope also used probabilistic or Bayesian reasoning to make determinations about musical parameters like harmony, rhythm, and structure (Cope, 1991, 2005).

Bayesian/Connectionist Hybrids

In many connectionist systems, the outputs of neural networks are shaped by Bayesian reasoning such that network weights are evaluated as probabilistic distributions, rather than fixed values. This approach is much more flexible compared to purely connectionist approaches, as these Bayesian networks can update themselves continually depending on the context of their inputs.

Some music transcription systems (systems that listen to polyphonic music and transcribe the sound as written notation or MIDI data) and chord recognition systems (that listen to multi-note simultaneities and determine the appropriate nomenclature to use) often use Bayesian methods since it is often difficult for such systems to parse and evaluate every note in a chord. An example of this would be a piece of music that has thus far been in C major that would rarely include a G minor chord, so if a chord recognition system detects a G and a D, it is likely that the chord being evaluated is a G major. However, upon the evidence (E) of the note Bb, the hypothesis (H) that the chord is a G major must be changed. The AI Duets app developed by Magenta seems to make use of Bayesian logic in this way (Hernandez-Olivan et al., 2022).

Holograms

Holographic systems are those that involve projected images, sometimes involving optical illusions, to give the impression of a 3-dimensional image. While systems like those seen in science fiction media like Star Trek, Star Wars, the Alien franchise, and Westworld can be projected in and around real environments, extant systems capable of projecting holograms as of this writing always have an extremely limited field of view and often also involve an extremely limited area to be viewed by an audience.

The Pepper's Ghost illusion (an image projected onto an angled pane of glass to create the illusion of a three-dimensional, spectral presence) was first demonstrated by John Henry Pepper and Henry Dircks in the 1860s. This nineteenth-century stage trick laid the conceptual groundwork for modern holographic performance. In 2007, Crypton Future Media's *Hatsune Miku* concerts revived and reimagined the technique through digital means, using rear-projection screens and LED panels to render a holographic avatar performing alongside live musicians. A decade later, the effect gained renewed attention at the 2012 Coachella Music Festival, where a digital simulacrum of Tupac Shakur appeared onstage through a modified Pepper's Ghost setup. The illusion was enhanced using a body double and a voice actor performing newly recorded material in Tupac's style 16 years after his death. Similar "resurrections" followed for Elvis Presley and Michael Jackson, revealing both the technical sophistication and the ethical ambiguities of digitally embodied performance. More recently, the technique was further refined by Industrial Light & Magic to produce *ABBA Voyage* (2022), a live event in which motion-capture technology, CGI modelling, and digital de-ageing combined to produce "ABBAtars" that perform nightly as their younger 1970s selves.

While the productions and systems listed above are some of the most striking and exciting projects in live performance happening today, these systems have all the same problems of connectionist systems, plus all the cost and complications of a robotics approach, plus the difficulties of an extremely complicated visual projection system. These systems tend to not be real-time in design but instead tend to mix a limited amount of real-time input (as with the

Tupac illusion) with mostly fixed or pre-recorded videos and sound. However, these systems are decreasing in cost, so it's not out of the question that 3D projection systems will make more of a musical impact over time.

When Gil Weinberg visited my Indiana University, Indianapolis in 2019, he told me that every robot his lab ever made started out as an animation first. My own Emergent Musical Hologram (EMH) system was an attempt to make a real-time face AI-based interactive musical output systems (Figure 11.5).

The initial versions of the EMH project were based on prerecorded videos of my dancer collaborators Maddie and Margo Korn recorded in front of a green screen. Later, I incorporated this system into concerts with my student performing group DISEnsemble utilising videos of the students. In the right circumstances, the effect for the audience is astoundingly eye-catching, but the concept is still in the prototype stage with a new version using real-time digitally rendered avatars coming hopefully soon (Figure 11.6).

There are, of course, more effective ways to make a hologram, but the EMH project was an attempt to achieve similar effects without the associated costs and inflexibilities inherent in most adaptations of the Pepper's Ghost technique.

Figure 11.5 A picture of the Emergent Musical Hologram in action (a DIY hologram of the author overlaid on a Yamaha Disklavier).

Figure 11.6 DISEnsemble, performing with the EMH (real Sarah Lopez on the right, holographic Sarah Lopez on the left, image reprinted by permission).

Datalore

Due to the fast-developing nature of the AI field, writing this book has at times been maddening, as I struggled to stay on top of AI news, late-breaking developments, and the constant updates to Max and its associated packages. Should this version of the text become obsolete at some point in the future, I hope it is of a high enough level to serve as a testament to the historical perspective we are living through regarding AI at this moment. If not, this will not be a tragedy. Even Lieutenant Commander Data eventually succumbed to the passage of time.

I owe a massive debt to many people who contributed in knowing and unknowing ways to the production of this text including: first and foremost Evie Evans, who originated the idea for me to write a book like this and stayed positive and helpful to the bitter end, and Emily Tagg, Editorial Assistant for the Audio list at Routledge; my wife and children who put up with me missing meals and Saturdays for more than two years; my friends at Plainfield Christian Church; the baristas at Cabin Coffee who put up with me showing up early, staying past closing time, and always taking the good table; my students (especially Chloe Golden, Regan Wakeman, Drew Hampton, Sarah Lopez, and Liam Boyle), who not only filled my brain with different perspectives and new ideas, but also put up with me ending class early, not getting my grading done promptly, or blowing off one-on-one meetings; my dancer collaborators *The Architects* (Jennifer Kayle, Kathy Couch, Katherine Ferrier, Lisa Gonzales, and Pamela Vail), Maddie Korn, and Margo Korn; my colleagues at IU Indianapolis in the music technology program: Jordan Munson, Dan Walzer, Tim Hsu, Robin Cox, Chuiyuan Meng, and Michael Drews. Finally, I would like to dedicate this book to my friend and long-time partner on the AVATAR Project, and composer of the AI Opera: Lexia, the late Scott Deal. Outside of my collaboration with Scott, no one would be interested in talking to me about my thoughts on AI. From the day I met him, Scott was always a mentor, a good friend, a role model, and a great promoter of me and my work, for which I can't thank him enough.

If you have questions about this text or the tutorials within or just want to talk about cool AI music-related stuff, send me an email at the address below. I will respond to all serious inquiries as time permits.

-Jason Palamara,
japalama@iu.edu
Assistant Professor of Music Technology
Director of DISEnsemble
& The Machine Musician Lab
Herron School of Art and Design
Indiana University, Indianapolis

References

Ableton. (2016). *Max for live connection kit – take live beyond sound.* Ableton Blog. https://www.ableton.com/blog/max-for-live-connection-kit/

Bastan, D. (2021). *MC movement studies* [Computer software package]. Cycling '74. https://cycling74.com/articles/mc-movement-studies-in-the-package-manager

Bastan, D. (2022). *Inspired by nature* [Ableton Live Factory Pack]. Ableton. Retrieved November 23, 2024, from https://www.ableton.com/en/packs/inspired-nature/

Bray, R. (2012, November 12). Interview: Kim Thayil (of Soundgarden). *Consequence of Sound.* https://consequence.net/2012/11/interview-kim-thayil-of-soundgarden/

Constanzo, R. (2025, October 14). *Data Knot* [Computer software]. https://rodrigoconstanzo.com/data-knot/

Cope, D. (1991). *Computers and musical style.* A-R Editions.

Cope, D. (2005). *Computer models of musical creativity.* MIT Press.

Dalugdug, M. (2025, October 21). Suno and Udio face another lawsuit from indie artists over AI training, echoing major labels' stream-ripping allegations. *Music Business Worldwide.* https://www.musicbusinessworldwide.com/suno-and-udio-face-another-lawsuit-from-indie-artists-accusing-them-of-stream-ripping-and-market-harm/

Dolan, J. (2012, November 13). Album review: King Animal, by Soundgarden. *Rolling Stone.* https://www.rollingstone.com/music/music-album-reviews/king-animal-122563/

Fiebrink, R. A. (2011). *Real-time human interaction with supervised learning algorithms for music composition and performance* (Doctoral dissertation, Princeton University). ProQuest Dissertations Publishing.

Gillian, N. (2014). *ml.lib: Machine learning library for Max* [Computer software]. https://github.com/nickgillian/ml-lib

Hawthorne, C., Elsen, E., Song, J., Roberts, A., Simon, I., Raffel, C., Engle, J., Oore, S., & Eck, D. (2018). *Onsets and frames: Dual-objective piano transcription.* Proceedings of the 19th International Society for Music Information Retrieval Conference (ISMIR 2018). Paris, France.

Hernandez-Olivan, C., Hernandez-Olivan, J., & Beltran, J. R. (2022, November 3). *A survey on artificial intelligence for music generation: Agents, domains, and perspectives.* ArXiv. https://doi.org/10.48550/arXiv.2210.13944

Neely, A. (2024, April 30). *Why AI is doomed to fail the musical turing test [Video].* YouTube. https://www.youtube.com/watch?v=N8NyEjB_XeA&t=1201s

Over the Bridge. (2021). *Drowned in the sun [Song]. On the lost tapes of the 27 club.* Over the Bridge. https://www.youtube.com/watch?v=cE4-8P509Ms

Savery, R. (2020). *Robotic musicianship: Embodied artificial creativity and mechatronic collaboration.* Springer.

Schnell, N., Schwarz, D., & Bevilacqua, F. (2023). mubu.knn [Max object help file] (Version 1.10). Ircam – Centre Pompidou. In *MuBu for Max* [Computer software]. https://forum.ircam.fr/projects/detail/mubu/

Schwarz, D. (2007). Corpus-based concatenative synthesis. *IEEE Signal Processing Magazine, 24*(2), 92–104. https://doi.org/10.1109/MSP.2007.323274

Schwarz, D. (2013). *CataRT-MuBu: Corpus-based concatenative sound synthesis in Max* [Computer software]. Ircam – Centre Pompidou. https://ismm.ircam.fr/catart/

Small, C. (1998). *Musicking: The meanings of performing and listening.* Wesleyan University Press.

Stewart, A. (2012, November 12). Album review: 'King Animal,' by Soundgarden. *The Washington Post.* https://www.washingtonpost.com/entertainment/music/album-review-king-animal-by-soundgarden/2012/11/12/c8b6aaba-2cf6-11e2-9ac2-1c61452669c3_story.html

Temperley, D. (2004). Bayesian models of musical structure and cognition. Musicae Scientiae, 8(2), 175–205. https://doi.org/10.1177/102986490400800204

Weinberg, G., Raman, A., & Mallikarjuna, T. (2009). Interactive jamming withShimon: A social robotic musician. In *Proceedings of the 2009 4th ACM/IEEEInternational Conference on Human-Robot Interaction (HRI)* (pp. 59–66). IEEE.https://doi .org /10 .1145 /1514095 .1514152

Weinberg, G. (2021). Robotic musicianship. *Communications of the ACM, 64*(5), 58–60. https://doi.org/10.5772/5206

Index

Note: Page numbers in **bold** denote tables, those in *italic* denote figures

For Product Safety Concerns and Information please contact our EU representative GPSR@taylorandfrancis.com Taylor & Francis Verlag GmbH, Kaufingerstraße 24, 80331 München, Germany

Batch number: 10722136

Printed by Printforce, the Netherlands